CHINESE
AUTOBIOGRAPHICAL
WRITING

Chinese Autobiographical Writing

AN ANTHOLOGY
OF PERSONAL ACCOUNTS

Edited by
Patricia Buckley Ebrey,
Cong Ellen Zhang,
and Ping Yao

University of Washington Press | Seattle

The open-access edition of Chinese Autobiographical Writing was made possible in part by an award from the James P. Geiss and Margaret Y. Hsu Foundation.

Additional support was provided by the McLellan Endowment, established through the generosity of Martha McCleary McLellan and Mary McLellan Williams.

UNIVERSITY OF WASHINGTON PRESS | uwapress.uw.edu

LIBRARY OF CONGRESS CATALOGING-IN-PUBLICATION DATA

Names: Ebrey, Patricia Buckley, 1947– editor. | Zhang, Cong, 1967– editor. | Yao, Ping (Professor of history), editor.
Title: Chinese autobiographical writing : an anthology of personal accounts / edited by Patricia Buckley Ebrey, Cong Ellen Zhang, and Ping Yao.
Description: Seattle : University of Washington Press, [2023] | Includes bibliographical references and index.
Identifiers: LCCN 2022032466 (print) | LCCN 2022032467 (ebook) | ISBN 9780295751221 (hardcover) | ISBN 9780295751238 (paperback) | ISBN 9780295751245 (ebook)
Subjects: LCSH: Autobiography—Chinese authors. | Biography as a literary form. | China—Biography—History and criticism.
Classification: LCC CT34.C6 C45 2022 (print) | LCC CT34.C6 (ebook) | DDC 808/.06692—dc23/eng/20220713
LC record available at https://lccn.loc.gov/2022032466
LC ebook record available at https://lccn.loc.gov/2022032467

∞ This paper meets the requirements of ANSI/NISO z39.48-1992 (Permanence of Paper).

CONTENTS

PREFACE AND ACKNOWLEDGMENTS

This volume has many points of origin. One is the work Patricia Ebrey did in the late 1970s with support from an NEH grant that led to *Chinese Civilization and Society: A Sourcebook* (New York: Free Press, 1981). Over a period of about three years, a group of graduate students at the University of Illinois working with Pat looked for texts that would make good classroom reading, then drafted translations. Pat went over them all, did some translations herself, wrote the introductions, and tested them in class. So many pieces were translated that publishing them all in a single volume became impossible, so Pat set aside several longer autobiographical pieces, thinking they might one day be published in a set of personal accounts. Four of the pieces included here were resurrected from the old paper copies that had been sitting in file folders for decades. They had to be shortened to be included here but are still among the longer pieces.

Another point of origin is our history together. This goes back to the 1990s, when first Ping Yao and later Cong Ellen Zhang entered the graduate program at the University of Illinois, took courses with Pat, and became good friends with each other. Although we have since scattered, a quarter century later we still read and discuss each other's work. Together, the three of us edited *Chinese Funerary Biographies: An Anthology of Remembered Lives* (Seattle: University of Washington Press, 2019). That volume, having begun with a workshop, contained translations by nineteen different scholars. This time we thought we would try doing most of the translations ourselves, making consistency easier to achieve. Ping largely did the first drafts of the pieces through the Tang, and Cong and Pat the ones for later periods, but we each spent quite a bit of time going over the others' work, so have not credited translations to one person. In the end, we also chose to include four translations by other scholars.

Since we were happy with the University of Washington Press's handling of the earlier anthology volume and enjoyed working with Lorri Hagman and her team, we turned to them with this volume as well. We were particularly impressed this time by the highly qualified readers they found to review our manuscript. We would like to publicly thank them for the obvious care they took in going through both the Chinese and English texts and the many suggestions for better phrasing they offered, almost all of which we happily adopted.

TRANSLATION CONVENTIONS

Translators always aim for a balance between conveying the meaning and capturing the style, between achieving fluency and minimizing inaccuracies. Here are some of the principles we tried to follow in seeking such a balance.

In Chinese, it is not necessary to supply the subject for a sentence, especially when it is obvious from context, but subjects are needed in English, so we routinely supply them. In addition, in Chinese it is not odd to refer to oneself in the third person, and in some cases would be considered respectful (referring to oneself as "your subject" when addressing the ruler, for instance). In Chinese, repeated use of "I" can seem egotistic or self-centered. In English, by contrast, referring to oneself in the third person can come across as pretentious or evidence of mental illness. This creates a tricky situation for the translator, as authors wrote about themselves in the third person for a variety of reasons, sometimes to make fun of themselves, sometimes simply because it suggested to them greater objectivity: they were giving not just opinions but facts. Here we have often switched to the first person in keeping with English style but have kept some in the third person so that readers can get a better sense of the flavor of the original, especially in cases where gentle self-mockery was involved.

Since our primary goal was to prepare translations that people would enjoy reading, we made an effort to translate as much as possible, rather than supply Chinese terms in romanization, with just four exceptions:

jinshi, the highest rank conferred in the civil service examinations, literally "presented scholar"

li, a unit of distance, approximately one-third of a mile or half a kilometer

mu, a unit of area about a sixth of an acre

qi, a now widely recognized philosophical term that refers to energy, including energy that courses through the body

In the case of other common units of measurement, we supply conventional translations, but it should be kept in mind that these are only roughly equivalent and there was, moreover, considerable change over time and regional variation. Thus we translate *chi* as foot, *cun* as inch, *jin* as catty, *dou* as peck, *hu* as bushel, and *shi* as picul. For units of currency, we translate *qian* as cash and *liang* as tael.

We normally supply the name of the modern province in brackets after place names. We translate *xian* as county in all periods. When office titles are listed in Charles Hucker's *A Dictionary of Official Titles in Imperial China* (1985), we use his translation. We give dates and reign periods in their original form, putting in brackets the Western year with which it overlaps the most, but we do not convert to the Western calendar. We similarly do not convert people's ages, simply giving their age in *sui*, which on average will make them seem a year older than if the count followed Western convention, but can be almost two years, as *sui* counts people as one at their birth and two on the next New Year's Day.

CHRONOLOGY OF IMPERIAL CHINA
WITH AUTHORS OF AUTOBIOGRAPHIES

Shang (ca. 1500–1045 BCE)

Zhou (1045–256 BCE)

    Warring States period

       (475–221 BCE)

Qin dynasty (221–206 BCE)

Western Han (202 BCE–9 CE)

    Emperor Wu (r. 141–87 BCE)

Eastern Han (25–220 CE)

    Wang Chong (27–ca. 97 CE)

    Zheng Xuan (127–200)

    Cai Yan (ca. 177–ca. 249)

    Cao Cao (155–220) and his son

       Cao Pi (187–226)

Three Kingdoms period (220–265)

    Zuo Fen (ca. 253–300)

Western Jin (265–316)

Eastern Jin (317–420)

Southern Dynasties (317–589)

    Emperor Wu (r. 502–549)

    of the Liang

Northern Dynasties (386–581)

    Northern Wei (386–534)

Sui dynasty (581–618)

Tang dynasty (618–907)

    Han Yu (768–824)

    Bai Juyi (772–846)

    Lu Guimeng (ca. 836–881)

Five Dynasties (907–960)

Liao dynasty (916–1125)

Song dynasty (960–1279)

    Northern Song (960–1126)

    Liu Kai (948–1001)

    Han Qi (1008–1075)

    Southern Song (1127–1279)

    Lou Yue (1137–1213)

    Yelü Chucai (1190–1244)

    Yuan Haowen (1190–1257)

Yuan dynasty (1234–1368)

    Wen Tianxiang (1236–1283)

    Xie Yingfang (1296–1392)

Ming dynasty (1368–1644)

    Tan Yunxian (1461–1556)

    Xu Wei (1521–1593)

    Ai Nanying (1583–1646)

    Madame Zhong (fl. 1570–1620)

    Chen Qide (fl. 1640s)

Qing dynasty (1644–1912)

    Pu Songling (1640–1715)

    Luo Fenpeng (b. 1726)

    Wang Huizu (1730–1807)

    Zeng Guofan (1811–1872)

    Liu Tang (1844–1929)

CHINESE
AUTOBIOGRAPHICAL
WRITING

INTRODUCTION

Today, the memoir is a very common form of literature. Celebrities of all sorts—performers, athletes, novelists—write accounts of their lives before and after gaining fame. Aspiring politicians write about their lives to introduce themselves to potential supporters. Those who complete terms as president generally write memoirs of their time in high office and how they managed crises and opportunities. Those who served under them also often write about their experiences, evidence that facts are slippery—people remember the same event differently, even when they were in the same room, and readers must always consider the possibility of self-serving distortions. Today even relatively unknown people write about their lives, knowing that there are readers interested in compelling stories written in the first person, especially if they bring them into worlds quite different from their own. Humorists, too, often draw extensively on their own experiences, making fun not of families or workplaces in general but the family or workplace they had to put up with. Memoirs today are often book-length, but magazines and newspapers regularly publish shorter pieces that are written in the first person. Reporters, for instance, when covering wars or catastrophes, regularly put themselves in the story, reporting where they were, what they saw, whom they talked to, trying to convey the moment they lived through. The popularity of this sort of writing, which draws attention to the author as a person, reflects modern notions of the self and authenticity but also draws on Western literary traditions going back centuries. Early examples include such works as the *Letters* of Pliny the Younger and the *Confessions* of Saint Augustine.

In China before modern times, it was less common for authors to write book-length memoirs or even to write shorter pieces that center on their own thoughts, feelings, and experiences. But the personal accounts that were written are well worth reading. They differ in many regards from modern memoirs and have their own history of conventions, but they share some of the immediacy of personal testimony that we expect from memoirs. They help us understand notions of self, interpersonal relations, and historical events. Of course, like memoirs today, they need to be read critically. Not every piece that presents itself as a person's own account should be taken at face value, and people writing about themselves are not always fully honest.

Many excellent examples of Chinese autobiographical writing have already been translated into English and are widely available (a list is included as an appendix). The central goal of this volume is to make more such personal accounts accessible to readers of English. The pieces selected for translation belong to many literary genres—poetry, letters, diaries, brief anecdotes, reports, confessions, prefaces or postfaces to books, self-written funerary biographies, not to mention a few works explicitly identified as autobiographies. In choosing pieces to translate, we looked above all for engaging works that draw us into the past or provide vivid details of life as it was lived. Some focus on a person's entire life, others on a specific moment. Some have an element of humor; others are entirely serious. In our choices we put a priority on capturing the diversity of what survives: pieces from different periods, different genres, by both men and women, by more obscure people as well as more famous ones. We also looked for pieces that would help illuminate the history and conventions of writing about oneself in the Chinese tradition. For the earliest period, we retranslated pieces that already were available in English in order to illustrate key facets of the development of ways of writing about oneself, many of them relatively short, but for later periods, with more works available, we have chosen pieces not previously translated, some of them substantially longer.

In this book, each selection begins by introducing the author and the piece. Readers will want to keep in mind the circumstances of the author and his or her purposes in writing. To help readers place it within the larger Chinese tradition of writing about oneself, basic features of that tradition are sketched below. Key developments took place in the Zhou and Han periods, but much more survives from later periods, as rising literacy, the expansion of the printing industry, and the flourishing of literati culture encouraged more people to write about their personal experiences and made preservation of their writings more likely.

Writing about Oneself in Verse

Perhaps the most common way to express one's innermost thoughts was through poetry. Many of the poems in *The Classic of Poetry* (Shijing) can be read as expressions of personal feelings or experiences, but we rarely know anything about the author outside the poem itself. A new stage was reached with the poems traditionally attributed to Qu Yuan (ca. 340–278 BCE), an aristocrat in the state of Chu who lost the favor of his king and eventually killed himself. "Sorrow" (Lisao) is taken to represent his laments about his fate, his defense of his virtues, and his attacks on those who defamed him. Whether or not actually written by Qu Yuan, the poem is ranked as a masterpiece and read as an expression of personal feelings. Among its best-known lines are "Long did I sigh and wipe away tears, sad that men's lives lay in such peril" and "On and on stretched my road, long it was and far, I would go high and go low, in this search that I made."[1] Both have been understood as the poet's passionate expression of his lofty aspirations.

Poetry remained a dominant genre for writing about oneself well into the nineteenth century. Many examples could be cited, among them quite a few by women writers, beginning with three in the Han period (202 BCE–220 CE), Ban Zhao (45–117), Ban Jieyu (Consort Ban, 48 BCE–2 CE), and Cai Yan (Cai Wenji, ca. 177–ca. 249). Ban Zhao was born to one of the most prominent scholarly families of the Eastern Han (25–220). She is best known for serving as adviser to the palace ladies; helping her father, Ban Biao (3–54), and brother Ban Gu (32–92) finish *History of the Han* (Hanshu); and authoring *Lessons for Women* (Nüjie), one of the most important texts for women's education in imperial times. In the history of autobiographical writing, Ban Zhao's *Rhapsody on a Journey to the East* (Dongzheng fu) occupies an important place. The rhapsody (fu) depicts a trip she took with her son in 113 when he was assuming a position in Henan. Ban wrote:

Now, in the seventh year of Eternal Renewal
I accompanied my son on his eastern journey.
On an auspicious day in the first month of spring
We chose a good time and set out on our way.

I then lifted my foot and climbed into the carriage
And that night we lodged in the town of Yanshi.

Leaving our friends there, we headed for strangers,
My mind was disturbed and my heart full of grief.
By the time dawn broke, I'd still not been able to sleep,
And my lingering heart still refused to obey.

After describing her reluctance to leave the capital, Ban describes the changes of scenery, the hardships she endured, and the sufferings of the common people that she witnessed. Ban Zhao recalls Confucius's misfortunes on the road and declares that "great virtue will never decay." At the end of the rhapsody, she adds, "The Classics and Canons teach only one thing: The Way and its virtue, humanity and wisdom."[2]

Ban Zhao perhaps wanted to avoid seeming to feel too sorry for herself. Her great-aunt, Consort Ban, a century earlier, had shown no such reluctance. Once favored by Emperor Cheng (r. 32–7 BCE), she became the target of other consorts. Afraid that she might be framed through palace politics, she asked to serve the empress dowager instead of the emperor. Her "Self-Mourning Rhapsody" (Zishang fu) starts with her entrance into the palace and selection as the emperor's favorite, then depicts her determination to follow the examples of the virtuous women in the past and her grief over losing a son. The focus of her writing, however, is on her sad, solitary life after demotion:

My mind dissolves in this place so silent,
If you do not grace me, who is my glory?
I gaze down at the vermilion steps,
And imagine Your embroidered shoes.
I gaze up at Your mist-covered house,
And tears course down my cheeks.[3]

Consort Ban's rhapsody is one of the earliest pieces in the tradition of the lament of the neglected woman (often, in later times, written by men in the voice of a woman). Another Han woman, Zhuo Wenjun, the wife of the famous scholar Sima Xiangru, was credited with contributing to this topic in her own words. Years after Zhuo, a widow, eloped with Sima, an event that made them celebrities, Sima decided to take a concubine. Disheartened by her husband's "betrayal," Zhuo composed "White Hair Lament" (Baitou yin), in which she bemoaned:

As brilliant as the snow on yonder mountain,
As splendid as the moon amidst the clouds—
I have been told that you now love another,
And so I've come to say goodbye forever.

....

How sad and lonely, oh, how sad and lonely!
When one gets married, there's no need to cry:
Just hope to find a man who'll always love you,
And will not leave you when your hair turns white.[4]

Several of our selections build on this tradition of using poetry to narrate defining moments or dramatic events in women's lives. Selection 7 includes two poems attributed to Cai Wenji, a woman captured by the Xiongnu and later able to return but without her sons. Selections 9 and 23 are by neglected consorts, Zuo Fen in the Western Jin and Consort Zhong in the Ming. Men were just as active. Among the works of Tang and Song poets are thousands of works with "self" (*zi*) in the title (such as laughing at myself, warning myself, pitying myself, and so on). Su Song (1020–1101) offers a good example. One of his autobiographical poems has a long title: "For many years, my request for retirement was refused, but a recent imperial edict granted me a sinecure position and I returned home. Living in leisure and having little to do, I thought back over my whole life and was moved to write a hundred-line poem. I have done this to enable my sons and grandsons to understand what I have lived through. I also intend this poem to serve as family instructions. For this reason, I have chosen to use plain language." Three-fourths (74 out of 100 lines) of the poem recollects Su's life from boyhood to retirement, touching on his studies, travels, official appointments, mourning his parents, and imperial favors.

Many other Tang and Song poets used verse to depict their daily life, joy and grief, family and friends, travels and spiritual life, and career and pursuits. They muse over the most personal, private, enjoyable, embarrassing, or regretful moments of their lives and sometimes address weighty topics such as poverty, career setbacks, death, and old age (see selection 15).

Recounting One's Life as a Preface or Postface to a Book

The earliest autobiography presented as a supplement to a book was written by China's first great historian, Sima Qian (145–ca. 86 BCE). The last chapter of his monumental *Historical Records* (Shiji) recounts his own story. He starts with his family's glorious past, rich traditions of scholarship, and his own early education. Sima then details his extensive travels to different parts of China in his twenties and later as an official during Emperor Wu's (r. 141–87 BCE) reign. Above all, Sima Qian highlights his role and that of his father, Sima Tan, as court historians; their ambition to write a general history of China; and the structure of The *Historical Records*. One episode of Sima's self-narration has remained powerful and memorable. It features a conversation between the father and son at the father's deathbed, when Sima Tan entrusted Sima Qian with his writing project. Sima Qian wrote, "I bowed my head and wept, saying, 'I, your son, am ignorant and unworthy, but I shall endeavor to set forth in full the reports of antiquity that have come down from our ancestors. I dare not be remiss.'"[5] Both the father and son understood this undertaking as a filial gesture from a son to his father and the duty of a historian.

Later authors often took advantage of the precedent set by Sima Qian to write about themselves at the beginning or end of a book they wrote. Many are included in this book (selections 5, 8, 10, 18, 20, 22, and 27). Clearly, taking advantage of the completion of a book to write about oneself remained attractive to writers throughout the imperial period. We do not include perhaps the most famous example, Li Qingzhao's (1084–ca. 1115) "Afterword to *Records on Metal and Stone*," as it is already available in multiple excellent translations (see the appendix). Today it is often cited in discussion of female talent and marital relations.

Adapting Conventions of Biography

Chinese autobiographical writing also is heavily indebted to the biography tradition. Here the great figure is once again Sima Qian, who established biographical accounts (*zhuan*) as a legitimate and powerful form of historical writing. Seventy of the 130 chapters of *Historical Records* contain biographies of about 150 individuals, some just a few lines long, others dozens of pages in length. Although the majority of Sima's subjects were rulers and their ministers, he compiled biographies of men and women notable for other achievements, ranging from philosophers and businessmen to assassins and private advisers. Biographical accounts in this tradition became standard features of dynastic histories and gazetteers in subsequent centuries.

From early on, this form was adapted by writers who wrote about themselves, often in an ironic or mocking tone. Here the most influential early work was by the Eastern Jin poet Tao Qian (Yuanming, ca. 365–427). Written in the last year of his life, Tao's "Biography of Master Five Willows" begins with the following sentences: "We don't know what age the master lived in, and we aren't certain of his real name. Beside his cottage were five willow trees, so he took his name from them."[6] It then lists the three things that were central to Tao's life: reading, drinking, and writing. In contrast to Sima Qian's commitment to politics, morality, family obligations, and scholarly achievements, Tao Qian focused on the individual and private life. Using plain language, he claimed to be contented with a simple life and indifferent to tangible gains and losses. Many of Tao's poems similarly projected himself as a wine-loving, carefree person in perfect harmony with his surroundings, nature, and the Way. Tao Qian also composed his own eulogy, writing as though he was already dead, in which he declared that, after a life following the Way, he left this world with no regrets. After imagining his own death and funeral, he concluded, "Life was truly difficult. I wonder how death will be?"[7]

Self-written biographies that followed in Tao Qian's tradition tended to avoid the author's real name and were customarily written in the third person. The use of the third person gave the author important narrative freedom. It also drew on the custom of acquiring multiple names: in addition to their given and courtesy names, traditional Chinese scholars often acquired one or more *hao* (sobriquets) at different stages of their lives. Tao Yuanming became known as Master Five Willows because of the willow trees next to his residence. Bai Juyi (772–846) entitled his autobiography "Biography of Master Drunken Poet" and Liu Kai "Biography of the Country Fellow of the Eastern Suburb" (selections 11 and 13). In the Song and later, some authors centered their accounts on their studio or residence, describing not only the physical structures but also their symbolic meanings. These accounts often highlighted the author's family and educational background as well as philosophical affiliations and spiritual life (selection 19).

Chinese biographical writing continued to develop and grow richer in later centuries, and these new developments continued to also shape autobiographical writing. Two important developments were the prominence of funerary biographies (especially funerary inscriptions, *muzhiming*) in Tang and Song times and the development of a form of book-long biographies organized year by year (*nianpu*) in the Song period. As writing funerary biographies for friends, relatives, and acquaintances became common among literati, some men, often in a humorous vein, drafted ones for themselves. An example included in this volume is Xu Wei's (1521–1593) "Self-Authored Funerary Biography" (selection 21).

In the Song period the first book-length biographies were written. These annalistic biographies were at first done for important Tang men of letters in an effort to associate their writings with what was going on in their lives when they wrote the piece, listing both events and literary works in chronological order, year by year. By the end of the Song period one prominent figure (Wen Tianxiang) wrote an autobiography using the year-by-year style. This became more common in the late Ming and especially the Qing periods. By then the authors did not have to be major writers and the events listed for each year could be relatively ordinary ones (see selection 26 for Wang Huizu's autobiography in this style).

Letters and Diaries

Personal letters afford authors opportunities to write about key events in their lives in a revealing manner. Sima Qian once again provided a model for later writers. In 98 BCE, Sima was imprisoned and later endured castration for defending the general Li Ling (134–74 BCE) following Li's defeat by and surrender to the Xiongnu, the Han's most formidable enemy. In a personal letter to Ren An, Sima Qian wrote:

> A man has only one death. That death may be as weighty as Mount Tai, or it may be as light as a goose feather. It all depends on the way he uses it.... It is the nature of every man to love life and hate death, to think of his relatives and take care of his wife and children. Only when a man is moved by principle is this not so. Then there are things he must do.... The brave man does not always die for honor, while even the coward may fulfill his duty. Each takes a different way to exert himself. Though I might be weak and cowardly and seek shamefully to prolong my life, yet I know full well the difference between what ought to be followed

and what rejected.... The reason I have not refused to bear these ills and have continued to live, dwelling among this filth, is that I grieve that I have things in my heart that I have not been able to express fully, and I am ashamed to think that after I am gone my writings will not be known to posterity.[8]

In order to achieve great things in life, Sima asserted, one should be ready to make large sacrifices.

In this volume, some of the earliest pieces included are letters that have been accidently preserved, dating to Qin and Han times (selection 4). These do not have the high drama of Sima Qian's letter, but do show that even ordinary letters help us imagine daily life in the past. We also have a letter from a prominent Confucian teacher and scholar, Zheng Xuan (127–200), to his son (selection 6). With the survival from late Tang on of individual authors' collected works, personal letters exist in great abundance. The literary giant Su Shi (1037–1101) left behind more than two thousand letters. They allow us to appreciate, among other things, the many gifts that he sent to relatives, his favorite foods, his coming to terms with living in exile, and his circle of friends. Another voluminous-letter writer, the Qing (1644–1911) statesman Zeng Guofan (1811–1872), wrote thousands of letters to family members, friends, and colleagues (selection 29).

The emergence of diary or journal writing provided another literary form for writing about one's experiences. Most of the earliest extant diaries were written to record observations made during trips and stress the author's first-hand knowledge. Several have been translated in full, among them Lu You's (1125–1210) A Journey into Shu (Ru Shu ji) and Fan Chengda's (1126–1293) Diary of a Boat Trip to Wu (Wuchuan lu). Here we have excerpts from Lou Yue's (1137–1213) diary of his trip to the Jin court (selection 16).

The Song period also witnessed the beginning of private journal writing. The historian and statesman Sima Guang (1021–1086), for example, kept a journal in the late 1060s and 1070s. His focus was on the major events at Emperor Shenzong's (r. 1067–1085) court, including announcements, appointments, promotions, examinations, and so on. Many of his contemporaries claimed to have maintained regular journal entries to help them remember more casual yet memorable aspects of daily life, such as gathering with friends, hearing an amusing story, or trying a new fruit. In Ming times, individuals committed to Confucian moral cultivation also often kept diaries full of self-reflection. They wrote of the temptations they faced, their thoughts and efforts to act in a right and responsible manner, aiming to monitor their shortcomings and their efforts to avoid them in the future. An early example is that of Wu Yubi (1392–1469), whose diary covers much of his adult life and records not just his efforts to improve himself but also his struggles to make ends meet as a teacher in a rural community.

The Testimony of Witnesses

There are many reasons people may bear witness. Sometimes they have observed a crime and report what they saw to the authorities. The authorities, in turn, can compel those accused of the crime to account for their own actions. The ones that are extant today usually began as oral statements, transcribed by government clerks. Here we include a few from the Qin, Han, and Tang periods that survived by accident (selection 2). Thousands more survive in the Qing government archives and have proven a rich source for historians doing research on rebellions, legal practice, marriage customs, and similar issues. These are usually fairly straightforward, perhaps reflecting the government clerk's editing. Normally, of course, the person testifying tries to make the best case for him or herself. Consider the 1748 confession of a tenant farmer charged with murdering a monk named Chengyuan who lived nearby.

> I'm from Lijiayuan of Xiaogan County and am fifty-five years old. My parents and my wife died a long time ago. I have only one son named Li Yifei and he left home to be a laborer in the seventh month of last year. The house I rented was returned to the original owner and since I had no place to live, I lived by myself in my brother Li Mingzhi's place. I made a living on my own. My brother is a trader and doesn't live at home. In his family, there's only my sister-in-law and nobody else.
>
> Originally I rented two *dou* of land from Chengyuan. We split the grain equally and I never owed him anything. In 1745, he suddenly refused to let me rent the land. I asked him several times but he wouldn't give in and I began to hate him. In the fall of 1746, I again begged him to be able to rent but he would not agree and said I was no good. I was really angry and had a quarrel with him but still never expressed my

anger. In the spring of 1747, he dug soil from my land to build up his paddy dike. We had another quarrel then. And so I hated him for a long time. Later he bought a few catties of wine to sell to others. I asked him if I could buy wine but he deliberately said he was sold out. Even though he had it, he refused to sell it to me. He was a monk! But he was an old, cunning, wicked man. He had no sense of compassion. He always insulted and bullied me. I really hated him and wanted to teach him a lesson. But I never had a chance, I couldn't do anything until the evening of the 26th day of the 8th month of 1747. I had had some drinks and ran into Chengyuan who was coming home from drinking. I saw he was a little drunk and then remembered all the mean things he'd done to me in the past. I got furious and under the influence of the wine wanted to hurt him. I figured that since he was an old man, was drunk and slept by himself, he would go to bed early that night and would not have any protection. I tied a rope made of bark around my waist and intended to strangle him in his sleep.

His confession then narrates many grizzly details of his hitting the monk with a club and an ax and trying to cover up his crime.[9] In this case it is easy to imagine that the tenant farmer did not say all of this as a monologue, but rather that the scribe made a single tale by stringing together his responses to the questions he was asked. For instance, to make it easier to convict him of premeditated murder, the investigator may well have repeatedly tried to get him to admit long-standing enmity between him and his victim.

Here we include a confession in a case that did not involve violence, but rather a type of fraud. An unsuccessful teacher dressed as an official and was able to get many people to offer him aid when they heard his hard-luck story (selection 25).

Another type of testimony is written accounts of what the author observed during times of disorder, especially war and natural calamities. Believing that there should be some record of the suffering or harrowing experiences they witnessed or learned about, they tried to get the basic facts down on paper. A well-known example is Wang Xiuchu's (17th c.) account of the slaughter of the population of Yangzhou during the Manchu invasion, "Ten Days in Yangzhou" (Yangzhou shiri). We include here writing by two key witnesses to the Mongol conquests of the Jin and the Song (selection 18). Their accounts are not as graphic, but they do help us imagine what living through these invasions could mean. In the case of Wen Tianxiang, he was an active player in the drama who had devoted himself to the probably impossible task of stopping the Mongols from conquering the Song.

Perceived social ills could also motivate men to write about what they learned, bearing witness against miscarriage of justice or inhumane treatment. An eighteenth-century example is Fang Bao's account of what he learned about the spread of disease in a Beijing prison. Natural disasters and the hardships they created also motivated some to put on paper what they had observed. The two authors whose records are included in selection 24 tried to appear as objective witnesses, recording what the larger population in their home region suffered during weather-induced famines without drawing attention to how the disaster impacted their own lives. We also have the account of a young man captured by rebels who recorded his experiences and what he learned of the rebels (selection 28).

Writing for Heirs

When an author wrote about himself in a book that he expected to circulate widely—either before or after the spread of printing—he was anticipating an audience for his words that included people he did not know. In daily life, of course, people are most likely to talk about themselves with people they are close to, especially, perhaps, their own family members. Fathers in China, as elsewhere, drew on their own experience when giving advice to their sons and grandsons, and some of them took to writing this down, a genre referred to in Chinese as "family instructions" (jiaxun). They could do this briefly in the form of a letter (such as the letter by Zheng Xuan included here, selection 6). In the sixth century, Yan Zhitui (531–591) wrote a full book directed to his descendants that provided advice on such subjects as avoiding political dangers and cultivating both Confucian and Buddhist virtues. He often supported his arguments with examples from his own eventful life. Here are a few examples:

> Some people let books pile up on their desk or allow the scrolls to scatter all over the place; their young children, maids, or concubines often get the books dirty; wind, rain, dogs, and mice may spoil them. This is truly a blemish on their virtue. When I read the writings of the sages, I have always treated them with solemn respect. If an old piece

of paper happens to contain phrases and principles of the Five Classics or the names of worthy men, I would not dare use it for irreverent purposes....

In our family, as you boys have seen, we do not ever speak of praying and making pleas to the gods through male or female spirit-mediums, nor do we ever resort to Daoist talismans and sacrifices. Do not waste your time on such ridiculous superstitions....

Education must be carried out early so as not to lose the opportunity. When I was seven *sui*, I memorized the "Rhapsody on the Hall of Numinous Brilliance," and even today I can still recite it if I review it once every ten years. As for the classics I read after turning twenty, I will forget them if I put them aside only for one month....

I once suffered from a loose tooth that was about to fall out; any cold or hot food or drink made it ache. I read about the method of preserving teeth in *Master of Embracing Simplicity*, that one should click one's teeth three hundred times every morning. I did it for a number of days and my tooth was healed. Now I do it constantly. Such minor techniques are completely innocuous and you may very well try them....

The sons and daughters of my family, even during their early childhood, are drilled and corrected little by little. If they ever pronounce one thing wrong, I consider it my fault. As for objects and vessels made in our household, I will not presume to name them arbitrarily without consulting books and records first, as you boys know well....

You should pay some attention to the formal script and the draft script.... Since my early childhood I have followed our family tradition [in calligraphy]; in addition, I am fond of the art and value it. Thus I have seen many model calligraphies and also spent considerable time on appreciation and practice. Even though in the end I am unable to achieve excellence, it is simply because I have no talent for it.[10]

As there are two full translations of this important book, we do not include any extracts from it here. But we do have a set of letters from the leading nineteenth-century political figure Zeng Guofan (1811–1872) (selection 29) to his son that while filled with details of what was happening in the military campaigns clearly keeps in mind that he is addressing a family member he hopes to have an influence on. He brings in his own experience that he sees as most relevant to his son's moral and intellectual development.

Recounting Relations with Loved Ones

The individual self does not develop in isolation but rather is fashioned within a nexus of personal relations: relations to parents, siblings, other relatives, friends, teachers, colleagues, lovers, and even sometimes enemies. Thus, authors who wrote about their relationships with people they were close to might reveal as much about themselves as about the subjects of their essays. Poetry provides us with the richest material about intimate relations between loved ones. A good example is the numerous exchanges between the most famous brothers in Chinese history, Su Shi (1037–1101) and Su Zhe (1039–1112). In a poem entitled "In Response to Ziyou's [Su Zhe] Poem on Suffering from Cold Weather," Su Shi describes the closeness he felt toward his younger brother and Su Zhe's unrivaled place in his heart, even though the two spent most of their adult lives away from each other.

> Human beings live less than a hundred years.
> You and I have spent three years apart.
> How many more three years do I have?
> Once gone, I'll never get them back.
> I fear that our separation
> Is speeding up the aging of my face and hair.
> In the past, I loved to write letters,
> Ever since we parted, I haven't finished anything.
> Thinking back on all the fun we had together,
> I realize today's sorrow was inevitable.
> Socializing with the leading talents in the world,
> Means less to me than sharing a good time with you.
> I am envious of your long period without official duties,
> Having spent so much time reading, lice live in your felt rug.[11]

Many elegies and funerary biographies can be read as personal accounts in addition to accounts of others. In this volume we have an elegy by Han Yu for his nephew and two by Han Qi for friends that can be read this way (selection 12). We also have a tribute a woman wrote for her husband and one a man did for his elder sister (selection 27). These are all relatively short. Better known are two considerably longer works written by men in the seventeenth and eighteenth century for women they were very close to. The first is Mao Xiang's (1611–1693) *Reminiscences of the Plum Shadows Convent* (Yingmei an yiyu), about his relationship with the courtesan Dong Bai, who died at the age of twenty-eight. The other memoir that can be read as a love story is Shen Fu's (1763–1808?) *Six Records of a Life Adrift* (Fusheng liuji), in which he describes his life with his wife Yun and their many trials and tribulations, including estrangement from his parents.

....

Altogether, this book contains works by fifty authors grouped into twenty-nine selections. The earliest, dated to the Western Zhou (1046–771 BCE), is a short bronze inscription, and the last, from the 1850s and 1860s, is a set of letters by the Qing statesman and scholar Zeng Guofan. Less than half of the authors were people of national stature based on their political, literary, or scholarly credentials; at the other end, a few of the authors are known solely from the piece we translate. Only nine pieces were written by women, which reflects the reality of literacy, education, and publishing. The three of us did all of the translations with four exceptions: selection 23, which was translated for this book by Zeyuan Wu; and three that had been previously published, selections 7, by Beata Grant and Wilt Idema; 9, by David Knechtges; and 25, by Mark McNicholas. Our own translations were fully collaborative, each of us going over the others' drafts and offering corrections and suggestions.

We invite readers to peruse these personal accounts in any order, as each can stand on its own. There is also an argument for reading them in chronological order, as that conveys a picture of Chinese history with individuals at the center and highlights cultural change by showing how people kept exploring ways to represent themselves in writing.

Notes

1. Translated in Stephen Owen, *An Anthology of Chinese Literature: Beginnings to 1911* (New York: W. W. Norton, 1996), 165, 169.

2. Wilt L. Idema and Beata Grant, *The Red Brush: Writing Women of Imperial China* (Cambridge, MA: Harvard University Asia Center, 2004), 23–25.

3. Idema and Grant, *The Red Brush*, 82.

4. Idema and Grant, *The Red Brush*, 111–12.

5. William T. de Bary and Irene Bloom, eds., *Sources of Chinese Tradition*, vol. 1 (New York: Columbia University Press, 2000), 370.

6. Owen, *An Anthology of Chinese Literature*, 314–15.

7. Owen, *An Anthology of Chinese Literature*, 616.

8. De Bary and Bloom, *Sources of Chinese Tradition*, 371–72. For more on this letter, see Stephen Durrant, Wai-yee Li, Michael Nylan, and Hans van Ess, *The Letter to Ren An and Sima Qian's Legacy* (Seattle: University of Washington Press, 2018).

9. Pei-kai Cheng, Michael Lestz, and Jonathan D. Spence, *The Search of Modern China: A Documentary Collection* (New York: Norton, 1999), 82–85.

10. Yan Zhitui, *Family Instructions for the Yan Clan and Other Works by Yan Zhitui (531–90s)*, trans. Xiaofei Tian (Boston: Walter de Gruyter, 2021), 49, 51, 135, 279, 401, 415.

11. Beijing Daxue Guwenxian Yanjiusuo, ed., *Quan Song shi* (Beijing: Beijing Daxue Chubanshe, 1986–1998), 14:788.9132.

Further Reading

Bauer, Wolfgang. "Time and Timelessness in Premodern Chinese Autobiography." In *Ad Seres et Tungusos: Festschrift für Martin Grimm zu seinem 65. Geburtstag am 25. Mai 1995*, edited by Lutz Bieg, Erling von Mende, and Martina Siebert, 19–31. Wiesbaden: Harrassowitz, 2000.

Chaves, Jonathan. *Every Rock a Universe: The Yellow Mountains and Chinese Travel Writing*. Warren, CT: Floating World Editions, 2013.

———. "The Yellow Mountain Poems of Ch'ien Ch'ien-i (1582–1664): Poetry as Yu-chi." *Harvard Journal of Asiatic Studies* 48, no. 2 (December 1988): 465–92.

Cochran, Sherman, and Andrew Hsieh. *The Lius of Shanghai*. Cambridge, MA: Harvard University Press, 2013.

Dolezelova-Velingerova, Milena, and Lubomir Dolezel, "An Early Chinese Confessional Prose: Shen Fu's *Six Chapters from a Floating Life*." *T'oung pao* 58, no. 1/5 (1972): 137–60.

Dryburgh, Marjorie, and Sarah Dauncey, eds. *Writing Lives in China, 1600–2010: Histories of the Elusive Self*. London: Palgrave MacMillan, 2013.

Durrant, Stephen. "Self as the Intersection of Traditions: The Autobiographical Writings of Ssu-ma Ch'ien." *Journal of the American Oriental Society* 106, no. 1 (1986): 33–40.

Fong, Grace. "Auto/biographical Subjects: Ming-Qing Women's Poetry Collections as Sources for Women's Life Histories." In *Overt and Covert Treasures: Essays on the Sources for Chinese Women's History*, edited by Clara Ho, 369–410. Hong Kong: Chinese University Press, 2012.

———. *Herself an Author: Gender, Agency, and Writing in Late Imperial China*. Honolulu: University of Hawaii Press, 2009.

———. "Inscribing a Sense of Self in Mother's Family: Hong Liangji's (1764–1809)

Memoir and Poetry of Remembrance." *Chinese Literature: Essays, Articles, Reviews* 27 (2005): 33–58.

———. "Private Emotion, Public Commemoration: Qian Shoupu's Poems of Mourning." *Chinese Literature: Essays, Articles, Reviews* 30 (2008): 19–30.

Fong, Grace, and Ellen Widmer, eds. *The Inner Quarters and Beyond: Women Writers from Ming Through Qing.* Leiden: Brill, 2020.

Grant, Beata. *Eminent Nuns: Women Chan Masters of Seventeenth-Century China.* Honolulu: University of Hawaii Press, 2009.

Hardie, Alison. "Conflicting Discourse and the Discourse of Conflict: Eremitism and the Pastoral in the Poetry of Ruan Dacheng (c.1587–1646)." In *Reading China: Fiction, History and the Dynamics of Discourse. Essays in Honour of Professor Glen Dudbridge*, edited by Daria Berg, 111–46. Leiden: Brill, 2007.

Hardy, Grant. *Worlds of Bronze and Bamboo: Sima Qian's Conquest of History.* New York: Columbia University Press, 1999.

Hargett, James M. *Jade Mountains and Cinnabar Pools: The History of Travel Literature in Imperial China.* Seattle: University of Washington Press, 2018.

Hawes, Colin S. C. *The Social Circulation of Poetry in the Mid-Northern Song: Emotional Energy and Literati Cultivation.* Albany: State University of New York Press, 2005.

Ho, Clara, ed. *Overt and Covert Treasures: Essays on the Sources for Chinese Women's History.* Hong Kong: Chinese University Press, 2012.

Holzman, Donald. *Poetry and Politics: The Life and Works of Juan Chi, AD 210–63.* Cambridge: Cambridge University Press, 1976.

Huang, Martin. *Literati and Self-Re/presentation: Autobiographical Sensibility in the Eighteenth-Century China Novel.* Stanford, CA: Stanford University Press, 1995.

Idema, Wilt L. "The Biographical and the Autobiographical in Bo Shaojun's *One Hundred Poems Lamenting My Husband*." In *Beyond Exemplar Tales: Women's Biography in Chinese History*, edited by Joan Judge and Hu Ying, 230–45. Berkeley: University of California Press, 2011.

Judge, Joan, and Hu Ying, eds. *Beyond Exemplar Tales: Women's Biography in Chinese History.* Berkeley: University of California Press, 2011.

Kindall, Elizabeth. *Geo-narratives of a Filial Son: The Paintings and Travel Diaries of Huang Xiangjian (1609–1673).* Cambridge, MA: Harvard University Asia Center, 2017.

Ko, Dorothy. *Teachers of the Inner Chambers: Women and Culture in Seventeenth Century China.* Stanford, CA: Stanford University Press, 1994.

Li, Wai-yee. *Women and National Trauma in Late Imperial Chinese Literature.* Cambridge, MA: Harvard University Asia Center, 2014.

Li, Xiaorong. *Women's Poetry of Late Imperial China: Transforming the Inner Chambers*. Seattle: University of Washington Press, 2012.

Lu, Weijing. *Arranged Companions: Marriage and Intimacy in Qing China*. Seattle: University of Washington Press, 2021.

——. "Personal Writings on Female Relatives in the Qing Collected Works." In *Overt and Covert Treasures: Essays on the Sources for Chinese Women's History*, edited by Clara Ho, 411–34. Hong Kong: Chinese University Press, 2012.

Mann, Susan. *Precious Records: Women in China's Long Eighteenth Century*. Berkeley: University of California Press, 1997.

McDowall, Stephen. *Qian Qianyi's Reflections on Yellow Mountain: Traces of a Late-Ming Hatchet and Chisel*. Hong Kong: Hong Kong University Press, 2009.

Owen, Stephen. "The Self's Perfect Mirror: Poetry as Autobiography." In *The Vitality of the Lyric Voice: Shih Poetry from the Late Han to the T'ang*, edited by Shuen-fu Lin and Stephen Owen, 71–102. Princeton, NJ: Princeton University Press, 1986.

——. "Wit and the Private Life." In *The End of the Chinese "Middle Ages": Essays in Mid-Tang Literary Culture*, edited by Stephen Owen, 83–106. Stanford: Stanford University Press, 1996.

Richter, Antje. *Letters and Epistolary Culture in Early Medieval China*. Seattle: University of Washington Press, 2013.

Shields, Anna M. "Words for the Dead and the Living: Innovations in the Mid-Tang 'Prayer Text' (Jiwen)." *Tang Studies* 25 (2007): 111–45.

Smith, Paul Jakov. "Impressions of the Song-Yuan-Ming Transition: The Evidence from *Biji* Memoirs." In *The Song-Yuan-Ming Transition in Chinese History*, edited by Paul Jakov Smith and Richard von Glahn, 71–110. Cambridge, MA: Harvard University Asia Center, 2003.

Spence, Jonathan. *Return to Dragon Mountain: Memories of a Late Ming Man*. London: Quercus, 2008.

Struve, Lynn A. "Confucian PTSD: Reading Trauma in a Chinese Youngster's Memoir of 1653." *History and Memory* 16, no. 2 (2004): 14–31.

——. "Dreaming and Self-Search during the Ming Collapse: The Xue Xiemeng Biji, 1642–1646." *T'oung Pao* 92 (2007): 159–92.

——. "Self-Struggles of a Martyr: Memories, Dreams, and Obsessions in the Extant Diary of Huang Chunyao." *Harvard Journal of Asiatic Studies* 69, no. 2 (2009): 73–124.

Waltner, Ann. "Life and Letters: Reflections on Tanyangzi." In *Beyond Exemplar Tales: Women's Biography in Chinese History*, edited by Joan Judge and Hu Ying, 212–29. Berkeley: University of California Press, 2011.

Wang, Yanning. *Reverie and Reality: Poetry on Travel by Late Imperial Chinese Women*. Lanham, MD: Lexington Books, 2013.

Wells, Matthew. *To Die and Not Decay: Autobiography and the Pursuit of Immortality in Early China.* Ann Arbor, MI: Association of Asian Studies, 2009.

Widmer, Ellen. "Women as Biographers in Mid-Qing Jiangnan." In *Beyond Exemplar Tales: Women's Biography in Chinese History,* edited by Joan Judge and Hu Ying, 246–61. Berkeley: University of California Press, 2011.

Widmer, Ellen, and Kang-i Sun Chang, eds. *Writing Women in Late Imperial China.* Stanford, CA: Stanford University Press, 1997.

Wriggins, Sally Hovey. *The Silk Road Journey with Xuanzang.* Rev. ed. Boulder, CO: Westview, 2004.

Wu, Pei-yi. "Self-Examination and Confession of Sins in Traditional China." *Harvard Journal of Asiatic Studies* 39, no. 1 (1979): 5–38.

———. *The Confucian's Progress: Autobiographical Writings in Traditional China.* Princeton, NJ: Princeton University Press, 1989.

Zhang, Cong Ellen. *Transformative Journeys: Travel and Culture in Song China.* Honolulu: University of Hawaii Press, 2010.

1

....

A SON'S TRIBUTE TO HIS MOTHER
An inscription on a bronze vessel (10th c. BCE)

....

This inscription on a tenth-century BCE bronze vessel recounts a successful campaign against a neighboring Rong tribe. The leading commander dedicated the vessel to his mother in gratitude for her guidance and protection.

Ancestor worship was a central religious practice in China from early times. During the Shang dynasty (ca. 1500–1045 BCE), pleasing and seeking instructions from the ancestors dominated every aspect of Shang society, and both male and female ancestors were assigned a date to be worshipped individually. With the Zhou dynasty (1045–256 BCE), patrilineal principles took priority and attention to female ancestors declined. While 97 percent of Shang dynasty sacrifices to a mother honored her in her own right, during the Western Zhou, this figure dropped to 64 percent. By the Han dynasty, female ancestors rarely received individual sacrifices.

The inscription on the bronze vessel known as the *Dong gui* is one of the longest dedicated to a mother from the Shang or Zhou period. The narrator, Dong, had the bronze food vessel made to "express his filial piety," evidence that the ideal of filial piety was firmly established by the tenth century BCE.

The importance of women in ancestor worship may have declined over time, but the moral principle of filial respect for mothers, so vividly reflected in this text, persisted throughout Chinese history.

This inscription can also be read as an autobiographical account. Dong tells us not only the date, locations, opposing forces, and weapons of the battles he waged but also how he felt about fighting them. From the list of the war spoils, we learn something of the hostility between the Zhou kingdom and its neighboring states, the scale of the battles, the types of weapons involved, and the disposal of the dead and the captives. At the time, it was a common practice that the severed heads of those killed in battle were brought back to be presented to ancestors during worship ceremonies, during which many of the captives would also be sacrificed.

Dong *Gui*

On the first day of the sixth month, the day of *yiyou*, at the Tang encampment, the Rong attacked [illegible]. I, Dong, led the supervisors and marshals to chase them a long distance. We stopped the Rong at Yulin and fought them off at Hu. My magnificent mother saw to everything, guiding my heart and protecting my body, enabling me to resolutely defeat the enemy. We returned with one hundred severed heads, two prisoners of war, and 135 of the enemy's weapons and other equipment, including shields, spears, daggers, bows, quivers, arrows, garments, and helmets. We also brought back 114 Rong captives. All through the battle, my body was never harmed. I clap my hands and kowtow repeatedly in gratitude and praise my magnificent mother's blessings and glory. I made this precious *gui* vessel for my magnificent mother, whose worship day is on the *geng* day. It will bless her son to live ten thousand years and to express his filial piety by presenting sacrificial offerings to the magnificent mother day and night. May my sons of sons and grandsons of grandsons use and cherish it.

SOURCE: Institute of Archaeology, Chinese Academy of Social Sciences, *Yin Zhou jinwen jicheng* 殷周金文集成 (Beijing: Zhonghua Shuju, 2007), #4322. Another version of the translation can be found in Constance A. Cook and Paul R. Goldin, eds., *A Source Book of Ancient Chinese Bronze Inscriptions* (Berkeley, CA: Society for the Study of Early China, 2016), 69.

Further Reading

Brashier, K. E. *Ancestral Memory in Early China*. Cambridge, MA: Harvard University Press, 2011.

Li Feng. *Early China: A Social and Cultural History*. Cambridge: Cambridge University Press, 2013.

Rosemont, Henry, and Roger T. Ames. *The Chinese Classic of Family Reverence: A Philosophical Translation of the Xiaojing*. Honolulu: University of Hawaii Press, 2009.

Zhou, Yiqun. "The Status of Mothers in the Early Chinese Mourning System." *T'oung pao* 99, nos. 1–3 (2013): 1–52.

2

....

CRIME AND PUNISHMENT
Personal testimony given in four legal cases
(3rd–2nd c. BCE)

....

These accidentally preserved case records include personal
testimony written down by scribes, providing glimpses
of ordinary people's lives.

From early times, even ordinary people were asked to tell their own stories or
account for themselves in legal disputes. Victims, witnesses, and the accused
would give oral testimony of what occurred. Bureaucratic practice necessi-
tated making written records of their testimony, and in rare instances this has
survived. Although one must often wonder to what extent coercion shaped
the testimony, surviving examples do provide glimpses of how people unable
to write presented themselves to others in words.

The earliest surviving case records date to the Qin and Han periods.
Although the Han dynasty turned away from the harshest features of Qin
Legalism, it retained much of its legal system. Offenses punishable by law
ranged from immorality to theft, bodily harm, and defiance of the civil authority. Punishments included exile, hard labor, flogging, castration, and
death. The Han law code, like its Qin predecessor, allowed nobles, officials,
and their family members to have their penalties reduced by giving up their

titles or property. Legal documents unearthed during the second half of the twentieth century show that both dynasties developed complex and sophisticated procedures to ensure full review of the sentencing process.

In this selection, we present four legal cases that record personal testimony by those involved. The first three cases were included in a bamboo strip text discovered in a 217 BCE tomb in Shuihudi, Hubei, for a Qin administrator. The text, titled "Forms for Sealing and Investigating" (Fengzhen shi), consists of twenty-three cases to use as precedents for conducting investigations. These documents recorded personal narratives by the accusers, the accused, and the investigators, and they show that by Qin times, a son's filial piety had become so imperative that he would be harshly punished if his father filed a formal complaint against him and that Qin women could file criminal reports on their own.

The fourth document is from *The Book of Submitted Doubtful Cases* (Zouyan shu), a bamboo slip document discovered in 1983 in a Han official's tomb in Zhangjiashan, Hubei. The book contains twenty-one legal cases dating between 246 and 196 BCE. "Officials Zhuang and Xi Submitting a Doubtful Case" (Hu Zhang Cheng Xi gan yan an) shows that by the early Han, elaborate legal procedures were established to uphold the institution of marriage.

Three First-Person Accounts
in Shuihudi Qin Bamboo Strips

1. BANISHING A SON

Transcript: A, a commoner of X Village, said in his denunciation, "Request to have the foot of my own son, C, a commoner of the same village, amputated and to have him banished to a border county in Shu, with the injunction that he must not be allowed to leave the place of banishment. This is my statement." I inform the head of Feiqiu [modern-day Xingping, Shanxi, first stop from Xianyang to Shu], "The commoner from Xianyang, living in X Village, named C, has been adjudicated because his father, A, requested to have his foot amputated and have him banished to a border county in Shu, with the injunction that to the end of his life he not be allowed to leave the place of banishment. We have banished C according to A's denunciation. His family members are banished along with him, as the statute stipulated. Now we have amputated C's foot. We ordered officers and conscripts to carry out the transfer. They will carry travel permits and a case report and hand them over to the county clerk. Be sure to replace the clerks and the conscripts, and do so through successive prefectures up to Chengdu. In Chengdu, the case report is to be presented to the governor. He is to be fed according to the Statutes. Once the Feiqiu staff transfer him, a report is to be made." This I report to the head.

2. DENOUNCING A SON

Transcript: The commoner A of X Village said in his denunciation, "My, A's, own son, the commoner C of the same village, is unfilial. I request to have him executed. This I report." Forthwith the prefectural clerk E was ordered to go and arrest him. Transcript of prefectural clerk E's report: "Together with the prison bond servant X, I seized C; we caught him in the house of X." The assistant prefect X interrogated C; in his statement he said, "I am A's biological son; I have been truly unfilial toward A at home. I am currently not being prosecuted for any other crime."

3. A STILLBIRTH

Transcript: A, the wife of a commoner of X Village, made a denunciation, saying, "I, A, had been pregnant for six months. Yesterday, in the daytime, I fought with the adult woman C of the same village. C and I grabbed each other by the hair. C threw me on the ground. A fellow villager, the grandee of the first order D, came to the rescue and separated us. As soon as I had reached home, I felt ill and my belly hurt; by the evening, the child was stillborn. Now I have wrapped up the child, and I have come to bring it, to report it in person and to denounce C." Forthwith an order was given to the prefectural clerk X to go and arrest C. Immediately I inspected the baby's sex and whether it had grown hair, as well as the condition of the placenta. Furthermore, an order was given to a bondwoman who had several times given birth to inspect the blood coming out of her front part as well as the condition of her wounds. I also interrogated the members of A's household about A's situation when she had reached her house, as well as the circumstances of the pain in her belly and of the child's coming forth.

Transcript of the assistant prefect B's report: Order was given to the prefectural clerk X and bond servant X to inspect the child that A had brought along. Before, it had been wrapped in a hemp cloth; it had the appearance of congealed blood, as large as a hand; it was not recognizable as a child. When it had been placed in a basin with water and shaken, the clotted blood was recognizable as a child. Its head, body, arms, fingers, and from the thighs down to its feet and toes, all resembled those of a human being. Its eyes, ears, nose, and sex were not yet recognizable. When taken out of the water, it again had the appearance of clotted blood.

Another report [on the examination of the wound] says: An order was given to the bondwomen XX, who had several times given birth, to inspect A. They said, "There is dried blood on the sides of her front part. At present blood is still coming out of her, but [only] a little; it is not menstruation." One said, "When I once was pregnant and miscarried, I lost blood from my front part the same way as A did."

SOURCE: Shuihudi Qinmu Zhujian Zhengli Xiaozu, *Shuihudi Qinmu zhujian* (Beijing: Wenwu Chubanshe, 1978), 155, 156, 161–2. For other translations of these cases, see A. F. P. Hulsewé, *Remnants of Ch'in Law* (Leiden: Brill, 1985), 195, 196, 205.

Officials Zhuang and Xi Submitting a Doubtful Case

In the tenth year of Emperor Gaozu [197 BCE], on the *guisi* day of the seventh month, whose first day fell on a *xinmao* day, Magistrate Zhuang and Assistant Magistrate Xi of Hu County [Henan] dare to submit this case for decision by higher authorities:

The official accusation states, "Judiciary clerk Lan, from Linzi [Shandong], commanded the woman, Nan, to wear a man's cap of undyed silk, feign illness, and lie inside an official carriage. He appropriated the travel permit of grandee of fifth-order Yu and brought her out of the Hangu Pass without authorization."

Now, Lan stated, "Nan is a member of the [former] Tian royal family of Qi. She had been ordered to reside in Chang'an. I had been assigned to accompany her on her journey and married her as a legal wife. We were to return to Linzi. We had not yet exited the pass when we were caught." Everything else is as stated in the official accusation. Nan's statement was similar to the official accusation and to Lan's statement.

Lan was cross-examined: "You were not allowed by law to marry Nan as your legal wife but did it anyway and together with her were returning to

Linzi. This is a case of 'coming to lure' as well as 'engaging in illicit intercourse.' Nan is an absconding aristocrat, yet you 'hid her.' How do you explain this?"

Lan stated, "I was traveling to the capital on assignment for Nan's relocation, but then married her as my legal wife. It is not a case of 'coming to lure.' The officials consider this to be 'engaging in illicit intercourse' as well as 'hiding Nan as an absconder.' I am guilty of these charges; I have no excuse to give."

Lan was cross-examined: "One of the reasons the statutes prohibit people 'coming from the kingdoms to lure' is to prevent persons from one kingdom from marrying persons from another kingdom. Although you did not intentionally come to lure, in reality, you lured a person of Han to go to Qi; this, in fact, is 'coming from the kingdom to lure.' How do you explain this?"

Lan stated, "I am guilty. I have no explanation to give."

An inquiry was conducted; it is in the statements.

The case was tried; everything was carefully verified: that Lan had accompanied Nan for her relocation, married her as his legal wife, and together with her was returning to Linzi, and had not yet exited the pass, and was apprehended.

There is no doubt as to what crime Lan is guilty of. He has been detained. We suspended the sentencing and dare to submit this case to higher authorities for decision.

In another case, the private female slave named Qing assisted in the walling of Handan City in Zhao [Hebei]. Shortly after this work was done, she absconded and followed her older brother to the territory of Zhao, and that was judged as absconding and going to the kingdoms.

Now Lan had arrived because he had been assigned to transport a relocated person; then he "lured" Nan.

The commandery official deliberated: "The case of Lan and Qing belong to the same category. Lan's case should be treated as a case of 'coming from a kingdom to lure.'"

Another opinion was that "Lan's case should be treated as 'engaging in illicit intercourse' and 'hiding a person guilty of a crime that matches undergoing tattooing and being made a grain-pounder.'"

In the tenth year of Emperor Gaozu, on the *guihai* day of the eighth month, whose first day fell on a *gengshen* day, Gongshang Buhai, the minister of the imperial stables and acting chamberlain for law enforcement, informed the bailiff of Hu County, "Regarding the submitted doubtful case involving judiciary clerk Lan, the submitted doubtful case has been fully investigated and submitted to this court." The decision: "Lan should be tattooed and made a wall-builder. The other individual should be sentenced according to the statutes and ordinances."

SOURCE: Zhangjiashan 247 Hao Hanmu Zhujian Zhengli Xiaozu 張家山二四七號漢墓竹簡整理小組, *Zhangjiashan Hanmu zhuji (247 hao mu)* 張家山漢墓竹簡 (247 號墓) (Beijing: Wenwu Chubanshe, 2006), 93. For another translation of these texts, see Anthony J. Barbieri-Low and Robin Yates, *Law, State, and Society in Early Imperial China: A Study with Critical Edition and Translation of the Legal Texts from Zhangjiashan Tomb no. 247* (Leiden: Brill, 2015), 1199–201.

Further Reading

Barbieri-Low, Anthony J., and Robin Yates. *Law, State, and Society in Early Imperial China: A Study with Critical Edition and Translation of the Legal Texts from Zhang-jiashan Tomb no. 247*. Leiden: Brill, 2015.

Sanft, Charles. "Law and Communication in Qin and Western Han China." *Journal of the Economic and Social History of the Orient* 53, no. 5 (2010): 679–711.

Selbitschka, Armin. "'I Write Therefore I Am': Scribes, Literacy, and Identity in Early China." *Harvard Journal of Asiatic Studies* 78, no. 2 (2018): 413–76.

3

....

A HAN EMPEROR ACCEPTING
THE BLAME
Edict by Emperor Wu 武帝 (r. 141–87 BCE)

....

In the "Edict on Luntai," considered the first Rescript for Accepting
Blame in Chinese history, Emperor Wu recounts the failures of his
Central Asian campaigns against the Xiongnu.

Emperor Wu had one of the longest reigns in Chinese history. He presided
over a great expansion of Han territory, sending armies into Korea to the east,
Vietnam to the south, and Central Asia (the Western Regions) to the west.
Near the end of his reign, however, he had a change of heart. In 89 BCE, he
issued the "Edict on Luntai," rejecting his advisers' suggestion to establish
new agricultural colonies at Luntai in the Western Regions. In the edict, he
took responsibility for recent military failures and blamed himself for the
consequent suffering of the soldiers.

This edict established a precedent for the ruler to take the blame when a
policy failed or a natural calamity occurred, often as a way to deflect criticism. In the Han period alone, a total of eighty-two Rescripts for Accepting
Blame are recorded. In many cases, an official probably drafted the edict,
using conventional language, but the ruler had to consent to the wording. As
Emperor Wu's "Edict on Luntai" was the first of its kind, it is easier to imagine

it as conveying Emperor Wu's own feelings. Some see it as reflecting his turn toward Daoism in his late years.

Edict on Luntai

To shore up the funding for the frontiers, some officials proposed increasing the poll tax by thirty cash per person, which would have excessively burdened the old, weak, orphaned, and alone. Now they propose sending soldiers to set up an agricultural colony in Luntai [Xinjiang], which is located more than one thousand *li* west of Jushi [northwest of Turpan]. Previously, when Duke Kailing led the expedition to Jushi, the royal families of the six local kingdoms who lived in the Jushi capital quickly joined our side. They prepared livestock and food for the Han troops and raised armies of tens of thousands of troops. The princes served as generals and participated in the siege of Jushi, which led to the king of Jushi surrendering. After the armies of the six kingdoms were disbanded, they could no longer supply provisions for the Han army. When the Han army arrived at Jushi, there was still plenty of food, but the soldiers had not brought enough supplies for the subsequent military operation. As a result, the strong ones kept all the food and livestock for themselves while the weak ones died by the roadside by the thousands. I ordered Jiuquan [Gansu] to arrange a donkey and camel convoy to carry food supplies to meet the army at Yumen [Gansu] and to get officers and soldiers from Zhangye [Gansu] to handle the logistics. Even though the distance was not great, the soldiers became separated and many failed to reach their destination.

At first, the facts were kept from me. The military official Hong's memorial to the court stated that "the Xiongnu tied up a horse's four legs and left it outside of the city gate, with a note saying, 'This horse is a gift for the Chinese.'" In addition, the Xiongnu retained Han envoys and refused to let them return. Therefore, I sent General Li Guangli of Ershi [Osh, Kyrgyzstan] to attack the Xiongnu to secure the release of the Han envoys. In ancient times, when officials gave advice, they first had divinations performed and would not act if the results were not auspicious. At the time, I shared the letter on the tied-up horse with my top officials—the counselor-in-chief, imperial censors, all officials with a salary of two thousand piculs, all grand masters and scholars, even commandants of subordinate states and commanderies such as Cheng Zhong and Zhao Ponu. They said things like, "The barbarians tied up their own horse, which is an extremely bad omen," or "the Xiongnu want to look strong; they lack supplies but pretend to have plenty."

Divination based on *The Book of Changes* (Yijing) came back with the hexagram "Great Excess" as well as lines that indicated a flying dragon (imperial throne) and the Xiongnu's defeat. Military astrologists observed the stars and meteorological phenomena, and grand diviners conducted yarrow stalk and turtle shell divinations. All agreed that the results were auspicious: the Xiongnu would definitely be defeated; the timing was perfect and should not be missed. They also predicted, "As long as it is a general-led northern expedition, the Xiongnu will be defeated at the Fu Mountains." The divinations also pointed to General Li as the best choice for general. Therefore, I personally sent off General Li to the Fu Mountains, though I ordered him not to march too deep into the territory. With hindsight, we can see that the plans were wrong and divinations misinterpreted. The Xiongnu intelligence gatherer captured by Duke Chonghe reported, "Upon hearing that the Han military forces were coming, the Xiongnu leaders ordered shamans to bury sheep and cows by the roads and waterways where the Han armies would travel as a curse. Whenever the Chanyu [the Xiongnu ruler] gave the emperor a leather robe, he ordered the shamans to put a curse on it. The tied-up horse was intended as a curse against Han military action." A divination result showed "inauspicious" for a Han military general. The Xiongnu often say, "The Han Empire is large, but the Han people are incapable of resisting hunger and thirst. If we lose one wolf, they will lose a thousand sheep." Subsequently, General Li was defeated and many soldiers were killed and stranded. This has caused me no end of grief.

The current request to set up agricultural colonies and military fortresses in Luntai would greatly burden the empire without bringing any benefit to the people, making it totally unacceptable. The chamberlain for dependencies and others also suggested recruiting prisoners to accompany the Xiongnu envoys back to Xiongnu territory. They also proposed that we promise the title of duke to anyone who successfully assassinates the Chanyu as our revenge for the Li Guangli fiasco. Such a scheme is so appalling that it would have been shunned even by the five hegemons in the Spring and Autumn period. Besides, when Han subjects surrender to the Xiongnu, the Xiongnu often frisk and interrogate them. Currently, the borders are disorganized and there are no restrictions on border crossing. Officers, clerks, and soldiers who guard the border hunt animals and sell animal skin and meat to support themselves [so might inadvertently stray into Xiongnu territory]. The soldiers are hard-pressed and can barely maintain the beacon fire system. Nevertheless, previous reports to the imperial court made no mention of their miserable conditions. I learned about them only after reports from captured or surrendered Xiongnu.

We now should shore up our military defenses by prohibiting brutality, stopping unauthorized taxes, encouraging agriculture, and replenishing our supply of horses by offering tax incentives to those who raise them. Throughout the country, officials with pay above two thousand piculs should submit proposals for raising horses and increasing supplies at the border. They should send them to the court along with their routine reports.

SOURCE: Ban Gu 班固, *Hanshu* 漢書 (Beijing: Zhonghua Shuju, 1970), 96B.3912–14.

Further Reading

Bo, Chen, and Gideon Shelach. "Fortified Settlements and the Settlement System in the Northern Zone of the Han Empire." *Antiquity* 88 (2014): 222–40.

Cai, Liang. *Witchcraft and the Rise of the First Confucian Empire*. Albany: State University of New York, 2014.

Chin, Tamara T. *Savage Exchange: Han Imperialism, Chinese Literary Style, and the Economic Imagination*. Cambridge, MA: Harvard University Asia Center, 2014.

Di Cosmo, Nicola. *Ancient China and Its Enemies: The Rise of Nomadic Power in East Asian History*. Cambridge: Cambridge University Press, 2002.

4

....

LETTERS HOME
Three letters sent by ordinary men and women
(3rd c. BCE and 9th–10th c. CE)

....

*Three private letters that survive from the early imperial
period reveal bits and pieces of the lives and concerns
of ordinary people away from home.*

When people are separated for lengthy periods, they naturally crave news
from home. And such separations were not rare occurrences. The vast size of
the Qin and Han empires and the practice of universal conscription meant
that many men spent long periods away from home. Women who married
into families some distance from their own could also try to keep in touch
by sending letters.

This selection introduces accidentally preserved private letters from ordinary people to their relatives. Because the letters have not survived in
perfect condition, there are often gaps in what can be deciphered today,
but there is still much that can be learned from them. "Heifu and Jing's
Letter to Zhong and Mother," written on wooden strips and discovered in
a Qin dynasty tomb in Yunmeng, Hubei, is generally considered to be the
earliest extant "letter home." The second letter, "Zheng's Letter to Youqing
and Junming," from the Han period, and the third letter, "Second Daughter's

Letter to Home," from the ninth or tenth century, were written on silk and discovered among the documents found in a Dunhuang cave temple. Each can be read as a personal account, as they reveal close emotional bonds between the senders and their family members and their hometown friends and neighbors, as well as their experiences away from home. Brothers Heifu and Jing were part of the Qin conquest of the Chu state, yet their army provisions do not seem to have been sufficient, and the soldiers often ran out of money. Zheng, the author of the second letter, was frustrated by the fact that he had been stationed in the middle of nowhere for more than five years and had no hope for a transfer or promotion. Second Daughter, author of the third letter, was fascinated by the variety of silks she could find in the eastern capital. Taken together, these letters remind us that ordinary people may not have left behind poetry or travel diaries, but their letters allow us to piece together aspects of their lives.

1. Heifu and Jing's Letter to Zhong and Mother (ca. 223 BCE)

On the *xinsi* day, the second month, Heifu and Jing send their warmest greetings to Brother Zhong and Mother. How are you? We are both fine here. Recently we were separated, but now we are together again. Heifu begged me to see that this letter is delivered:

> Send Heifu cash, not summer clothes. Once this letter arrives, Mother, look in Anlu [Yunmeng, Hubei] for cheap silk cloth that can be made into an unlined skirt and shirt, which you should make and have sent here together with the cash. If silk cloth is too expensive, just send the cash, and I will buy cloth here and tailor them myself. We are stationed in Huaiyang [Henan] to attack rebel cities. I am not sure if I will be sick or injured during this tour. I hope that Mother will send enough provisions for me. When the letter arrives, please, all of you, reply. In the reply, be sure to say whether Xiang Jiajue has come or not. If he has not, please tell me what's going on. Have you heard whether Wang De is all right? Has Wang De bid farewell to Xiang Jiajue? When the letter and clothes arrive at the Southern Army . . .

> Give Aunt [father's elder sister], Elder Sister Kangle [possibly married], Eldest Aunt Gushu, and her husband . . . our sincere regards. . . . How are they? Give Sister at the eastern wing our sincere regards. We hope she is all right.

Give young Ying Fan our sincere regards. What has happened with that matter? Is it settled?

Give the elders of Lü Ying's family in Xiyang Lane and the elders of Yan Zheng's family in Bing Lane our sincere regards. How are they? Yin and Zheng are all fine here, though they have run out of money and clothes.

Jing gives his wife and daughter his sincere regards. How are you? My wife, do your best to look after our parents. Don't give... Yuanbai [possibly Jing's brother-in-law] does not know when he will be back. My wife, please do your best.

SOURCE: Chen Wei 陳偉, *Qin jiandu heji—shiwen zhushi xiudingben* 秦簡牘合集 · 釋文註釋修訂本 (Wuhan: Wuhan University Press, 2016), 1:2.592. For another translation of the letter, see Enno Giele, "Private Letter Manuscripts from Early Imperial China," in *A History of Chinese Letters and Epistolary Culture*, ed. Antje Richter (Leiden: Brill, 2015), 457–62.

2. Zheng's Letter to Youqing and Junming (Former Han Dynasty)

Zheng prostrates himself, bows repeatedly, and states:

Your Honors, Youqing and wife Junming, how are you? We have not seen each other for a long time. It is the hot season, and I prostrate myself to offer my sincere wish that Youqing and Junming clothe yourselves appropriately, eat enough food, and stay informed about the prefect's affairs. I have been stationed in Chengle [Shanxi] for more than five years and have not been transferred or promoted. The place is in the middle of nowhere, and transportation is minimal. My official position is insignificant, and my status low, so I cannot write you often. I kowtow in respect. Since a young colleague of mine, Wang Zifang, is now promoted to become an assistant to Duke Yuze of Dunhuang, I respectfully beg you to look after him.... [Yang] Junqian did not participate in the defense or stay in the northern border region. Therefore, when he returned, he did not submit a report. I kowtow in respect. Governor Mr. Ren got sick in the middle of the first month of the year and unfortunately passed away. Governor.... I often receive your admonition [letters] and know that your sons are all fine, which makes me feel very fortunate. I hereby respectfully send my greeting to your honors, Youqing and Junming.

Please convey my greetings to Brothers Zhangshi, Zizhong, and Shaoshi.

SOURCE: Yang Fen 楊芬, "Du Dunhuang boshu Zheng yu Youqin Junming shu zhaji" 讀敦煌帛書《政與幼卿、君明書》劄記, *Dunhuangxue jikan* 94, no. 1 (2011): 120. For another translation of the letter, see Enno Giele, "Private Letter Manuscripts from Early Imperial China," in *A History of Chinese Letters and Epistolary Culture*, ed. Antje Richter (Leiden: Brill, 2015), 442–44.

3. Second Daughter's Letter Home

... I have been away for a long time and miss you deeply. Unfortunately, we are separated by clouds and rivers... I long for you helplessly. The last month of summer is extremely hot ... I wish you good health and every comfort, as if I am serving you at your side. Outside... How have you been since we parted? I hope you are adapting to the change of seasons. Take great care of yourself. This is my humble wish.

Since leaving home, I, Er'niangzi, accompanied the imperial commissioner and minister of works of the Guiyi Circuit and arrived at the eastern capital, Luoyang, on the seventh day of the intercalary third month of this year. The trip went well. My stay here is also peaceful and pleasant; please do not worry from far away. Since the season is now at its most sweltering, I earnestly hope Mother and everyone else in the family rest well and eat regularly. Please do take it easy, and don't worry about me, Er'niangzi, here.

I am sending a piece of red brocade to Elder Sister as a gift; it is *tuan* brocade. The plain violet undergarment is also for Elder Sister. The half bolt of white damask silk is for Mother. I thought about sending other goods but worried that they might not reach you, so I do not dare to send them with this letter. Please forgive the paucity of my gifts. [Since I have been away for so long], I respectfully write this letter of greeting, though it is nowhere near sufficient.

Daughter Er'niangzi writes, with respectful bows to Mother, on the twenty-first day of the sixth month.

PS. As for my sister's sons, Mosi and Huaizhu, I assume they are well and happy. I am sending two pieces of red Tuanchao brocade and a small mirror as gifts for them.

SOURCE: Li Zhengyu 李正宇, "Anhuisheng bowuguan cang Dunhuang yishu Er'niangzi jiashu" 安徽省博物館藏敦煌遺書《二娘子家書》, *Dunhuang yanjiu* 69, no. 3 (2001), 91.

Further Reading

Richter, Antje. *Letters and Epistolary Culture in Early Medieval China*. Seattle: University of Washington Press, 2013.

——, ed. *A History of Chinese Letters and Epistolary Culture*. Leiden: Brill, 2015.

Rong, Xinjinag, and Imre Galambos. *Eighteen Lectures on Dunhuang*. Leiden: Brill, 2013.

Sanft, Charles. *Literate Community in Early Imperial China*. Albany: State University of New York Press, 2019.

5

········

A NATURAL PHILOSOPHER'S ACCOUNT OF HIS LIFE
Last chapter of his collected essays
by Wang Chong 王充 (27–ca. 97 CE)

········

In around 88 CE, the philosopher Wang Chong added
an account of his life to his philosophical treatise.

One of the earliest autobiographies in Chinese history was written by Wang Chong as the final chapter of his *Balanced Discussions* (Lunheng), best known for its analyses of natural phenomena. An original thinker, Wang Chong rejected key elements in the theory of correspondences between Heaven and mankind, popular among the Han intellectuals and favored by the Han court. He also denied the existence of ghosts and ridiculed commoners who believed in demons and other supernatural powers. Eager to debunk false-hoods, Wang wrote in an iconoclastic and combative style, earning him many enemies during his lifetime and a long list of detractors in later centuries. During the twentieth century, however, Western scholars saw in his skepticism harbingers of scientific thinking, and the Chinese Communist government celebrated him for his materialistic explanation of the origin of the cosmos, with its echoes of Marxist materialism.

From his biography in *History of the Later Han* (Hou Han shu), we learn that

Wang Chong was born to a poor family in Shangyu (Zhejiang) and studied at the Imperial University in Luoyang under the renowned Confucian historian Ban Biao (3–53). During his time in Luoyang, we are told, Wang Chong read widely while standing at bookstalls. He was assigned a few official positions but did not rise high due to his combative attitude toward his superiors and aloofness toward his colleagues. We also learn that in his later years, Wang Chong became very interested in the Daoist theory of qi and ways of prolonging life, hoping to live long enough to complete his mission of spreading "impartial" assessment of the cosmos.

Autobiography of Wang Chong

I, Wang Chong, am a native of Shangyu in Guiji [Zhejiang]; my courtesy name is Zhongren. My ancestors (family named Wangsun) hailed from Yuancheng in Wei Commandery [Hebei]; some branches used the family name Sun. Men of early generations joined the military, and because of their accomplishments, the family was enfeoffed in Yangting in Guiji. However, just a year later, the fief was suddenly rescinded. Nevertheless, the family settled down there and engaged in farming and sericulture. My great-grandfather was bold and wayward and did not get along with the local people. During a famine, he assaulted and killed people like a ruffian, making many enemies. As the dynasty was in turmoil, my grandfather Wang Fan worried that my great-grandfather would be abducted by those he had wronged, so he led the entire household to seek safety in Guiji. They settled down in Qiantang County, where he took up trade. He had two sons, the older one Meng, the younger Song. Song is my father. My ancestors had always been an unruly bunch, but it got worse in Meng and Song's generation. Both Meng and Song bullied people left and right. Eventually they feuded with local magnates like Ding Bo, so the family moved again to Shangyu.

I was born in the third year of the Jianwu reign period [27 CE]. In playing with other children, I was not inclined toward mischief. My friends loved trapping birds, catching cicadas, gambling, and climbing trees; I was the only one unwilling to join in, much to my father's amazement. My education began at the age of six. I was polite, honest, kind, obedient, and well mannered. Both serious and on the quiet side, I aspired to become a person of significance. My father never once flogged me, nor did my mother ever chastise me or my neighbors scold me. At the age of eight, I started school. There were more than a hundred boys there, and all of them were at times punished for their misbehavior or thrashed for their bad handwriting. I was the only one who not only made daily progress in learning to write but also did not commit any major offenses. Once I had learned to write, I bid farewell to that teacher and began to study *The Analects* (Lunyu) and *The Book of Documents* (Shangshu), reading aloud a thousand words a day. Once I understood the classics and ethical principles, I left my classics teacher and began my private studies. Everyone was amazed at my writing ability. The books I read became increasingly wide-ranging. Despite my many talents, I did not get sloppy, and even though I could talk eloquently, I preferred not to get into arguments. If there was no one around I considered worth talking to, I would stay silent all day. When people heard me talk, they often found my ideas bizarre at first, but by the time I had finished, I had won them over. Such was the way I developed my writing and cultivated my character.

I rose to be an administrator in the personnel department of a county, then held the same office under a chief commandant. Under a governor, I was one of the five chief administrators, with the added duty of overseeing affairs of the Personnel Department. At a prefecture, I was an aide. I was not interested in seeking fame, nor did I work for personal gain. I spoke often about people's strengths and rarely of their weaknesses. I especially recommended those scholars who had not had a career break and reprimanded only those who made mistakes after being promoted. If I found something reprehensible, I would not praise it. Yet if a mistake was not corrected, I would not condemn the offender any further. I could forgive people's grave mistakes and take pity on their minor errors. I aimed to be irreproachable but would never boast about it.

Wanting to establish my reputation on the basis of my conduct, I was ashamed that I was recognized mainly for my talents. In company, I would not speak unless spoken to. When superiors received me, I would not respond unless I was addressed. As a commoner, I modeled myself after Ju Boyu's [Spring and Autumn period] steadfastness in moral principles; at court, I tried to attain Shi You's [courtesy name Ziyu, Spring and Autumn period] honesty. When attacked, I did not make excuses, nor did I harbor resentment when passed over for promotion. Although I was too poor to have much of a house, I was more content than dukes or kings. My official positions were among the lowest, but to me, they were cushy ones. I did not celebrate when I was assigned an office nor resent it when I lost one. When life was comfortable, I did not indulge myself; nor did I give up hope when life was harsh. I found pleasure in ancient texts and loved to hear different opinions about them. Current books and popular theories tended to annoy me. Living alone, I thought hard about truth and reality.

I am honorable and serious by nature and selective in making friends, and I do not associate with people carelessly. If a person's conduct is admirable, even if his position is low or he is much younger than me, I definitely treat him as a friend. I love people with exceptional grace and have no interest in knowing people with poor taste. If mediocre people slander me behind my back for some insignificant mistake, I make no effort to explain myself, nor do I bear a grudge against them.

Some might say, "You are so talented, and your writings are so excellent. Why don't you defend yourself when you are falsely slandered? In the past, Yang Sheng's [d. 148 BCE] slanders sent Zou Yang [d. 120 BCE] to jail. Without defending himself, Zou would not have been released. Even though you have done nothing wrong, still you should not allow people to defame you. Furthermore, given your ability to clear yourself, you should certainly not let yourself be wrongly accused."

My response would be that this is to be expected: dirt only shows in clear water; only at high places does one feel danger; only large spaces can be shrunk; empty buckets have nothing in them to be taken. It is only natural that capable gentlemen are slandered. People defend themselves because they want to move up; people justify themselves because they are afraid of being demoted. Since I have no such desires or concerns, I choose to keep quiet. Yang Sheng probably made false accusations because someone made him do it; Zou Yang was probably pardoned because someone intervened. Confucius spoke of submitting to destiny, and Mencius talked of Heaven. People cannot control what may befall them, good or bad. The ancients knew this, so they attributed their lot to destiny or the times they lived in. This gave them peace of mind, as they had nothing to worry about or rail against. When they met good fortune, they did not think it was due to their own effort, nor did they blame themselves when misfortune fell. They felt neither proud when by chance their careers advanced nor discouraged when career setbacks occurred. They did not use straitened circumstances as a reason to seek wealth nor seek security because they dreaded danger. They did not trade their knowledge for salaries, nor did they decline positions to boost their reputations. They did not obsess over advancing their careers just to show off, nor did they blame others when demoted. To them, there was no big difference between safety and danger, life and death. They saw good fortune and adversity as equivalent, failure and success as similar. Therefore, even if they encountered ten Yang Shengs, they would say, "It does not matter." Realizing this, I leave everything to Heaven and have no need to explain anything.

I am a calm and mild-tempered person with no craving for wealth and power. If a higher-up recognizes me and promotes me ahead of others, I do not cling to my position. If a higher-up does not recognize me and demotes me unjustly, I do not let my low position bother me. None of the times when I was assigned as a county clerk did I ask for a transfer or decline the post. Someone might say, "Your mind is lofty, yet your actions are simple. You only befriend the like-minded and are not selective when it comes to assignments. Since this casts doubt on your integrity and conduct, how can you expect people to follow your model?" My response is that there is no better paragon of virtue than Confucius. Yet Confucius did not mind what official position he was offered. When he was a low-level clerk in charge of the staff at stables and granaries, he did not complain. Confucius was once the minister of works of the state of Lu, and during the peace treaty negotiations between Lu and Qi, he took on the role of a grand councillor, yet he did not appear overjoyed when making the arrangements. When the sage Shun was tilling the land in Lishan, he did not act as if this were temporary. When Yao abdicated and handed over responsibility to him, he acted as though it were nothing exceptional. We should worry about whether we are virtuous enough, not the respect we get. We should be ashamed if our names are blemished, not if our careers stagnate. Fine jade might be placed in a box of tiles, bright pearls in a bag of gravel; however, no one in the world would fail to distinguish these precious gems from the tiles or gravel. A person that the world recognizes for his goodness is esteemed no matter how low his place in society, just as someone occupying a high post can be held in disrepute. If a person conducts himself consistently no matter how high his position and preserves his character no matter what his social status, that should be enough.

Common people tend to admire the successful and ignore the failures. They fawn on the victor while snubbing the loser. When I was promoted to a powerful position, people attached themselves to me like ants, but when I was dismissed and lived in poverty, my old friends and acquaintances abandoned me. During my time of "retirement," I wrote a twelve-chapter book, *A Critique of Common Morality* (Ji su jie yi), in the hope that by reading the book, common people would gain insight. Toward that end, I wrote in a straight-forward style and used as many common words as possible. When someone criticized the work as shallow, I responded that quoting the classics to little kids or talking to country people using refined language does not enlighten them. On the contrary, it turns them off. When Su Qin [d. 284 BCE] lobbied at the Zhao court, his fancy words failed to convince the powerful Li Dui [fl. 295 BCE]. When Shang Yang [ca. 395–38 BCE] proposed adopting the way of the true king at the Qin court, Duke Xiao of Qin rejected his advice. This is because if you don't understand how a person thinks and feels, nothing you say can convince him, not even if you use the words of Yao and Shun. It is like giving a cow fine wine to drink or feeding a horse salted dried meat. Therefore, elevated and profound words are suitable only to the high and mighty, not the ordinary folk. People will not take your message to heart even if you force them to listen. When Confucius lost his horse in the countryside, local folk locked it up and refused to give it back. His disciple Zigong tried to get it back with fancy talk but only angered them. When Confucius's groom went and talked to them in country folk language, by contrast, things went fine. Common people only understand simple and concrete words. Forcing them to read something lofty and profound is like mixing an elixir to cure a cold or wearing a fur coat to fetch firewood or vegetables.

In addition, there are times when propriety is not a must and niceties can be omitted. To make a decision about someone who is clearly guilty, it is not necessary to call on sage Gao Tao [minister to Yao and Shun]. And to prepare a simple vegetable dish, there is no need for renowned chef Di Ya [Spring and Autumn period]. To entertain the common people, there is no need for majestic musical pieces such as *Shao* [enjoyed by Shun] and *Wu* [enjoyed by King Wu of the Zhou dynasty]. To worship a village god, there is no need to sacrifice a whole cow. What is unnecessary is also inappropriate, like carving a chicken with a cleaver for an ox, digging up wild vegetables with a long halberd, cutting chopsticks with an iron battle-ax, or using a large basin as a wine cup. Few would think the size was appropriate.

What is eloquence? Using common language to illuminate the profound. What is wisdom? Using simple language to explain difficult issues. The sages and the worthies were good at gauging the reader's ability, and they wrote accordingly.

I wrote *A Critique of Common Morality* because I deplored popular senti-ment. I also worried about the ruler's approach to governing, which was solely focused on controlling the people without understanding the right way to do it. After struggling with this, I still could not find the right path. Therefore, I wrote *On Government Affairs* (Zhengwu). I was also disgusted at the fact that most deceitful books and popular literature lack substance and truth, so I wrote *Balanced Discussions*. After the deaths of the sages, the interpretation of their works diverged, and with time, many scholars established their own schools. Even an erudite scholar could not judge these scholars' reliability simply by careful reading of their works. Their teachings were passed down haphazardly. Some were written down, others passed down orally, all more than a hundred years ago. With the passage of time, people began to think that since these are so old, they must be close to the truth. Such belief was so deeply rooted in their minds that they were not able to think otherwise. Therefore, I wrote this book [*Balanced Discussions*] to reveal the truth. Its contents are rich, its arguments combative. Furthermore, it examines and refutes every preposterous and specious argument. It eliminates empty words and preserves what is simple and solid. It corrects the loose language of this age and revives the honest customs of ancient times....

My official career has been a bumpy one, and the only thing I have accomplished is writing books to express my ideas. Some might jeer at me, "The great talents are respected because they do well in office, get important positions, have their opinions accepted, get things done, and have outstanding achievements. This is what people consider noble. Now you are down and out in the world; you were repeatedly demoted or dismissed from your posts. You had no opportunity to apply your talents to your official career or use your ability to fulfill official duties. Therefore, the only thing you can do is rack your brain and write essays and books. What good do fancy words do? What do you hope to get from your extensive writings?"

My response would be that no one was more talented than Confucius, yet his talents were not appreciated. He was expelled [by the ruler of Lu]; [a Song official] chopped down the tree [where he practiced rites with students]; [when a Qi assassin came for him], he ran for his life with washed rice [since he had no time to cook]; [for five days in the Kuang region of the Song], he was besieged; [in the state of Wei], his traces were obliterated; when he was tormented by hunger between the states of Chen and Cai, his disciples looked famished. Now my talents do not come anywhere near those of Confucius, and the hardships I suffered in employment do not equal his either, so why is it that I am despised? Besides, the successful are not necessarily wise, nor the distressed ignorant. If you meet someone who appreciates you, you thrive; otherwise, you languish. With good luck, a simpleton can achieve celebrity status; with bad luck, an outstanding man can find himself in dire straits. If you judge a person's talent and virtue based on his position, then those local officials and fief holders must have been more talented than Confucius and Mozi [470–391 BCE]. A person who has high official rank but low reputation, talks of purity but acts corruptly, has a high salary but does not possess one single virtue, this kind of person really deserves contempt. If someone possesses great virtue and a pure reputation but his official position is low and his salary meager, this is not the fault of his talents, and no one should be burdened by it. Scholars would love to share the hut with Yuan Xian [Confucius's disciple who was known to be upright and frugal] but are not eager to ride a chariot with Duanmu Ci [Confucius's disciple who was known to be an eloquent, rich merchant]; they would be happy to be Bo Yi's [Shang dynasty] companion but are not eager to share the road with [the bandit] Liu Xiazhi [Spring and Autumn period].

High-minded people cherish different things than ordinary people do, so the fame they seek is different from what the rest of the world seeks. Their bodies decay like grass and trees, but their reputations shine along with the sun and the moon. Their condition might be as down and out as Confucius's, but their writings are ranked with Yang Xiong's [53–18 BCE]. This is what I consider glorious. Some people have successful careers but mediocre intelligence, high position but little virtue. They might think this is glory, but I consider it problematic. The honor and comfort a person can gain by ingratiating himself with those in power will be gone within a hundred years like everything else. His name will not be passed down to the next generation, nor will a single work by him be known to anyone. Even though his emoluments filled his coffers, his writings and virtues came to little. That is not what I prize. If one's virtue is excellent and his knowledge extensive, if his ink flows like rain and his words gush up like a spring, if his talent is rich, his knowledge erudite, his conduct noble, and his mind lofty, then even if he lives only one lifetime, his name will be passed down for a thousand years. This is what I consider extraordinary.

I came from a poor and humble family. Some might deride me, saying, "Your ancestors did not build a foundation of virtue for you, nor did they leave any literary work. Even though you wrote some beautiful books, you are nobody's disciple, so you can never be considered brilliant. A sudden eruption of *qi* we call a monstrosity, a creature that cannot be categorized, a freak, an unusual occurrence, an abnormality, a violation of common sense, an aberration. Who are your ancestors? Their names have not been recorded in historical texts. Not to mention that you have never studied Mozi's theories or associated yourself with scholarly circles. All of a sudden, you produced treatises that are thousands and thousands of words long. This must be considered an unnatural transformation. How can we possibly treasure your writings and praise your virtues?"

My answer would be that the phoenix is a bird without a pedigree, a unicorn an animal without a family, a sage a man without forebears, and a precious treasure a thing without a peer. If men of great talents are stifled, the fault lies with the era in which they live. Scholars of worth rise one by one; precious things grow in isolation. Asserting that literature improves from imitating the worthy is as absurd as asserting that the wine spring must have a source and fine grain comes from an old root. When a remarkable scholar appears, his exceptional writings should not be compared to typical literature, and common people will be unable to evaluate them. The exceptional deserves to be written down or engraved on bronze vessels. The Five Emperors did not rise only in one generation; Yi Yin and Taigong Wang [advisers to the Shang and Zhou founders] came from different families. The regions they lived in are a thousand *li* apart, and their lives were separated by hundreds of years. The value of scholars lies in their refined talents and their caution in the work. They do not bask in their high rank or reputations because they are descendants of a noble line. The calf of a black and yellow cow may be reddish, but he still can be used for sacrificial offerings. The ancestors of a pure scholar may be undistinguished, but this does not prevent him from becoming an exceptional person. Guan was wicked, yet his son Great Yu was a sage. Sou was perverse, yet his brother sage Shun divine. Bo Niu was bedridden with illness, yet his son Zhonggong [Confucius's disciple] was fine and fit. Yan Lu was mediocre and stubborn, yet his son Yan Hui [Confucius's disciple] excelled all his peers. Confucius and Mozi had ignorant ancestors, yet they themselves were sages. The Yang family was not eminent, yet Yang Xiong was brilliant. The house of Huan was not distinguished, yet it produced the amazing Huan Tan [23 BCE–56 CE]. A man must be endowed with more than the ordinary dose of original *qi* to become an able writer.

In the third year of the Yuanhe reign period [86 CE], I was called upon to serve in Danyang [Jiangsu], Jiujiang [Jiangxi], and Lujiang [Anhui] in the Yangzhou region and moved my family there. Later I was appointed assistant governor. My abilities were small, my responsibilities huge. My chief duties were related to personnel affairs, including selection and evaluation. For years, all my plans for writing had to be set aside. In the second year of the Zhanghe reign period [88], I resigned from this position and returned home. As I was approaching seventy, it was time to give up my official carriage.

With my official career definitely over, I could not help but feel that I had not realized my aspirations. Some things went well, others badly, and my health had ups and downs. My hair turned white, and my teeth fell out. I was getting older day after day. My peers went elsewhere, and I had no one to rely upon. Too poor to afford much, I found little to enjoy. The Geng and Xin years passed; my time was drawing near. Even though I was afraid of dying, my mind was still full of silly ideas. I wrote a book, *On Macrobiotics* (Yangxing), in sixteen chapters. To preserve oneself, one needs to cherish the vital *qi*, eat moderately, drink less, close one's eyes and ears to shut out worldly affairs, and garner one's energy. With the help of medicines and exercise, one can hope to briefly prolong life and stop aging. It may be too late for me but should be useful for future readers. The duration of human life is limited, and people, like animals, live for a while and then die.

To whom can I entrust all the books I have written over the years in the hope that they will be passed down? Human beings must descend to the Yellow Springs and become earth and ashes. Employing the doctrines of the sages and the analytical approaches of the wise men, I have commented on everything from the Yellow Emperor and Tang Yao to the Qin and the Han dynasties. My assessments are as impartial as a scale and as clear as a mirror. I have discussed in great detail every issue from youth and old age to life and death and ancient and present times. How unfortunate that life cannot be prolonged!

SOURCE: Liu Pansui 刘盼遂, ed., *Lunheng jijie* 论衡集解 (Beijing: Beijing Guji Chubanshe, 1957), 579–92. Another translation was published by Alfred Forke in 1907 in his *Lun-Heng: Philosophical Essays of Wang Ch'ung*, vol. 1 (repr., New York: Paragon Book Gallery, 1962), 64–82.

Further Reading

Brown, Miranda, and Uffe Bergeton. "'Seeing' Like a Sage: Three Takes on Identity and Perception in Early China." *Journal of Chinese Philosophy* 35, no. 4 (2008): 641–62.

Csikszentmihalyi, Mark. *Readings in Han Chinese Thought*. Indianapolis: Hackett, 2005.

Loewe, Michael. *Chinese Ideas of Life and Death: Faith, Myth and Reason in the Han Period (202 BC–AD 220)*. London: George Allen and Unwin, 1982.

Wang Ch'ung. *Lun-Heng: Philosophical Essays of Wang Ch'ung*. Translated by Alfred Forke. 2 vols. 1907. Reprint, Chicago: Paragon Book Gallery, 1962.

6

A FATHER WRITING TO HIS SON
A letter by Zheng Xuan 鄭玄 (127–200)

A letter from a Han Confucian scholar to his son combines
autobiography and family instruction.

Zheng Xuan was one the most accomplished scholars of the Confucian classics in Chinese history. Born to a family of modest means, he studied diligently and was admitted to the Imperial University, where he studied both the New Text and the Old Text versions of the Confucian classics. After being banished from court due to factional politics, Zheng Xuan devoted himself to writing commentaries on the classics. His interpretations of the classics drew on both the New Text and Old Text schools and were regularly read along with the classics themselves through the rest of Chinese history.

The letter translated here was written when Zheng was seventy *sui* and is considered the first to combine autobiography with family instruction. In detailing his life experience, Zheng Xuan stressed that his lifelong goal was "to illuminate the original ideas of the sages, to compile, compare, and analyze different schools of thought of the Spring and Autumn and Warring States era." Zheng Xuan's instructions also touch on family ethics, household management, and family tradition, key elements in the family instruction tradition that matured during the following centuries.

The letter, dated 196, is addressed to Zheng Xuan's only son, Zheng Yi, referred to by his courtesy name, Yi'en. Zheng's fatherly love is apparent in his concern that Yi'en will have to take over the "affairs of the family." He admonishes him "to seek the Way of the gentleman, to study and explore incessantly." He even reminds his son to "eat lightly and wear simple clothes." Unfortunately, Zheng Yi would soon be murdered by the Yellow Turban rebels, most likely before Zheng Xuan's own death of illness four years after he wrote this letter.

Letter Admonishing My Son Yi'en

Although my family was poor, my parents and siblings tolerated my aspirations and allowed me to quit my job as a county assistant and pursue learning. I visited capitals of the Zhou and the Qin [Chang'an, Xianyang, Shaanxi] and traveled around You [Hebei], Bing [Shanxi], Yan [Shandong], and Yu [Henan]. I was able to meet influential people who were in power as well as great scholars who did not serve the government. They accepted my request to study with them, and I learned a great deal. I studied the Six Arts, read broadly in the commentaries on the classics, and had the opportunity to access and understand astrological and augury texts. After reaching forty, I returned home to serve my parents. I tilled the land to support my family and enjoyed my life.

At that time the eunuchs were in control of political power; I was implicated in factional politics and banished from the court. Fourteen years later, I was pardoned. Afterward, I was recommended through the Worthy, Excellent, Straightforward, and Upright category and summoned by the general-in-chief and the office of three ministers [the minister of education, the defender-in-chief, and the minister of works]. If I agreed to have my name listed for consideration, my rank would be equal to a grand councillor a long time ago. Of course, these gentlemen (general-in-chief and the three ministers) were virtuous, refined, and capable of assisting the emperor; it was appropriate that they were where they were. Reflecting on myself, I know very well that I did not have what it takes to do the job. My goal was to illuminate the original ideas of the sages, to compile, compare, and analyze different schools of thought of the Spring-Autumn and Warring States era. This alone would exhaust my capability. Therefore, I did not accept the appointments. Then the Yellow Turbans rose up; I wandered from place to place, fleeing the destruction. In the end, I returned to my hometown.

This year, I reached seventy. My past work is in shambles, and I still find mistakes here and there. I will make some changes based on the classics so that I can pass them down to you. Hereby I inform you that I will retire and leave day-to-day affairs to you. I will lead a leisurely and peaceful life and focus on completing my work. Aside from receiving an order from the emperor, consoling relatives in distress, paying respect at the ancestors' tombs, or observing wild animals, have I ever grabbed my cane and walked out of the door?

The great and small affairs of the family, you must now shoulder them all on your own. Ah, you solitary man, you never had a sibling to depend on! You should make every effort to seek the Way of the gentleman, to study and explore incessantly. You should be respectful to those with dignity and stay close to those who are virtuous. Illustrious reputations come from colleagues and friends, but virtuous conduct comes from one's own aspirations. If one achieves fame and acclaim, this will also bring honor to one's parents. Won't you keep this in mind? Won't you keep this in mind! Even though I did not leave behind the accomplishment of high office, my refusal of an appointment was high-minded. I am content with the fact that in completing all those commentaries and annotations of the ancient texts, I will not bring embarrassment to later generations. In the end, what really upsets me is the fact that I have not been able to complete my parents' tombs, and that the books I love are crumbling and I did not manage to get them into the Imperial University so they could be passed down. With the sun setting, do I still have time to make it up?

Our family is now a bit better off than in the past. If you work diligently and follow the farming seasons closely, you will not have to worry about being hungry or cold. You should eat lightly and wear simple clothes; moderation on both matters will lessen my worries. If you forget or do not understand what I said, then I give up.

SOURCE: Fan Ye 范曄, *Hou Han shu* 後漢書 (Beijing: Zhonghua Shuju, 1971), 35.1209–10.

Further Reading

De Crespigny, Rafe. *Fire over Luoyang: A History of the Later Han Dynasty 23–220 AD*. Leiden: Brill, 2016.

Gardner, Daniel K. "Confucian Commentary and Chinese Intellectual History." *Journal of Asian Studies* 57, no. 2 (1998): 397–422.

Henderson, John B. *Scripture, Canon and Commentary: A Comparison of Confucian and Western Exegesis*. Princeton, NJ: Princeton University Press, 2014.

Zhao, Lu. *In Pursuit of the Great Peace: Han Dynasty Classics and the Making of Early Medieval Literati Culture*. Albany: State University of New York Press, 2019.

7

....

AN ABDUCTED WOMAN
ON RETURNING HOME
Poems by Cai Yan 蔡琰 (ca. 177–ca. 249)

....

The daughter of a prominent family, forced to become the consort
of a Xiongnu chief, tells of her experiences and describes her
complex emotions on returning home without the sons she bore.

Most writings by women that have been preserved from the early imperial period dwell on the hardships or frustrations they faced. Few, however, had as much to lament as Cai Yan, or Cai Wenji, as she was commonly known. The daughter of Cai Yong (132–192), one of the most distinguished Han dynasty scholars, she had a string of bad luck. Her father got caught up in factional struggles and died in prison. Her husband died early, and without children she returned to her natal home. As the Han fell into chaos, she was abducted first by followers of General Dong Zhuo (132–192) and later by armies of the Southern Xiongnu. She was forced to marry a commander of the Southern Xiongnu and gave birth to two sons during her twelve years as a captive. Cao Cao (155–220), the eventual victor of the civil wars and military dictator of northern China, was an admirer of Cai Yong. In 207, he paid a handsome ransom to the Xiongnu to redeem Cai Wenji, but she had to leave her sons behind. Upon returning to the capital, Cao Cao arranged a marriage for her to a military official.

In the two poems below, Cai Wenji recounts in detail her experience and the emotional toll of captivity. The first poem was written in the pentasyllabic style, new during the Han dynasty, the second in the style of *The Songs of Chu* (Chu ci).

Grief and Indignation

POEM ONE

At the end of the Han, the court lost its power
And Dong Zhuo upset the natural order.
As his ambition was to kill the emperor,
He first did away with the wise and good.
Asserting his force, he moved the old capital
And controlled his lord to strengthen himself.
All through the world loyal troops arose
And together vowed to quell this disaster.
When Dong Zhuo's troops descended on the east,
Their golden armor glistened in the sun.
The people of the plain were weak and timid,
The troops that came were ferocious barbarians!
They plundered the fields, surrounded the cities,
And wherever they went, conquered and destroyed.
They killed and slaughtered, spared not a soul,
Bodies and corpses propped up one against the other.
From the flanks of their horses they hung men's heads,
And behind them on their horses they sat the women.
In this way they sped through Hangu Pass,
On a westward journey so perilous and far!
Looking back I only saw a distant haze,
And my innards turned to rotten pulp.
The people they abducted were in the thousands,
But we were not allowed to stay together.
At times flesh-and-blood relatives were reunited,
Who would have liked to talk but did not dare.

If you displeased them even in the slightest way,
They'd shout right out: "You dirty slaves.
We really should just kill you off,
Why should we even let you live!"
How could I still have clung to life and fate?
Their swearing and cursing was too much to bear.
At other times we were whipped and beaten,
All the bitter pains rained down on us at once.
At dawn we set out, weeping and crying,
At night we sat down, sadly moaning.
One longed to die, but that was not allowed,
One longed to live but that too could not be.
Blue heaven up above, what was our sin
That we should suffer this great calamity?

The border wilds are different from China,
And their people's customs lack propriety.
The places where they live are full of snow,
And the Hun winds rise in summer and spring,
Tugging at my robes in all directions,
And filling my ears with their wailing sounds.
Moved by the seasons, I recalled my parents,
And my sad laments went on without end.
Whenever guests would arrive from afar,
That news would always give me great joy.
But when I sought them out for tidings,
They would never turn out to be from my home.
Then out of the blue my constant wish was granted,
As relatives showed up to take me home.
So finally I was able to make my escape,
But at the cost of abandoning my sons!

A bond of nature ties them to my heart,
Once separated there could be no reunion.
In life or death: forced forever apart.
I could not bear to bid them farewell!
My sons flung their arms around my neck,

Asking: "Mother, where are you going?
The people are saying that our mother has to leave,
And that you will never come back to us.
Oh mother, you were always so kind and caring,
How come you are now so cold and cruel?
We still are children, not grown-up men,
Can *it* really be you do not care?"
When I saw this, my heart broke into pieces,
And I felt as if I'd lost my mind, gone mad!
I wept and cried and stroked them with my hands,
And as I was about to depart, was filled with doubt.

The people who had been abducted with me,
Came to see me off and say goodbye.
Jealous that I alone could go home,
Their sad laments tore at my heartstrings.
Because of this the horses did not move,
Because of this the wheels refused to turn.
All those who watched heaved heavy sighs
And we travelers choked back our sobs.

Going and going I deadened my feelings,
The journey took us day by day further away.
And so, on and on, the full three thousand miles:
When would I ever meet with them again?
Memories of the children born from my womb
Completely tore me to pieces inside.
Arriving home, I found I had no family,
No relatives of any kind remained!
The city had become a mountain forest,
The courtyard was overgrown by thorns,
And white bones, who knows of whom,
Lay scattered around in the open field.
Outside the gate no sound of human voices:
Just the yelps and howls of dholes and wolves.
Lonely I faced my solitary shadow,
As I cried out in anguish, my heart was shattered.

I climbed to a high spot, and gazed into the distance,
And my soul and spirit seemed to fly away.
It was as if my life was over and done,
And those around me had to comfort me.
Because of them I forced myself to live,
But even so, on whom could I rely?
To my new husband I entrust my fate,
I do my best to make an earnest effort.
A victim of the wars, I lost my honor,
And always fear that I will be discarded.
How many years are in a human life?
This pain will haunt me till my dying day!

POEM TWO

How poor my fate, alas, to meet such dismal times!
My relatives were massacred and I alone survived.
I was captured and abducted to beyond the western pass,
The journey perilous and long to that barbarian land.
Mountains and valleys stretched endlessly, the road went on and on,
Lovingly I looked back east and heaved a heavy sigh.
At night when I should have slept, I could not find rest,
When hungry I should have eaten, but could not swallow a thing.
Constantly awash in tears, my eyes were never dry.
Weak in resolve, alas, I was afraid to die,
And though I clung to life, I was dishonored and abased!
Now those regions, alas, are far from the essence of yang,
As yin's breath congeals, snow falls even in summer.
The desert is darkened, alas, by clouds of dust,
And its grasses and trees do not flower in spring.
The people like beasts feed on rancid flesh,
Their speech is gibberish, their faces unsightly.
At the end of the year as the seasons pass by,
The nights stretch endlessly behind the locked gates.
Unable to sleep in my tent, I would get up,
Ascend the barbarian hall, look out over the wide courtyard.
Dark clouds would gather, obscuring moon and stars,

And the piercing north wind would coldly howl.
At the sound of the barbarian reed pipe, the horses whinnied,
And a lone goose returned, honking forlornly.
The musicians arose and plucked their zithers,
Their notes harmonized so sadly and clear.
My heart spewed out its longings, my breast filled with rage
How I longed to let it all out, but I feared to give offense,
And as I suppressed my sad sobs, my tears soaked my collar.

As my relatives had come to fetch me, I had to go home,
But setting out on this journey meant abandoning my children.
My sons cried "Mother!" till their voices grew hoarse,
I covered my ears as I could not bear to listen.
Running they tried to cling to me, so alone and forlorn,
They stumbled, got up again, their faces all bleeding!
Looking back at them, I felt utterly shattered,
My heart stunned, I fainted but did not die.

Translated by Wilt Idema and Beata Grant

SOURCE: Wilt Idema and Beata Grant, *The Red Brush: Writing Women of Imperial China* (Cambridge, MA: Harvard University Asia Center, 2004), 114–18.

Further Reading

Chang, Kang-i Sun, and Haun Saussy. *Women Writers of Traditional China: An Anthology of Poetry and Criticism.* Stanford, CA: Stanford University Press, 1999.

Frankel, Hans H. "Cai Yan and the Poems Attributed to Her." *Chinese Literature, Essays, Articles, Reviews* 5, no. 1/2 (1983): 133–56.

Hinsch, Bret. *Women in Early Imperial China.* Lanham, MD: Rowman & Littlefield, 2010.

8

....

MILITARY MEN TOUTING THEIR MERITS

Essays by Cao Cao 曹操 (155–220)
and his son Cao Pi 曹丕 (187–226)

....

In the final decade of the Han, two key figures
present themselves as highly capable military men.

Disordered times call for individuals willing to take action. When the Han fell into disorder after major rebellions broke out in 184, even many well-educated men rose to the challenge of leading armies. Good examples are Cao Cao and his son Cao Pi, both excellent poets but also skilled in the arts of war. Cao Cao and other officials assigned to suppress the rebels soon were competing among themselves for supremacy, their rivalry immortalized in the stories associated with the subsequent Three Kingdoms period (220–265). Cao Cao became the dominant figure in the north, but it was Cao Pi who, after his father's death, finally arranged the abdication of the last Han emperor and established the Wei dynasty.

Cao Cao composed the first text below in 210, when he was fifty-six. By then, with the north firmly in his grip, he aspired to unify the entire empire. When his rivals attacked him at the court, claiming that he intended to depose the emperor, Cao Cao wrote this essay as a response. He asserted that he had many opportunities to declare himself emperor but had never harbored such ambitions.

The piece by Cao Pi that follows was written a few years later and is the preface to his *On the Standards for Literature* (Dianlun), only parts of which survive. In the preface, Cao Pi mentions his love for poetry only in passing. He devotes his account instead to his martial arts training and how his skills surpassed those of almost everyone he had ever encountered. Even when writing about literature, it would seem, he wanted to be thought of as a brash military man, not given to false modesty.

Relinquishing My Fiefs and Clarifying My Basic Aims, by Cao Cao

I was quite young when I was nominated as Filial and Incorrupt. Since I was not a famous recluse, I feared that prominent people would regard me as a stupid nobody. Therefore, I hoped to become a commandery governor, build my reputation through able governing and reforming the people, and become known to the world that way. When I was the governor of Ji'nan [Shandong], I began with eliminating cruelty and corruption and implementing a fair recommendation system. I offended quite a few palace attendants-in-ordinary. Worried that my actions had enraged the powerful local families and would cause harm to my family, I resigned on the pretext of illness.

At that time, I was still very young. Among my peers recommended as Filial and Incorrupt the same year, some were already fifty, yet they were not regarded as old. So I thought to myself, "If I wait for twenty years until the empire is peaceful and just, I will be no older than these peers are today." Therefore, I returned home with the intention to retire permanently. I built a fine study fifty *li* east of Qiao [Anhui, Cao Cao's hometown]. My plan was to read books during the summer and fall and go hunting during the winter and spring. I just wanted to have a mediocre plot of land, retreat from the world, and cut off all human contact. However, my wish was not fulfilled.

I was appointed as a commandant-in-chief and promoted to take charge of Control Army, my assignment to capture traitors and make a name for myself. I hoped to be enfeoffed and made the general who conquers the west, so that later my grave would have a tomb inscription titled "The Tomb of Marquis Cao of Han, the Late General Who Conquers the West." That was my ambition. When Dong Zhuo [132–192] rebelled, the call arose for a military expedition. At that time, I could easily organize a large army; however, I did not want too many soldiers, so I actually often reduced the number of my troops. This is because a large military force often becomes overconfident, thinking itself invincible, ready to take on a strong enemy, bringing on a new disaster. Therefore, in the Battle of Xingyang [190, Henan], I deployed only a few thousand soldiers. Later, when I returned to Yangzhou [Jiangsu] to recruit soldiers, I took less than three thousand because I had always wanted to limit the size of my forces.

When I was the governor of Yanzhou [Shandong] and defeated the Yellow Turban Rebellion, three hundred thousand Yellow Turbans surrendered. Then Yuan Shu [d. 199] declared himself emperor in Jiujiang [Jiangxi] and those under him all presented themselves as his subjects. He named the city gate Jianhao [Founding Reign] Gate and selected garments appropriate for an emperor. His two wives competed with each other for the title of empress. After Yuan decided on his plan, his subordinates advised him to assume the throne immediately and proclaim his act to the world. Yuan Shu replied, "Since Cao Cao is still a threat, I cannot do it." Later we captured four of his generals, after which his troops surrendered. Consequently, Yuan Shu became completely desperate, fell ill, and died. When his brother Yuan Shao [155–199] seized the region north of the Yellow River, he had a very powerful military force. In assessing my own strength, I knew very well that I could not compete with him. However, I figured that if I died for the country and for a just cause, then my name would be known throughout the ages. Fortunately, I defeated Yuan Shao and killed his two sons.

Then there was Liu Biao [142–208] who counted on his royal background. He harbored evil intent, made tentative moves, and waited for opportunities. After he occupied Dangzhou [Hubei and Hunan], I crushed him as well. By then I had pacified the realm. I was appointed the grand councillor, the most powerful position in the government. This already surpassed what I had aspired to. My words sound self-important, but the reason I recount these things is to forestall criticism; hence I do not hold anything back. If it had not been for me, who knows how many people would have proclaimed themselves emperors or kings.

Seeing that I am powerful and never believed the Mandate of Heaven, some people might privately comment that I harbor the intention of overthrowing the emperor. Such baseless conjectures disturb me to no end. The reason that both Lord Huan of Qi [d. 643 BCE] and Lord Wen of Jin [d. 628] are well-known throughout history is that even though they both had vast military strength, they were still loyal to the Zhou and served the Zhou court. *The Analects* (Lunyu) says, "The Zhou controlled two-thirds of the empire, yet continued to serve the Yin. The virtue of the Zhou may be said to be the utmost of virtue." This is because the Zhou, with its superior power, was willing to serve a weak king. In the past, when the Yan general Yue Yi [Warring States period] sought refuge in the state of Zhao, the king of Zhao wanted his help to conquer Yan. Yue Yi prostrated himself and declared that "I served the Yan king with the same sincerity as I serve you. If I committed a crime and was exiled to another state, I would never in my life do anything to hurt your people of Zhao, and not just because I am a descendant of Zhao!"

When the Qin emperor Huhai [230–207 BCE] was about to execute General Meng Tian [ca. 250–10 BCE], Meng said, "From my grandfather to his son and grandson, three generations of the Mengs were given commissions by the Qin court. I commanded more than three hundred thousand soldiers, making my military force strong enough to overthrow the emperor. Nevertheless, I know I have to protect the moral principle of the ruler-subject relationship, even if it means death. This is because I do not dare to dishonor my ancestors' teachings and betray the late emperor." Whenever I read about these two people, I break down in tears. My grandfather, father, and I were all high ministers of the Han emperors, fully trusted by them. If I count my son Cao Pi and his brothers, the trust has lasted more than three generations. This is not just what I say publicly; I say the same thing to my wife and concubines, ensuring that they understand my intentions as well. I tell them, "When I die, you all should remarry and make my intentions known to others." These words of utmost importance are from the bottom of my heart.

The reason that I am expressing my innermost thoughts so earnestly is because I read the "Golden Coffer" [a chapter in *The Book of Documents* (Shangshu)]. The chapter recounts how the Duke of Zhou placed his prayer for King Wu in a golden coffer, on the chance that if people came to doubt his loyalty, he could prove his innocence. It is unrealistic now for me to hand over my troops, resign from my office, and return to Wuping [Henan] as a duke. Why? Because I truly worry that destruction will descend if I give up my army. I need not only to consider how my children and grandchildren will fare but also to keep in mind that if I fall, the state will collapse. Therefore, I need to avoid seeking an empty name at the cost of putting us all in real danger.

The previous emperor made my three sons dukes, which I then resolutely declined but now plan to accept. This is not because I want the glory but because these trappings provide security. Whenever I read about Jie Zitui [d. 636 BCE] declining the fief offered by Jin and Shen Baoxu [fl. 506 BCE] avoiding the rewards granted by Chu, I put down the book and sigh. These stories made me think. Relying on the authority of the state, I led expeditions on behalf of the emperor. Though the weaker one, I defeated the stronger party, a case of the smaller army capturing the larger one. Once I took action, all my wishes came true, all my worries were set to rest. I pacified the realm and did not disgrace the emperor's command, all thanks to Heaven's showing favor for the Han, as human power alone could not possibly have achieved this. I was granted four counties with an income of taxes from thirty thousand households. What virtue did I have to deserve this!

Because the empire is still unstable, I cannot abandon my official position. However, my fiefs can be much reduced. I will relinquish the income from the Yangxia, Zhe, and Ku Counties [all in Henan], in total twenty thousand households. I will retain only the fief of Wuping County, with ten thousand households. I hope that this will quash baseless criticism of my actions.

SOURCE: Cao Cao 曹操, Cao Cao ji 曹操集 (Beijing: Zhonghua Shuju, 1959), 2.41–43.

Preface to *On the Standards for Literature*, by Cao Pi

In the first year of the Chuping reign period [190], Dong Zhuo murdered Emperor Shao [r. 189], poisoned Empress Dowager He (d. 189), and undermined the royal house. At that time, the entire empire was exhausted by Emperor Ling's rule and outraged by Dong Zhuo's vicious actions. Families were concerned about impending chaos, and everyone felt in grave danger. Governors in the east called for everyone to act on the principle articulated in *The Spring and Autumn Annals* (Chunqiu): that everyone has the responsibility to fight against villains, which was asserted by the people of Wei when they went out on campaign against Zhouyu in Pu. The governors began to raise armies. Many magnates, noble warriors, rich families, and powerful clans responded to the call, arriving from near and far, and congregated there. The troops of Yanzhou [Shandong] and Yuzhou [Henan and Anhui] fought in Xingyang [Henan]. The army of Henei [Henan] fought in Mengjin [Henan]. Dong Zhou then moved the emperor to the western capital Xi'an. In the east, the most powerful warlords annexed neighboring states, the lesser ones swallowed up cities, and weaker ones managed to amass lands. Everyone fought everyone else. Just then the Yellow Turban Rebellion erupted in the Haidai region [Shandong] and bandits rose in the mountains of Bing [Shanxi] and Ji [Hebei]. Following up a series of victories, the Yellow Turban forces shifted their target and moved to the south. Townsmen fled for safety at the sight of signal alarms; urban dwellers took flight on seeing the approaching rebels. People were slaughtered; their exposed bones were everywhere. At that time, I was five years old.

As the world was in such turmoil, my father decided I should learn archery. By the age of six, I had mastered the skill. Then he taught me to ride a horse. By the age of eight, I was very good at shooting from horseback. With military conflicts so frequent, I often joined my father on military campaigns. At the beginning of the Jian'an reign period [196], my father led a southern expedition to Jingzhou [Hubei]. When he reached Wan [Henan], Zhang Xiu surrendered. Then ten days later, he turned around and rebelled. My brother the Filial and Incorrupt Cao Ang (courtesy name Zixiu) and my cousin Cao Anmin were killed, but I managed to escape on horseback. At the time, I was ten years old.

Clearly, the usefulness of the civil versus military arts depends on the time in which one lives. I was born during the disastrous Zhongping era and grew up amid war. Therefore, from a very young age, I loved the bow and horses, and my passion has persisted to this day. I can still chase an animal for ten *li* and often practice shooting from horseback with a target a hundred feet away. My body grew stronger day after day, and I never tired of practice.

In the tenth year of the Jian'an reign period [205], Jizhou [Hebei] was finally pacified. The [ancient Korean] Wo and Mo peoples offered fine bows as tribute; the Yan and Dai regions [Hebei] presented famous horses. In the late spring of that year, the tree god Goumang was presiding over the season, so gentle breezes caressed the plants. The bow was warm, the hand deft, the grass short, the animals fat. My cousin Cao Zidan and I went hunting in Ye [Hebei] the whole day. We captured nine river deer and thirty pheasants and rabbits. Later, when the troops marched south and bivouacked at Quli [Henan], director of the imperial secretariat Xun Yu [163–212] came to present the troops food and goods on behalf of the emperor. We met, and at the end of our conversation, Xun Yu said, "I heard you are good at shooting arrows from both the left and right sides, which is so difficult." I replied, "Your honor has not seen how I can shoot down the targets on horseback from any position and angle." When Xun Yu, pleased, said, "Great!" I added, "Shooting targets in a practice range is not that impressive even if your score is perfect. What is really impressive is when you ride a horse on the plain covered in luxuriant grass and chase fleeing animals and birds in flight, each arrow hitting the moving target perfectly." At that time the military adviser Zhang Jing was present. He looked at Xun Yu and clapped: "Marvelous!"

I also studied sword-fighting with many masters. There are many different schools, but the best teachers are from Luoyang. During Emperors Huan and Ling's reigns [147–188], the warrior Wang Yue, an expert of the Luoyang school, was well-known around the capital. Shi A of Henan was said to have studied under him and learned the basics of Wang's methods. I studied with Shi A and became quite proficient.

One time, I drank with a group including Liu Xun, the pacifying barbarians general, and Deng Zhan, the courage and bravery general. I had long heard that Deng Zhan excelled at capturing adversaries through hand-to-hand combat and was skilled at all types of weapons. He was said to be able to fight an armed enemy with his bare hands. I discussed sword-fighting with Deng Zhan for a long time. I told him that his sword-fighting technique was not the best and that I had been interested in this sport for a long time and had become quite good at it. Deng Zhan begged to fight me. At that time, we were all quite drunk and were just about to eat sugarcane, so we used sugarcanes as swords and fought several rounds. I hit his arm three times. People around us burst out laughing. Unhappy, Deng Zhan begged for another round. I said, "Since I depend on speed, it is very hard for me to hit your face, so I only hit your arms." Deng Zhan again asked for one more round. I realized that he planned on suddenly hitting me in the front, so I pretended to move forward and attack. Sure enough, Deng Zhan came toward me, so I stepped back and struck him in the middle of his forehead. Everyone was amazed. I returned to my seat and said laughingly, "In the past, when Chunyu Yi [205–150 BCE] went to study with the famous doctor Gongsheng Yangqing [Han dynasty], Gongsheng forced Chunyu to abandon his old medical prescriptions. Only then did he teach Chunyu his secret methods. Now I also hope you, General Deng, will abandon your old techniques and adopt the real sword-fighting method." Everyone was excited.

An important thing to remember is not to regard yourself as the best. When I was young, I was skilled at double-halberd fighting and thought no one could beat me. People call such fighting "sitting in an iron room" and a decorated shield a "closed wooden cabin." Later, I studied with Yuan Min of the Chen region. He excelled at fighting double halberds with a single halberd. It was truly amazing; his opponents had no idea which direction the halberd would appear from. Had I met Yuan Min in a narrow road, we might have had a hell of a fight.

I rarely played games other than Shooting Go, which I mastered to some degree. I wrote a rhapsody about it when I was young. At the time, the masters of Shooting Go were the duke of Hexiang, Ma Lang; Dongfang Anshi; and Zhang Gongzi. I still regret that I did not get a chance to play against any of them.

My father loved poetry and books and always had a book in his hand, even during military campaigns. When I called on him or waited on him at leisure, he would often tell me, "If you love learning at a young age, you can really concentrate. Adults don't have as good memories. Yuan Yi [courtesy name Boye] and I are the only adults who are capable of studying diligently." Therefore, when I was young, I recited *The Classic of Poetry* (Shijing) and *The Analects*, and when I grew up I studied the five classics and read widely in other kinds of books, including *The Historical Records* (Shiji), *The History of the Han* (Hanshu), and the writings of all the philosophical schools, devouring them all. I composed sixty essays and poems. Whether I can be described as smart without showing off, brave but willing to retreat, kind to others, and fair to subordinates, I will leave to the judgment of the good historians of the future.

SOURCE: Xia Chuancai 夏傳才, *Cao Pi ji jiaozhu* 曹丕集校註 (Shijiazhuang: Hebei Jiaoyu Chubanshe, 2013), 247.

Further Reading

Besio, Kimberly, and Constantine Tung. *Three Kingdoms and Chinese Culture.* Albany: State University of New York Press, 2007.

De Crespigny, Rafe. *Imperial Warlord: A Biography of Cao Cao 155–220 AD.* Leiden: Brill, 2010.

Goodman, Howard L. "The Orphan Ts'ao P'i, His Odd Poem, and Its Historiographic Frame." *Asia Major* (Third Series) 22, no. 1 (2009): 79–104.

Wu, Fusheng. *Written at Imperial Command: Panegyric Poetry in Early Medieval China.* Albany: State University of New York Press, 2008.

9

THE PAIN OF SEPARATION
Poetic writings by Imperial Consort Zuo Fen 左芬
(ca. 253–300)

*A Jin imperial consort recounts her life and
her longing for her family in verse.*

For early periods, a disproportionate share of the surviving writings attributed to women were done by women in the palace, such as Lady Ban, discussed in the introduction. These women were brought to the palace in their teens and might have few opportunities to see their own relatives in later years. If they gained the favor of the ruler, that could lead to loss of friendship with other women in the palace, who saw themselves as rivals, and the ruler might in time lose interest in them, leaving them isolated. Although only a tiny proportion of women ever entered the palace, people saw in their circumstances something more universal: the pain of separation from loved ones, the plight of women who lose the love of the men they are mated with, and feelings of isolation. Men who perceived that their ruler had lost confidence in them would sometimes express their unhappiness through the voice of a neglected woman.

Discord in the imperial household and related noble families was at a high point during the brief Western Jin period (265–317), when princes and consort families sometimes took up arms against each other. It was in just this period that Zuo Fen (ca. 253–300) entered the palace. Born to a well-known family, both she and her elder brother, Zuo Si (ca. 255–ca. 306), were ranked among the most accomplished poets of the day. Zuo Fen's epitaph, excavated in 1930, referred to her as Emperor Wu's (r. 266–290) "Noble Lady" (Guiren), one of the three highest ranked consorts. Like her brother, Zuo Fen excelled in both rhapsody (*fu*), a verse form with lines of unequal lengths, and *shi* poetry, with lines of equal length. Rhapsodies first appeared during the Spring and Autumn period and by the third century had become a literary form considered especially appropriate for narratives rich in description.

With her position in the imperial palace and her literary reputation, it came as a surprise to archaeologists that Zuo Fen was buried very simply. Her epitaph recorded only her title, date of death, place of burial, and natal family members. Scholars surmise that by the time she passed away, the Jin was in the midst of political turmoil and the epitaph was hastily arranged by her brother's family instead of the imperial court. Fuller information is given in her brief biograph in *The History of the Jin* (Jinshu), compiled in the Tang dynasty, which claims that it was Zuo Fen's literary reputation that led to her selection as an imperial consort. During her years as Emperor Wu's consort, she was often summoned to compose poetry to commemorate special occasions, and the "Rhapsody of Thoughts on Separation" was reportedly written at the emperor's command. Nevertheless, from her poem written for her brother, "Heartfelt Feelings on Separation," it is clear that the raw emotion expressed in the rhapsody reflected her deepest feelings. Emperor Wu died in 290, and Zuo Fen lived in the palace as a "widow" for another ten years. She had no children.

In the poem and rhapsody translated below, Zuo Fen both recounts her experience in the palace and reflects on mundane problems and frustrations of women in imperial China.

HEARTFELT FEELINGS ON SEPARATION

From the time I left our parents,
Suddenly two years have passed.
The distance separating us has become gradually greater;

When shall I pay my respect to them again?
I have perused what you kindly told me in your letter,
And I savor the words of your sorrowful song of separation.
I can almost imagine your face before me,
And I sigh and sob out of control.
When will we meet again
To amuse ourselves with prose and verse?
How can I recount my misery?
I'll express my feelings in writing.

RHAPSODY OF THOUGHTS ON SEPARATION

I
Born in the humble seclusion of a thatched hut,
I knew nothing of state documents.
I never saw the splendid portraits painted on palace walls,
Or heard the canons and counsels of the ancient sages.
Despite my foolish vulgarity and meager learning,
I was mistakenly given a place in the purple chamber.
This is not a place for a rustic,
And I constantly tremble with worry and fear.
My breast is filled with the sadness of longing,
Redoubled by ten thousand unremitting cares.
Alas, heavy sorrows accumulate deep within me!
Alone in my torment, I have no way to vent them.
My mind is vexed and troubled, joyless;
My thoughts are tied in a tangle, and my longing increases.
At night I lie awake unable to sleep;
My soul is restless, fretful till dawn.
Wind, soughing and sighing, rises all around;
Frost, pure white, covers the courtyard.
The sun, dim and dark, casts no light;
The air is sad and gloomy, bitterly cold.
I hear many sorrowful feelings
And am afflicted by tears that fall of themselves.

II

Of old, Boyu, handsome and fair,
Always dressed in colored clothes to cheer his parents.
I grieve at the separation of today;
Like Antares and Orion, long have family and I been parted.
It is not that the distance is far—
It does not even exceed several rods.
How cold and confining the forbidden palace!
I wish to gaze into the distance but lack the means.
I look up at the moving clouds and sob;
Flowing tears soak my gown.
Qu Yuan was beset with sorrow;
Oh, how he grieved at separation!
He who wrote a song at the wall tower
Compared one day to three months.
How much more painful for parents and children who love each other,
Cut off so long and so far.
Long have I been laden with sorrow, afflicted with grief;
I look up the blue sky and weep tears of blood.

THE CODA SAYS:

Parents and children, the dearest of kin,
Have been transformed into strangers.
We bid a final farewell,
And I was sorrowful and sad.
I dream that my soul returns home,
And I see my loved ones.
I wake with a start and cry out:
My heart cannot comfort itself.
Copious tears pour down my face;
I pick up a brush and express my feelings.
Tear upon tear falls
As I make my plaint in this poem.

Translated by David R. Knechtges

SOURCE: This translation is in Kang-i Sun Chang and Haun Saussy, eds., *Women Writers of Traditional China: An Anthology of Poetry and Criticism* (Stanford, CA: Stanford University Press, 1999), 31–33. Other translations of this poem are included in Wilt L. Idema and Beata Grant, *The Red Brush: Writing Women of Imperial China* (Cambridge, MA: Harvard University Asia Center, 2004), 43–46, and Fusheng Wu, *Written at Imperial Command: Panegyric Poetry in Early Medieval China* (Albany: State University of New York Press, 2008), 51–52.

Further Reading

Chang, Kang-i Sun, and Haun Saussy, eds. *Women Writers of Traditional China: An Anthology of Poetry and Criticism*. Stanford, CA: Stanford University Press, 1999.

Hinsch, Bret. *Women in Early Imperial China*. Lanham, MD: Rowman & Littlefield, 2010.

Knechtges, David R., and Xiao Tong. *Wen Xuan or Selections of Refined Literature. Vol. 2, Rhapsodies on Sacrifices, Hunting, Travel, Sightseeing, Palaces and Halls, Rivers and Seas*. Princeton, NJ: Princeton University Press, 2016.

10

....

AN EMPEROR'S DISCOURSE ON KARMA AND VEGETARIANISM
Preface by Emperor Wu 梁武帝 (r. 502–549) of the Liang

....

Emperor Wu of the Liang dynasty recounts his life as a prince,
his political maneuvers and successes, and his Buddhist faith.

Buddhism entered China in the late Han as a religion of merchants from Central Asia. Its spread was slow at first, but by the Northern and Southern Dynasties (420–489) was gaining more and more followers at all social levels. This was a time of multiple regimes, with non-Han rulers in the north and a series of short dynasties in the south with capitals at Jiankang (modern Nanjing) whose ruling families were Chinese.

One of the greatest patrons of Buddhism was Xiao Yan 蕭衍, the founding emperor of the Liang dynasty, known as Emperor Wu of the Liang. Beginning as a military officer of the previous Qi dynasty, he rose quickly to the rank of general, widely praised for his valor and battlefield successes. At first he had strong interests in Daoist ideas of immortals and transcendence, but after joining a literary salon led by a Qi prince, he became fascinated by the prince's Buddhist practices and the lectures he arranged by renowned monks. By the time he took the throne himself in 502, he was fully committed to Buddhism. He chose the Buddha's birthday, the eighth day of the fourth month, as the first day of his dynasty and instituted vegetarian offerings to imperial ancestors instead of the traditional animal sacrifices, as Buddhism rejects killing animals or other sentient beings.

In his later years, Emperor Wu penned *Rhapsody of Good Karma* (Jingye fu) to express his Buddhist aspirations and his journey to enlightenment. In the preface, translated here, he recounts his decision to give up eating meat and to abstain from sexual activity. He seems to have exaggerated his sexual abstinence, however. His wife died before he ascended the throne, but he took at least seven concubines, who bore him eight sons and three daughters, the last born when the emperor was fifty. In the translation below, a few lines have been omitted because scholars believe that they were added after Xiao Yan's death.

Preface to *Rhapsody on Good Karma*

When I was young, I loved nature and aspired to be a recluse, but due to worldly ties I could not fulfill my wish. Still, I rectified my wayward conduct and veered away from self-indulgence. I was then selected to serve at court. That was a period of frequent crises, as the court fought wars all the time, not a year passing without a disturbance. The ruler [Xiao Baojuan, 483–501] was a brutal maniac, his underlings scheming and disorderly. The way of the gentleman declined while that of the scoundrel flourished.... Those in power held fast to their positions, barking demands day in and day out, running roughshod over the people, and handing out execution orders at will. The loyal and the worthy were beheaded, and officials with outstanding service were put to death for no reason. Donning clothes like those of officials, men of prowess set out to different regions, all claiming to represent the emperor and possess full authority. They used treacherous schemes to confuse and agitate the public. From morning to evening they made merry; day and night they sought to destroy the capital. The sick died by the roadside, their children unable to mourn them. Pregnant women gave birth by the side of the road, unable even to hold their newborns. The populace was in constant fear of imminent death.

Prince Xuanwu of Changsha [posthumous title of Xiao Yi, the author's elder brother] made great contributions to the Qi dynasty, yet he was not given the customary rewards. Instead he was persecuted, as were his brother [Xiao Chang] and nephews. Xiao Baojuan then sent Huan Shenyu, Du Bofu, and several other commissioners to Yongzhou [Hubei] to discuss collaborating with local military commanders to do me harm. However, their plan failed to gain any support and came to nothing. Afterward, Xiao Baojuan sent Liu Shanyang to capture me. With no personal guards, I expected to meet my death when fierce men with sharp weapons clad in armor appeared. Had that happened, I would have died at the hands of the lowest of the low and become the laughingstock of the world. However, on arriving in Jingzhou [Hubei], Liu Shanyang was captured by Xiao Yingzhou [462–501], who immediately sent a messenger to inform me of the news.

As a consequence of all this, I called for overthrowing Xiao Baojuan and formed my own army. People all over, sharing my hopes, responded to my declaration. In the first month of the second year of the Yongyuan reign of the Qi dynasty [500], my army set out from Xiangyang [Hubei]. The soldiers were like a huge cloud, and the boats were lined up tightly, stretching as far as one could see. Jingling [Hubei] governor Cao Jingzong, commander of the cavalry Yin Chang, and others led the infantry and cavalry under their command to wait on the banks to welcome me. The fleet going upstream against the current of the Han River extended forty *li* to my boat. Just then, a pair of white fish jumped into my ship, as if to declare that our expedition equaled the Menjin Declaration [in which King Wu mobilized Zhou forces and alliances to defeat the Shang dynasty]. This surely was a confirmation of Heaven's will. Our army marched with the force of thunder and the speed of wind. Soon we captured Yingcheng [Hubei] and forced Jiangzhou [Jiangxi] to surrender. The Gushu [Anhui] forces retreated as soon as they learned of our advance. Li Jushi of Xinting [fortress of the capital Jiankang] bowed his head and joined our forces.

After we eliminating the despot, the populace was able to breathe again, so I once more gave some thought to becoming a recluse and enjoying nature to my heart's content. Yet I felt pressured by the shared desire of the people and was awed by the mandate that Heaven had bestowed on me, giving me no alternative but to assume the throne. I conducted myself with caution, as if I were standing at the edge of an abyss or treading on thin ice. Still I hoped to abdicate and allow someone more capable to take over. However, if I yielded the throne, the country would fall into chaos once more. That would not only lead to my death and humiliation but also let down both the living and the dead who counted on me. I thus composed these lines: "Day and night I go over things in my mind, again and again, finding no solution. If I stop thinking about it, I might still be able to leave, but then things will not end well."

Once I was sitting on the throne and holding audiences, I reached out to all the people within the four seas. Day and night, I worked unceasingly, cautioning myself not to be complacent, as if I were driving six horses with a single rotten rein. Commentators of the time compared me to King Tang of the Shang and King Wu of the Zhou, an unfair appraisal. Tang and Wu were sages, and I am an ordinary person, unworthy of comparison to them. On the other hand, King Tang exiled his ruler (King Jie of the Xia dynasty) and King Wu beheaded his king (King Zhou of the Shang dynasty) before their ties to their sovereigns were severed. I eliminated the despot and removed the peril of the world only after our ruler-subject relationship had been broken. For these two reasons, my case is different.

Prior to taking the throne, I focused only on Confucian rites and duty and did not understand Buddhist faith and belief. I slaughtered and cooked sentient beings to entertain guests. I regularly ate meat and hardly knew the taste of vegetables. After I ascended the throne, the wealth of the entire empire was at my disposal. Delicacies from afar were presented to me one after another; exotic food was delivered to me all the time. Sumptuous feasts were a constant occurrence; the kitchen was well stocked with gourmet food. However, whenever I was about to eat, I would put down my chopsticks and sob. I was sorry that I could not fulfil the filial obligation of serving my parents day and night. How could I possibly enjoy a feast by myself? Hence, I started eating only vegetarian fare and would not take a single bite of fish or meat. At first, I did this secretly, without telling anyone. Then when I hosted banquets for court officials, I followed my dietary routine, but since I had not gotten used to a vegetarian diet, my body looked sallow and weak. That was when officials began to realize what I was doing.

Xie Fei, Kong Yanying, and others repeatedly urged me to give up my vegetarian diet. This reflected their loyalty to me but nevertheless was not what I wanted. Besides, I reminded myself that it had never been my ambition to become the ruler. Du Shu [197–252] once said, "If I cut off my heart and throw it on the ground, all I would lose would be a small piece of flesh." I am indebted to enlightened gentlemen who expressed their inner feelings in this way. In order for the people to know that I had not intended to take the throne, I would have to do something beyond the capacity of a normal person. Therefore, in addition, I abstained from sexual pleasure. For more than forty years now, I have not shared a bedroom with a consort.

Sometime earlier, when I had some minor physical problem, I asked imperial doctors Liu Chengzhi and Yao Puti for a diagnosis. Liu Chengzhi said, "I know for sure that the cause is overeating." I replied, "I always had delicacies before I took the throne." Liu Chengzhi said, "What you had back then cannot compare to what you have now." Yao Puti shook his head with a smile and said, "I am the only one who knows the cause: you go to excess in sexual activity." By then I had not eaten fish or meat or engaged in sexual intercourse for a long time. I realized that both of them lacked the wisdom of the legendary doctors He and Huan [Spring and Autumn period] and the skills of the legendary doctors Bian Que [Spring and Autumn period] and Hua Tuo [Han dynasty]. Therefore, I held my tongue and only asked for prescriptions.

Liu Chengzhi prescribed medicinal liquor, and Yao Puti prescribed pills, but my illness continued to worsen. Since they did not know the actual cause of my illness, I stopped the treatment. Afterward, whenever I got sick, I took care of it myself and no longer consulted physicians, a practice I have continued for more than forty years. I may not be a *vīrya* [diligent person], but since I don't eat sentient beings, I am not bothered by the killing hindrance, and since I don't touch consorts, I am no longer hindered by lust. After eliminating these two hindrances, my mind gradually became clear. I understood all the scriptures after just a quick read. From that time on, I knew exactly what my path would be. *The Book of Rites* (Liji) says, "At birth, a person is serene: this is his Heavenly nature. Through contact with other things, he is stirred and desire appears." Being stirred up contaminates the mind, while serenity purifies it. If outside interference is eliminated, the mind will be clear. Once you realize that, worries will have no way to take root. I thus compose this *Rhapsody on Good Karma* to express myself.

SOURCE: Liu Dianjue 劉殿爵, Chen Fangzheng 陳方正, and He Zhihua 何志華, *Liang Wudi Xiao Yan ji zhuzi suoyin* 梁武帝蕭衍集逐字索引 (Hong Kong: Chinese University Press, 2001), 24–25.

Further Reading

Chen, Jinhua. "'Pañcavārṣika' Assemblies in Liang Wudi's Buddhist Palace Chapel." *Harvard Journal of Asiatic Studies* 66, no. 1 (2006): 43–103.

Dien, Albert E. *Six Dynasties Civilization.* New Haven, CT: Yale University Press, 2007.

Strange, Mark. "Representations of Liang Emperor Wu as a Buddhist Ruler in Sixth- and Seventh-Century Texts." *Asia Major* (Third Series) 24, no. 2 (2011): 53–112.

Tian, Xiaofei. *Beacon Fire and Shooting Star: The Literary Culture of the Liang (502–57).* Cambridge, MA: Harvard University Press, 2007.

11

....

LATE TANG WRITERS ON LIFE BEYOND OFFICE-HOLDING
Accounts by Bai Juyi 白居易 (772–846)
and Lu Guimeng 陸龜蒙 (ca. 836–881)

....

Given the political climate, some men of letters in the ninth
century found it better to stay out of office and find meaning
in other ways, such as socializing with friends over wine
or pursuing a passion for tea.

In terms of culture, the ninth century was an exciting time, when many leading men of letters brought new energy to poetry, encouraged writing prose in
the "ancient style," and revitalized Confucian learning. Key figures included
Du You (735–812), Han Yu (768–824), Bai Juyi, and Liu Zongyuan (773–819).
In terms of politics, however, there was a sense that much had gone wrong.
Many of the provinces had become effectively independent of the central
government, and palace eunuchs had gained control of the throne. Men
continued to take the civil service examinations, but political advancement
was less straightforward.

The two essays below were written by poets who presented themselves as preferring the carefree life to the burdens of office. The first is by Bai Juyi, a *jinshi* holder who had had a relatively successful political career. He wrote this essay in retirement and claims in it to like his new identity as a master drinker, someone who prefers to drink wine with friends than worry about the problems of the government. Although Buddhists were enjoined to refrain from alcohol, offering wine had long been a common feature of entertaining guests and making sacrifices to gods and ancestors, perfectly acceptable in both Daoist and Confucian traditions. Among literati, drinking wine was also seen as a way to gain a higher level of insight and attain a carefree mindset, with Daoist overtones. It is said that after Bai Juyi's death, the "Biography of Master Drunken Poet" was inscribed onto a stele erected next to his tomb in Mount Longmen (Shanxi). For generations, people who came to pay respect would pour a cup of wine as a sacrificial offering, with the result that the tomb area was consistently damp.

The second essay was written a generation later by Lu Guimeng, who had failed the *jinshi* exams repeatedly and held only minor posts as a prefectural aide. After he gave up on an official career, he returned to his hometown and lived what was called the life of the recluse. He was an admirer of tea master Lu Yu (ca. 733–804) and his *The Classic of Tea* (Chajing) and enjoyed discussing tea and Lu Yu's work with eminent monks who visited him frequently. Lu Guimeng would go on to write *The Book of Tea Ranking* (Pindi shu), an important work on tea culture in the Tang. In his autobiography, Lu bragged about living near excellent sources of water for brewing tea, two of them at Buddhist temples, and, in fact, religion, especially Buddhism, was a key ingredient in the story of tea in China.

In these two essays, the authors are writing in a mildly humorous way, best captured by retaining the use of the third person.

Biography of Master Drunken Poet, by Bai Juyi

Master Drunken Poet cannot recall his name, place of origin, or official ranks and titles. As though in a trance, he has no idea who he is. For thirty years, he went from place to place seeking official posts. When approaching old age, he retired to Luoyang. His property has a five- or six-*mu* pond surrounded by thousands of bamboo trees, dozens of arbors, and all the typical features that make up an estate such as pavilions, terraces, boats, and bridges. He settled down there contently. Even though he is not rich, he does not suffer from cold or hunger, and even though he is old, he is not senile yet. He loves drinking wine, indulges himself in playing the zither, and is given to poetry. He hangs out mostly with wine imbibers, zither lovers, and poets. In addition, as a Buddhist he studies the Theravada, Mahayana, and Vajrayana traditions thoroughly. Monk Ruman of the Song Mountain is his best Buddhist friend. He sightsees with recluse Wei Chu of Pingquan. Liu Yuxi [772–842] of Pengcheng and he are poetry friends. Huangfu Shu [fl. 816] of Anding is his best drinking buddy. Seeing them brings him so much joy that he often forgets to return home. Within sixty or seventy *li* of Luoyang, he has toured every Daoist shrine, Buddhist temple, and mountain retreat, as well as every place with springs, rocks, flowers, or bamboo. He visits any family known for fine wine, music, book collections, or dancers. When he gets invitations to a meal, whether from a local official or a commoner, he always accepts. In fine moments in beautiful surroundings, or on a snowy day or moonlit evening, if a like-minded person comes by, he takes out his wine jar and poetry collections for their amusement.

After a bit of drinking, Master Drunken Poet pulls out the zither and plays "Autumn Longing." If he is in the mood, he has his servants form a musical ensemble and play "Rainbow Skirt and Feather Dress." If everyone is having a merry time, he calls his house courtesans over to sing "Song of Willows," with a dozen newly composed lyrics. They entertain themselves to their heart's content and do not stop until everyone is drunk. While in high spirits, he often walks to the neighbors, hikes around the countryside, or rides a horse into the city. Sometimes he travels in a sedan chair to see the countryside. A zither, a pillow, and few volumes of poetry by Tao Qian [ca. 365–425] and Xie Lingyun [385–433] are always placed inside the sedan chair. On the right and left poles, he hangs jugs of wine. He searches out rivers and gazes at mountains, visits them whenever he is in the mood, plays his zither and drinks wine during the journey, and returns home only after he has enjoyed himself to the fullest. He has lived like this for ten years now.

During this period, he has written poetry every day, perhaps a thousand or more poems in total. Every year, he makes several hundred jars of wine. He has lost count of how many poems he has written and the number of jars of wine he has filled over the past ten years. His family worries that he goes too far, but he just laughs and pays no attention. Only after their repeated expressions of concern did he respond this way:

It's human nature to have a special fondness for something—rarely do you find someone who is moderate in all matters. I am certainly not a temperate person. Imagine that unfortunately I was a greedy person intent on building up wealth, to the extent that I amassed valuables and grandiose houses, inviting disasters and endangering myself. In that case, would your advice have any impact on me? Or imagine that unfortunately I loved gambling, threw away tens of thousands of cash at will and lost the family fortune, so that my wife and children had to endure cold and hunger. In that case, would you be able to change my behavior? And what if unfortunately I was into elixirs, gave up on clothing and food, and focused only on transmuting lead and mercury, so that in the end I not only did not produce anything useful but also brought harm to myself. In that case, would your warnings make a difference? Now, fortunately, I am not into any of that; instead I am content with wine and poetry. Even if I indulge myself a bit excessively, what is the harm? Isn't it much better than being addicted to those three vices? This is why Liu Ling [ca. 221–300] would not listen to his wife's advice (on moderation in drinking) and Wang Ji [589–644] went to the Land of Drunkenness and did not return.

Afterward, he led his disciples into the wine cellar, where they circled around the wine jars. He sat on the floor with legs extended and his face looking upward. He let out a long and deep sigh: "I came to this world with talents and ability far inferior to those of the ancients. Yet I am wealthier than Qian Lü [Warring States period], have lived longer than Yan Yuan [521–481 BCE], have more food to eat than Bo Yi [late Shang], am happier than Rong Qiqi [595–500 BCE], and heathier than Wei Bin [286–312]. How extremely fortunate I am! What else do I need? If I give up on what I am fond of, how will I endure old age?"

He thus composed this "Poem on Expressing My Heart":

Holding a zither thrilled Rong Qiqi;
Drinking to excess freed Liu Ling.
Looking ahead I see blue mountains.
Readily I let my white hair grow.
I don't know
How many years I have left in this world,

So from now till the day I die,
Every day is a day to enjoy myself.

After reciting the poem, he smiled. He opened a wine jar and scooped out a cup of wine. After a few cups, he was drunk. From then on, he fell into an unending cycle of getting drunk, sobering up, reciting poetry, and getting drunk again. As a result, he came to the realization that life is really a dream, and wealth and high rank are as ephemeral as fleeting clouds. The sky is his tent, the earth is his mat; in the twinkling of an eye, a hundred years passes by. Joyfully, mindlessly, he forgets that old age is approaching. The ancients said that only in wine can one preserve oneself, hence he named himself Master Drunken Poet.

Written in the third year of the Kaicheng reign [838] at the age of sixty-seven. His beard may be completely white, his head half-bald, and his teeth all gone, but his passion for wine and poetry has not let up. Therefore, he says to his wife, "So far I have lived contently, but I don't know what will happen to my passion in the future."

SOURCE: Zhu Jincheng 朱金城, *Bai Juyi ji jianjiao* 白居易集箋校 (Shanghai: Shanghai Guji Chubanshe, 1988), 3782–83.

Biography of Mr. Fuli, by Lu Guimeng

No one knows where Mr. Fuli comes from. People saw him plowing in Fuli [Jiangsu] and gave him this name. Mr. Fuli is unrestrained by nature and loves books by the ancient sages. He has studied the six classics and understands their main ideas. Among the six classics, he is especially fond of *The Spring and Autumn Annals* (Chunqiu), picking out the parts that are profound and subtle. He read a book by Wang Tong [584–617] in which Wang commented, "After the Three Commentaries were written, parts of *The Spring and Autumn Annals* were scattered."[1] Mr. Fuli strongly agrees with this assessment. During the mid-Zhenyuan reign period, Han Huang [723–787] wrote *General Standards of the Spring and Autumn* (Chunqiu tongli) and had the text carved onto a stone tablet, acting as if study of the *Annals* was his responsibility. Even though his book is full of mistakes and shortcomings, for almost a century no one dared to criticize its faults. Fearing that later scholars might be misled by it, Mr. Fuli wrote a book to single out and criticize Han's missteps.

Mr. Fuli usually keeps himself amused by writing, not letting up even when suffering distress, illness, or other difficulties. He applies himself to revising, polishing, and making notes, and as the sheets of paper pile up, he tosses them into boxes. This goes on for years. After he finishes, even if an interested party leaves with his book and he later finds it in that person's home, he does not bother to claim authorship. In his youth, Mr. Fuli concentrated on poetry and wanted to challenge the authority of the rule-makers. His poems evolved over time, and his styles vary. His earlier poems were crushing and swirling, mobile yet strong, as if trying to seize monsters and shatter battle formations. In the end, however, he sought simplicity and tranquility.

Personally fastidious, his shelves, windows, desk, and seats are all neat without the slightest dust. When he acquires a book, he reads it thoroughly until he is completely familiar with its content before shelving it. He scrutinizes every book he puts his hands on, often going through it several times. Every day he has a red-ink brush and yellow-ink brush in hand.[2] Even though his collection is small, the books are all refined, reliable, checked against the authoritative texts, and suitable for wider circulation. When he borrows books from other people, if the bindings are broken or worn, he rethreads them; if there are errors in the texts, he corrects them. He enjoys hearing of other people's studies and does not stint on giving them well-thought-out feedback. When untrustworthy types carelessly damage or soil his books or fail to return them, Mr. Fuli sadly puts the blame on himself.

Mr. Fuli is not rich but he never talks about financial matters. When people bring up the subject, he responds, "Pursuing financial gain is what merchants do. For someone who is a scholar to pursue it, wouldn't that disturb the division of labor of the four classes? Besides, Confucius and Mencius would never approve." The place where Mr. Fuli lives has a pond several *mu* in size, a thirty-room house, fields measuring a hundred thousand paces [about four hundred acres], more than ten head of cattle, and a dozen farmhands. His fields are low-lying, and one summer, after a heavy summer rain, the flood water merged with the Yangzi River, so no one could tell whose land was whose. As a result, Mr. Fuli's crops failed and his granary did not have even a peck of stored grain. Mr. Fuli picked up a basket and shovel and personally led his farmhands to build a levee. From then on, every year, no matter how fierce the surge, the flood waters never came over the top of the levee to inundate the crops. When someone ridiculed him [for performing manual labor], Mr. Fuli said, "Both Yao and Shun were dark-skinned and wiry, and the Great Yu had callused feet, but weren't they sages? I am just a common person. If I don't work hard, how can I support my wife and children? Should I be just a flea on a precious vessel or a rat in a granary?"

Mr. Fuli loves tea. He owns a small tea plantation in the foothills of the Guzhu Mountain [Jiangsu]; the 10 percent of the crop that he takes for rent is just enough to cover his own tea consumption. He wrote *The Book of Tea Ranking* (Pindi shu) as a sequel to both *The Classic of Tea* (Chajing) and *The Tea Formulas* (Chajue).[3] Zhang Youxin [fl. 814] of Nanyang [Henan] had written *On Water* (Shuishuo), in which Zhang ranked the seven best sources for water suitable for brewing tea. Ranked number two is the water at the Stone Spring of the Huishan Temple, number three is the water of the Stone Well of Tiger Hill Temple, and number six is the Wusong River. All three places are less than one hundred *li* from Mr. Fuli's place. Eminent monks and recluses often visit, adding to his enjoyment.

Earlier, due to his fondness for wine, Mr. Fuli got really sick. For two years he was bedridden, as his vital energy and blood were depleted. Since then, whenever a visitor comes, he takes out a wine bottle and cups but no longer drinks much himself. Mr. Fuli does not like to socialize with vulgar types and often refuses to see them even if they show up at his door. He does not own a carriage and has no interest in paying social calls. He never joins his relatives for seasonal ancestral rites or funerals. When weather and health permit, he sets out in a tiny boat that is fitted out with an awning, table, and seat, and supplied with books, a tea set, writing supplies, fishing tackle, and a young boat hand. If the place he visits is not entirely to his liking, he returns without hesitation, more speedily than the flight of a water bird or a frightened mountain deer. Because people call him the Wanderer in Rivers and Lakes, he composed and chanted "Biography of the Wanderer in Rivers and Lakes." He pays no attention to what others say about him, good or bad, and glib tongues make no impression on him.

Mr. Fuli gets easily irritated and has trouble suppressing his anger. Even though he sees this as a failing, he has not been able to change. Because he has neither committed a major indiscretion nor held office, his name is not widely known. No one in the world really understands him. Could he be someone remarkable, like the anonymous old man fishing in the Pei River who invented acupuncture, the fisherman from Qu Yuan's parable, or the old man sailing on the Yangzi River who saved Wu Zixu?

SOURCE: Dong Gao 董誥, ed., *Quan Tang wen* 全唐文 (1814; repr., Beijing: Zhonghua Shuju, 1983), 801.24b–26b.

Notes

1. The Three Commentaries refers to *The Gongyang Commentaries of the Spring and Autumn Annals, The Guliang Commentaries of the Spring and Autumn Annals,* and *The Zuo Commentaries of the Spring and Autumn Annals.*

2. Red-ink brushes were often used for punctuating, commenting on, and annotating books, while yellow-ink brushes were used as "white-out" to correct the mistakes.

3. *The Classic of Tea* was written by Lu Yu, and *The Tea Formulas* was written by Monk Jiaoran (730–99).

Further Reading

Berkowitz, Alan J. *Patterns of Disengagement: The Practice and Portrayal of Reclusion in Early Medieval China.* Stanford, CA: Stanford University Press, 2000.

DeBlasi, Anthony. *Reform in the Balance: The Defense of Literary Culture in Mid-Tang China.* Albany: State University of New York Press, 2002.

Shields, Anna M. *One Who Knows Me: Friendship and Literary Culture in Mid-Tang China.* Cambridge, MA: Harvard University Press, 2015.

Yue, Isaac, and Siufu Tang, eds. *Scribes of Gastronomy: Representations of Food and Drink in Imperial Chinese Literature.* Hong Kong: Hong Kong University Press, 2013.

12

....

MOURNING FRIENDS
AND RELATIONS
Elegies by Han Yu 韓愈 (768–824)
and Han Qi 韓琦 (1008–1075)

....

*Read during mourning ceremonies, elegies addressed
recently deceased friends or relatives. The examples
by Han Yu and Han Qi relate intimate details about
their relationships with the deceased.*

Death rituals occupied an important place in Chinese life since ancient times. As a ritual and cultural practice, mortuary and sacrificial writing gained greater importance as forms of commemoration from the Tang dynasty (618–907) onward. This was seen in the popularity of funerary biographies, dirges, elegies, and related texts. An elegy (*jiwen*) was a communication between a mourner and a deceased person and was offered to the spirit of the deceased along with food and wine. In addition to those written for relatives, Chinese scholar-officials wrote elegies for friends, colleagues, and acquaintances. Elegy writing grew to be such an important obligation and symbol of a close relationship that those who were unable to attend a funeral or memorial service would compose one and have it delivered over long distances. Failure to do so was known to have caused endless speculation regarding souring friendship or political betrayal. Elegies written by and for famous people were routinely copied, compiled in collected works, and admired for their literary and artistic quality by those who had no direct connections with either the author or the deceased. As commemorative literature, elegies are often replete with allusions to classical works and hyperbolic language. They nonetheless can tell us much about the lives of both the deceased and the mourner: writing an elegy provided the perfect opportunity for the mourners to reflect on their most precious memories of the deceased and articulate their emotional responses to their losses.

The first selection below was written by the famous Tang scholar Han Yu for his only nephew, Twelfth Brother. Orphaned as a boy, Han Yu was brought up by his brother and sister-in-law, so grew up in the same household with Twelfth Brother. Han's narrative reveals nothing of Han Yu the great writer and Confucian thinker, only a middle-aged man lamenting the passing of a junior family member and longtime companion. It should be noted that Han's demonstration of intense grief was somewhat unconventional. Even though parents and senior family members composed elegies and epitaphs for their children, rarely did they allow themselves to express their emotions at such length.

The next two selections were composed by Han Qi, one of the most influential statesmen in the Northern Song (960–1127), both for social equals. The first one, dated 1052, was addressed to Fan Zhongyan (989–1052), one of the most revered political and literary figures in Chinese history. Han and Fan shared some of the greatest moments of their lives: they were co-commanders in the Song-Xia War (1039–1042), collaborated in a short-lived yet important reform movement (the Qingli Reform, 1043–1044), and considered each other good friends. They last saw each other in 1044 but kept in touch through letters and exchanging literary compositions.

Han Qi composed the second elegy in 1071 to mourn the passing of Zhao Ziyuan (999–1071), the husband of his wife's sister. Han and Zhao had known each other since both were junior officials in the capital, and even though their careers took different paths, they stayed in touch their whole lives and exchanged many poems over the years.

Elegy for Twelfth Brother, by Han Yu

It took me, your uncle Yu, a week after hearing of your death to gain enough control of my grief to compose this expression of my feelings. I am sending Jianzhong on the long journey to prepare the sacrificial food and drink and to report to your spirit the following.

Alas! I was orphaned when still a very small child and had little memory of my parents once I was grown. I depended completely on your parents [lit. my older brother and his wife]. When your father died in the south in the prime of life, you and I were still young. We accompanied your mother to Heyang [Henan], where she buried your father. You and I then moved to Jiangnan [lower Yangzi region].

We were miserable, lonely orphans who spent every day together. I had had three older brothers, but they had all died early, so you and I were the only descendants in our family, you in the grandchild generation, me in the son generation, each generation with a single survivor. Your mother once held you and pointed to me and said, "You two are the only ones left from two generations of the Han family." At the time you were very small, so you probably do not remember it. Although I remember what she said, at the time I did not comprehend the sadness of her statement.

I was nineteen when I went to the capital for the first time. Four years later, I returned home to see you. After another four years, I went to Heyang to visit the family graves, where I met you, there to bury your mother. Two years later, you came to see me while I was serving under Vice Director Dong in Bianzhou [Henan] and stayed for a year before leaving to get your family. But the next year, after Vice Director Dong died, I left Bianzhou, so you did not in the end return with them.

That year I was assigned to the military garrison at Xuzhou [Jiangsu]. The messenger I had sent to get you had just set off when I was reassigned, so again in the end you did not join me. I rationalized that if in fact you had joined me in the east, it would have been temporary, so if we wanted a more enduring arrangement, it would be better to go back west. I was going to set things up and get you. Alas! Who could have foretold that so soon after we separated you would die so suddenly! When we were both young, I assumed that even if we lived apart for a while, we would eventually live together permanently. On that basis I left you and traveled to the capital in my quest for a meager government salary. Had I in fact known how things would turn out,

I would not have tolerated living apart a single day, even to gain the highest post in the government.

Last year, when Meng Dongye was heading your way, I wrote a letter to you: "I am not yet forty, and yet my vision is dimming, my hair turning gray, and my teeth getting loose. Considering that the men in my father's generation and my own generation had seemed so strong and healthy yet died young, I wonder how a weakling like me can survive much longer. With me unable to leave and you unwilling to come, I worry that any day now I could die and you would be burdened with limitless pain." Who would have thought that the younger and healthier of us would die and the older and sicklier one would live on?

Alas! Can this really be true, or is it a dream? The report cannot be true, can it? How can I believe that my elder brother, who was so virtuous, would have his heir pass away so young? Or that you could be so brilliant but reap none of the rewards you deserved? It is unbelievable that the young and strong would die young and the old and decrepit would survive—it must be a dream, or the report must be wrong. Dongye's letter, Genglan's report, why are they here by my side?

Alas! It seems to be true—my elder brother was so virtuous, and yet his heir died young; you who were so brilliant and able to raise our family got none of what you deserved. This is what is meant by the saying that Heaven is truly unfathomable, the spirits impossible to understand. Or the saying that we cannot use reason to predict who will have a long life. From this year on, my silvery hair will turn whiter and my loose teeth fall out, my body will grow more feeble and my mental acuity decline. How long will it be before I follow you in death? If the dead are conscious, our separation will not last much longer. If they are not conscious, my sorrow will not last that much longer before I am without sorrow forever.

Your son is just ten and my son only five. If a strong young man like you failed to survive, is there hope that these children will achieve adulthood? Alas! Such sorrow!

Last year you wrote in a letter, "I have come down with beriberi, and often it is quite bad." I responded, "This is a disease that Jiangnan people often get." I did not get alarmed. Alas! Was this in the end what cut your life short? Or was another disease the cause? Your letter was dated the seventeenth of the sixth month. Dongye said you died on the second day of the sixth month, and Genglan's report did not mention the date. Probably Dongye's messenger did not think to ask your family members about the date, and Genglan did not realize that he should mention the date. When Dongye wrote to me, he must have asked the messenger, who made up something. What is the truth?

I am now sending Jianzhong to make the sacrificial offerings to you and offer my condolences to your orphans and the nursemaid. If they have enough food to remain there until the burial, then he will wait for them, then bring them here. If they do not have enough to get by until the funeral, he is to bring them here right away and leave the funeral arrangements in the hands of the servants. If I am able to arrange it, I will later move your grave to the family cemetery. Only once that is done will I feel I have done my part.

Alas! I do not know when you fell ill or on which day you died. While you were alive, I was not able to support you so we could live together, and with your death, I am unable to put my hands on you to exhaust my sorrow. I will not be supervising the encoffining or attending the burial. It must be my disregard of the spirits that brought on your early death. Neither filial nor loving, I have been unable either to support you in life or to take care of you in death. One of us is on the edge of Heaven, the other the margins of the earth. While you were alive, your shadow did not cross my body, with death your soul will not visit me in my dreams. It is all my fault! No one else is to blame! How vast is the blue Heaven! From this day forth, I will detach myself from the world of men. I will look for a few hundred *mu* of land at the confluence of the Yi and Ying Rivers to spend my remaining years. I will teach your son and mine and hope they grow to adulthood. I will provide for our daughters till they marry. I will make this my prime purpose in life.

Alas! I am out of words, but my emotions will never cease. Are you aware of this? Alas, the grief! I make this offering.

SOURCE: Han Yu, *Han Yu wenji huijiao jianzhu* 韓愈文集彙校箋注, ed. and annot. Liu Zhenlun 劉真倫 and Yue Zhen 岳珍 (Beijing: Zhonghua Shuju, 2010), 1:13.1469–71.

Elegy for Mr. Fan Zhongyan, the Cultured and Upright, by Han Qi

On this unspecified day, I have prepared clear wine and delicious food to sacrifice to the spirit of Mr. Fan, the academician.

Alas, the grief! Heaven definitely created you for the sake of the Song. It meant for you to assist his majesty in the manner of Yao and Shun, which you performed selflessly and loyally. You strove to reform popular customs to match the era of the Zhou kings Cheng and Kang, and you thought long and hard about how to treat the people with benevolence. You were promoted to the top ranks, so no one can say you were not recognized. On behalf of the court, you pacified the frontiers, so no one can say that you were not given important responsibilities. Then why did your goal of achieving peace and harmony fail, making your grand vision just a dream? This is what vexed you and pained everyone else in the world as well. How could my grief come only from losing a lifelong friend? The news of your death made me wail bitterly. Alas, the grief!

I had not had much contact with you when I first entered officialdom, yet we shared similar goals and principles. When I was appointed to lead the troops on the western borders, I finally got to work with you. United in our determination, we pledged to eliminate our enemies. Our bond was built upon our devotion to the dynasty. We were as close as brothers. Drawing on our loyalty and trustworthiness, we overcame innumerable difficulties and dangerous situations. I admired you but knew I would never match you, just as a nag looks up to a racehorse, and ten nags together would not be able to catch up with one racehorse. How could I dare to ride side by side with you? Yet people did not recognize this and referred to us as Han-Fan. In my heart, I knew I was not your match and felt greatly mortified. Largely due to you, we eventually conquered the barbarians.

After the rebellious Tanguts surrendered, we returned to the court together. You and I were both put in key positions to take charge of important matters. We took opposing stands on key issues concerning the dynasty's long-term fortunes, then reconciled as if nothing had happened. We were accused of forming factions, a dubious charge. In the end, our vision did not conform with the times, and people labeled you foolish and me ignorant. One after another, we were demoted to local positions. Slander made our lives harder. Grateful that you understood me, I remained your steadfast friend. Alas, the grief!

Dingzhou [Hebei], where I was posted, and Qingzhou [Shandong], where you held office, were not far apart. After you left the capital, you wrote regularly and we became even closer friends. Your letters were written in neat, small characters; the beautiful words and perfect calligraphy filled the sheets. You said that you were fit and healthy and sent me your regards. I assumed that you were doing fine and taking care of yourself.

Then suddenly you wrote that you were ill and asked for a doctor. Shocked, I immediately sent a messenger and waited to hear from you. At the time, you happened to have been reassigned to Yingzhou [Anhui] and traveled there by sedan chair. You even took the trouble of writing a few words to me. Thinking that you had somewhat recovered, I felt relieved. I was preparing a letter and medicine to send you when I heard from Cai Yuangui that you had passed away. Reading Yuangui's letter left me stunned. In shock, I couldn't breathe or taste my food.

Your way of serving the throne was consistent throughout. Life is bound to end—even the sages could not escape this. How unfortunate that at a time when the country needs wise and virtuous men, Heaven is so inhumane that it deprives us of one! Alas, the grief!

Throughout your life, you followed the model of Kui and Xie [who assisted the ancient sage king Shun]. Your outstanding writing and policies as well as your unparalleled loyalty and principles will be forever remembered. They match those of the ancients and will be examples for future sages. Your exceptional character and achievements will be recorded in the history books and widely recognized for tens of thousands of generations. In this sense, should your passing be counted as premature death or as long life? I trust the wise will be able to judge. How could I fully recount your lifelong accomplishments in one elegiac essay! What I can do is to think back on your life and mourn in silence. As long as I live, my grief will persist. Are you conscious of this?

SOURCE: Zeng Zaozhuang 曾棗莊 et al., eds., *Quan Song wen* 全宋文 (Shanghai: Shanghai Shiji Chuban Youxian Gongsi, Shanghai Cishu Chubanshe, Anhui Chuban Jituan, Anhui Jiaoyu Chubanshe, 2006), 40:860.133–34.

Elegy for the Retired Academician Mr. Zhao Ziyuan, by Han Qi

On a certain day in the eighth month of the fourth year of the Xining reign period [1071], I am sending my attendant Zhang Shichang to offer clear wine and delicious food to the spirit of the academician Zhao Ziyuan:

Alas! We were such intimate, like-minded friends. In terms of our relationship, we were both sons-in-law of the Cui family. In the early Mingdao reign period [1032–1033], we both served in the Hanlin Academy. Promoted at the same time, we became even closer. When on duty, we stayed at the same dormitory; when apart, we thought alike. We were like two fast horses riding on flat terrain, wanting to race for a thousand *li* and arrive at the destination at the same time. How would we know that, in the middle of our journey, our courses would diverge?

You were content with your lot in life so never haggled over it, but I was disappointed that your talent was not fully utilized. You served in multiple local offices as a conventional official. In old age, you sought a position in the censorate, then retired shortly afterward. In the capital, Luoyang, you built a house where you planned to enjoy a leisurely life and attain your lofty goals. Who would have thought that the quiet life would damage your body? From far away, you sent a messenger to inform me of your illness. Shocked, I sent a doctor out of concern. No sooner had the doctor arrived than you passed away. Alas, the grief!

You lived to over seventy, which is more than a long life. Your sons are doing exceptionally well in their government careers. Entering officialdom, you achieved a good reputation; retiring, you cut off worldly burdens. Nothing in your life caused any regret. What has saddened me is that our relationship was so profound and intimate, yet I will never see your face or hear your voice again, nor will I ever receive another letter from you. I am not at your funeral to offer this in person. Hollering into the wind, with tears streaming down my cheeks, I am sending a messenger to deliver this meager offering. If somehow you receive it, come to meet me in a dream. Please enjoy my offerings.

SOURCE: Zeng Zaozhuang 曾棗莊 et al., eds., *Quan Song wen* 全宋文 (Shanghai: Shanghai Shiji Chuban Youxian Gongsi, Shanghai Cishu Chubanshe, Anhui Chuban Jituan, Anhui Jiaoyu Chubanshe, 2006), 40:860.143–44.

Further Reading

Ebrey, Patricia Buckley, Ping Yao, and Cong Ellen Zhang, eds. *Chinese Funerary Biographies: An Anthology of Remembered Lives*. Seattle: University of Washington Press, 2019.

Hartman, Charles. *Han Yü and the T'ang Search for Unity*. Princeton, NJ: Princeton University Press, 1986.

Shields, Anna M. *One Who Knows Me: Friendship and Literary Culture in Mid-Tang China*. Cambridge, MA: Harvard University Asia Center, 2015.

——. "Words for the Dead and the Living: Innovations in the Mid-Tang 'Prayer Text' (Jiwen)." *Tang Studies* 25 (2007): 111–45.

13

AN ADVOCATE OF THE SIMPLE LIFE

Autobiography by Liu Kai 柳開 (948–1001)

In the early years of the Northern Song, Liu Kai was an important figure in the Confucian revival movement and the effort to promote ancient style writing, linking him to such prominent Tang predecessors as Han Yu. In this piece, he provides a description of his personality and his scholarly and intellectual ambitions.

The period from the mid Tang (618–907) through the Song (960–1279) was a time of major political, intellectual, social, and cultural transformations. Among the most important changes was the resurgence of Confucian scholarship. Troubled by the dominance of Buddhism, political decentralization, and other problems, thinkers such as Han Yu (768–824) and Liu Zongyuan (773–819) in the Tang and Zhu Xi (1130–1200) in the Song gave Confucian philosophy new meanings, new structures, and a new textual basis in their energetic promotion of its centrality in Chinese culture. This intellectual movement resulted in the establishment of a "new" type of Confucianism, the Learning of the Way or Principle, better known in the West as Neo-Confucianism.

The author of the following autobiography, Liu Kai, was an important link in this movement. Liu was a native of Hebei, a region that had suffered greatly from political fragmentation in the wake of the An Lushan Rebellion (755–763) and continued to be known for its "knight-errant" culture in the first decades of the Northern Song (960–1127). Anecdotes and Liu's own work portray him as an unruly young man who challenged the popular fear of ghosts. He once threatened to set fire to the family residence if his uncle did not give him money to aid a person in financial straits. Liu Kai earned the prestigious *jinshi* degree in 973 and served in over a dozen low-ranking civil and military positions, gaining recognition for his ideas on military and border affairs. Liu admired Han Yu and Liu Zongyuan so much that he later gave himself two courtesy names, Jianyu (supporting or standing on Han Yu's shoulders) and Shaoxian (carrying on the cause of the predecessors, or Shaoyuan, continuing the mission of Liu Zongyuan), thus revealing his intentions to "clear a path for the Sagely Way" (Kai, the meaning of his name).

This autobiography clearly owes a debt to earlier ones, such as those by Bai Juyi and Lu Guimeng (selection 11). While in those cases we retained the original third-person voice in our translation, this time we have used the first person.

Biography of the Country Fellow of the Eastern Suburb

I, who refer to myself as the country fellow of the Eastern Suburb, have the personal name of Jianyu [lit., standing on Han Yu's shoulders] and courtesy name of Shaoyuan [continuing the mission of Liu Zongyuan]. The reason why the sobriquet does not mention my clan name is because it is the same as my family name. I am a native of Wei [Hebei], but because I live to the left of one of the city wall gates, I use "Eastern Suburb" to identify myself as a country fellow.

Someone once said, "You live in a town but call it a suburb. You are a member of the scholar-official class yet call yourself a hick. Isn't this misleading?" I replied, "What I consider a suburb, you call a town; what I take as a country fellow, you think a scholar. How could I not understand that a suburb is not a town and a scholar is different from a rustic? But do these facts have any connections to the real meaning of the terms? When I live at home, I call where I live the eastern suburb. When I am away, I call it the suburb of Wei. This is to distinguish being inside and outside."

I am by nature an unsophisticated person. I am simple but not dull, innocent yet not ignorant. Although accommodating, I know when to move forward. Although tough, I know when to pull back. When pushed forward, I do not hesitate to advance. When called back, I do not resent the brave ones going forward. I do not refuse to see those who come to visit even if they are my enemies. Similarly, I do not chase after those who depart even if they are my intimates. Generally speaking, I focus on people's good qualities and disregard their shortcomings. Profit does not tempt me. Potential disasters do not deter me. An introvert, I am as though without ego. Unbounded, I am as though lacking a sense of self. I do not consider the Heaven and Earth as the only things that are vast. I do not take the sun and moon as the only things that are bright. I am not troubled by ominous weather patterns. I am not in awe of the power of the great mountains and rivers. Nobody fully understands me. I do not approve or disapprove of those who associate with me. Nor do I doubt or envy anyone. Whether they are virtuous or foolish, of high or low rank, I figure that it is a matter of luck that I know them. The more they interact with me, the more they see my profoundness. Some rascals, thinking I was an ignorant person just like them, tricked me. After succeeding once, they tried a second or third time to swindle me for their gain. Even though they failed in the end, I did not change in the slightest how I treated them or expose their deceptions. In the end, none of them was able to fool me again. My family elders used these incidents to caution me. I laughed, "Those petty rascals were trying in vain. I once caught a tiger in its cave. I blocked the entrance with a sharp knife in my hand. The tiger, stuck inside, was not able to leap to a better position. What could it do when I was in control of the narrow exit? Why should I worry about those stupid people!"

When guests come from afar, I go all out to entertain them, eating, laughing, and napping with them, indifferent to status differences. My family elders thought this unwise: "Why do you act this way? Isn't this taking things too lightly? Shouldn't you pay attention to what sort of people they are? I countered, "They are human beings. So am I. What separates us? Besides, are the realms of Heaven and Earth divided into insiders and outsiders? All within the four seas are my kin. If I start drawing boundaries, won't I end up treating my parents and brothers as outsiders? If I do not treat others as outsiders, will others treat me as an outsider?" My arguments proved persuasive.

In order to send my guests off with gifts, I do not hesitate to pawn my clothes for cash. Similarly, I cut back on my own food in order to help those struggling with hunger or hardship, worrying only that I cannot offer long-term help. By contrast, I give little thought to my own problems. Someone once said, "You are poor and of low rank but strive to be generous and upright. This is what Sima Qian ridiculed." I replied, "Alas! The true gentleman worries about other people's emergencies, not his own. When one is poor and lowly, it is difficult to be generous to others. For the wealthy and influential, it is easy. Besides, Sima was hardly the ideal gentlemen. The book he wrote is at odds with Confucian teachings. For example, he devalued recluses and celebrated villains, and he placed the Daoist Huang-Lao School above the Six Classics. I would be ashamed to act that way."

In cases where people were feuding, I sometimes would get them together and ask them why they hated each other. "You schemed against him but resent him for conspiring against you in response," I would say. "This cycle of retaliation has to stop for the animosity to end. You should not hate him for not being nice to you since it begins with your not treating him well. If you help others, they will want the best for you. Have you seen how robbers act? They commit cruel, dishonest, foul, and evil crimes, to the extent that even their parents cannot stand them. Yet, among themselves, their bonds are strong. They would sacrifice their lives to protect each other and stay loyal through thick and thin. There is no other explanation than the fact that they understand each other and commit to each other. If bandits can act like this, shouldn't good people like you! Please change your ways." Some previous enemies reconciled after hearing my arguments.

My family was so poor that there was often no food for the next day and no clothes for the next season. At fifteen or sixteen, I took up writing. The following year, Mr. Zhao introduced me to the work of Han Yu. I liked it so much I took to reciting it. At the time, no one in the world talked about ancient-style writing. In addition, I was young and my friends did not share my interests. But I held Han's books in my hands all day long and on my own gradually deepened my understanding of them. My late father, seeing that I loved Han's work so much, indulged me and did not question whether my passions fit the times.

When I reached fifteen, the age of capping, my father passed away. By then I had achieved a deep understanding of the strong points and marvelous passages of Han's writing and was ready to pen my own compositions in his style. An uncle restored a bathhouse in a Buddhist temple in our hometown and asked me to compose an account of the deed as a test of my literary ability. Although at the time I was ill, one day I asked for paper and ink to be brought to my sickbed, then wrote the essay without having to make any revisions, to the amazement of my family. They circulated it among interested parties, who called it outstanding. Others, though, took offense. They laughed at me and said, "Foolish and arrogant boy, claiming, 'I will restore the ancient-style prose by myself.' How could his family be so indulgent?" Such carping was widely repeated. Upon hearing this, my uncles and brothers feared that the substance of my writing was not in accord with the time and urged me to follow the conventions of the day.

I completely ignored their advice and, if anything, became more determined to focus on the ancients. I talked exclusively about Confucius, Mencius, Xunzi, and Yang Xiong, taking them as my models. Everyone thought I had gone crazy, the unconventionality of my writing taken as evidence of its inferiority. In the *wuchen* year of the Qiande reign period [968], I began to compose *The Book of the Eastern Suburb* (Dongjiao shu), in one hundred chapters, trying to make it amusing. I was halfway through when, one day, I burned everything I had written, saying, "My late mentors would not have approved of this. I originally studied the classics. How did I turn around and become a writer of random notes?" When people heard what I said, they found me even harder to comprehend.

I set my mind on transforming conventional practice. My followers considered themselves the disciples of Mencius and Yang Xiong. Those who wanted to study with me all said, "Two hundred years after Han Yu, you, our master, have appeared." I always responded by saying, "I would not dare to refuse this mission and am willing to do my best." Someone said, "Should you share the responsibility?" I replied, "This is what is meant by not leaving to others what one ought to do oneself." Someone else asked, "Who was superior, Tuizhi [Han Yu] or Zihou [Liu Zongyuan]?" I replied, "Their writing is close, but their way is different." When asked to explain, I said, "Liu's ancestors were Buddhists. For this reason, he is inferior to Han Yu."

In the early years of the Kaibao reign [968–976], I wrote the ninety-chapter *Unofficial History and Biographies of Eastern Suburb* (Kaibao yeshi zhuan). When someone asked why I wrote it, I said, "I took it as my duty." When someone asked why I called it *Unofficial History*, I answered, "It gathers things that were not recorded in the state history." When someone asked, "How do you compare with Sima Qian [145–86 BCE], Fan Ye [398–445], and Ban Gu [32–92]?" I answered, "Sima was concise and argumentative. His work was broad, disordered but comprehensive. Ban's writing was refined in vocabulary and proper in its use of the classics. His work is remarkable, concise, and selective. The lowest of the three is Fan. His work is not as good as the other two and is profuse and in poor taste. My work falls closer to the two good ones." When someone questioned the usefulness of the book, I said, "If it is read, it will be useful to the world. Like the works of the earlier masters, if it is not read, it just exists. It is up to the world to decide whether to read it or not. What do I know?"

I wrote "Differentiating Heaven?," "On the Sea," and "Explaining the Classics" because I thought that the ancients had failed to investigate the truths underlying Heaven and Earth, the capacity of the sea, and the foundation of the classics. The three essays analyze the issues and expose fallacies, achieving insights the ancient worthies had failed to attain. Later, my writing style gradually shifted from Han Yu's and was modeled directly on the Six Classics. When someone asked, "Why did you first advocate then discard [Han Yu]?" I told him, "Mencius, Xunzi, Yang Xiong, and Han Yu were all disciples of the sages. They reached different levels by studying the masters. Those with less ability can choose one of them to reach his goal. That was the route I took. If you do what I did, you can get there too."

At the time, I was just twenty-four. Two years later, I wrote another autobiography, in which I called myself Mr. Restoring What Was Lost.

The commentator says:

The Country Fellow of the Eastern Suburb referred to himself as Standing on the Shoulders [Jianyu] of something because he loved the way of the ancients. He called himself Inheriting and Continuing [Kai] something as he revered ancestral virtues. Tuizhi is greater than Zihou. So he used Yu [Jian-yu] in his name. Zihou is second [to Han Yu], so he used Zihou's name [Zong-yuan] in his literary name [Shao-yuan]. In addition, because Han and Liu lived in the same era and followed the same way, he picked [the auspicious sign of] their accompanying each other, hoping that he would benefit from their good names. Having seen his writing and conduct, it is not an exaggeration to say that he matched the two masters.

SOURCE: Zeng Zaozhuang 曾棗莊 et al., eds., *Quan Song wen* 全宋文 (Shanghai: Shanghai Shiji Chuban Youxian Gongsi, Shanghai Cishu Chubanshe, Anhui Chuban Jituan, Anhui Jiaoyu Chubanshe, 2006), 6:127.390–93.

Further Reading

Bol, Peter K. *Neo-Confucianism in History*. Cambridge, MA: Harvard University Asia Center, 2008.

——. *"This Culture of Ours": Intellectual Transitions in T'ang and Sung China*. Stanford, CA: Stanford University Press, 1992.

Hartman, Charles. *Han Yu and the T'ang Search for Unity*. Princeton, NJ: Princeton University Press, 1986.

Zhang, Cong Ellen. "How Long Did It Take to Plan a Funeral? Liu Kai's (948–1101) Experience Burying His Parents." *Frontier of History in China* 13, no. 4 (2018): 508–30.

RECORDS OF THINGS
SEEN AND HEARD
Prefaces to five Song miscellanies (11th–13th c.)

*In these prefaces to their collections of miscellaneous notes, Song
writers reminisce about the long trips they had taken, what they
had learned over a lifetime, and their encounters with interesting
people, natural conditions, and social customs.*

In the history of Chinese literature, *biji* referred to a variety of collections of
miscellaneous writing about things "seen and heard." First appearing in the
Six Dynasties, *biji* production reached a high point in the Song dynasty due
to three major factors: the expansion of the publishing industry, the growing
size of the scholar-official class, and the rising level of literacy among the
general population. About five hundred *biji* collections have survived from
the Song. The sizes of these works vary greatly. Some contain only a few dozen
short entries. Others include lengthier episodes and dozens, even hundreds,
of chapters. Equally diverse are the backgrounds of *biji* authors. While tow-
ering scholarly and literary figures such as Su Zhe (1039–1112) and Huang
Tingjian (1045–1105) composed *biji*, the majority of *biji* authors, such as Wang
Dechen (1036–1116) and Zhang Shinan (fl. 1228), achieved neither high office

nor literary fame. Their *biji* collections were often their only surviving works, bearing witness to these men's travel records, social connections, scholarly and artistic inclinations, and everyday concerns.

A prominent feature of *biji* writing is that many items in them can be loosely categorized as autobiographical in nature. In fact, Song writers routinely stated in *biji* prefaces that their writing was the result of years of record-keeping of items acquired through hands-on investigation and personal experience. As a result, a typical *biji* would include direct observations about natural conditions and local customs as well as notes on encounters with interesting personalities and unusual occurrences. In keeping track of and compiling this miscellaneous information into books, Song *biji* authors elevated the importance of the empirical knowledge that they had gained over time.

The five *biji* prefaces below were written by four authors. Wang Dechen expressed the wish to record all the important things that he had learned over a long life. Su Zhe stressed that it was not until living in exile that he had the free time to recollect and write down his life experience. As an admirer and follower of Huang Tingjian, Fan Xinzhong (fl. 1104–1105) traveled long distances to meet Huang in exile in southern China, took care of Huang in his last year of life, and played a key role in preserving Huang's journal. Zhang Shinan not only presented himself as a knowledgeable person but also stressed that the things he had seen and heard should not be forgotten. Read together, these brief accounts give us glimpses of Song society and culture and the lives of Song scholar-officials.

Preface to *Zhushi*, by Wang Dechen 王得臣

When I was a boy, my father ordered me to accompany him and study in the capital. Ten years passed before I earned a degree. After that, pressed by official appointments, I traveled north and south for almost three decades. Whenever I learned something from the comments of teachers and friends, the pleasant conversation of my guests and colleagues, or my own eyes and ears, I would write it down without fail. In old age, after I reached sixty, I retired from the Ministry of Revenue and returned home. Living in reclusion to recover from an illness, with little to do, I took out what I had recorded, by then quite voluminous, and reedited it, ending up with 284 items.

My records touch on affairs in the capital and outside it in the prefectures and towns. To make the entries more convenient for careful study, I classified them into forty-four categories and assembled them into three chapters. I named the collection The *History of Zhu* (Zhushi), using "history" because its content is based on reliable records, not exaggerations, embellishments, or deceptions.[1] Although my writing belongs to the Lesser Way, it has items that make it worth leafing through. I hope those who read it do not laugh at me.

At age eighty, on the fifteenth day of the seventh month of the *yiwei* year in the Zhenghe reign period [1115] of the Great Song dynasty, I, Wang Dechen (master of Fengtai, courtesy name Yanfu) added this preface to my compilation.

SOURCE: Wang Dechen, *Zhushi* 麈史, ed. Huang Chunyan 黃純艷, in *Quan Song biji* 全宋筆記, ed. Zhu Yi'an 朱易安 and Fu Xuancong 傅璇琮, series 1, vol. 10 (Zhengzhou: Daxiang Chubanshe, 2006), 5.

Preface to *Brief Record at Longchuan,* by Su Zhe 蘇轍

From Yunzhou [Jiangxi], I was exiled to Leizhou [Guangdong], and from Leizhou to Xunzhou [also Guangdong]. Over the course of two years, a few dozen of us, young and old, traveled by land and water for tens of thousands of *li*, always needing to find ways to feed and clothe ourselves. My whole life my family never accumulated any rare things. I had several hundred volumes of books but had given them away beforehand.

Upon our arrival at Longchuan, the government did not even allow us to live in a Buddhist temple or Daoist shrine. Using our last fifty strings of cash, I purchased a ten-room house. Once we repaired the leaks and damage, it just barely protected us from wind and rain.

Past the north wall was an empty lot that could be used to grow vegetables and a well for irrigation. My son Yuan and I did the hoeing. After a few months with rainfall, chives, green onions, cluster mallow, and mustard sprouted up. They could be eaten fresh or pickled for later use. Once the field was clear, I no longer had anything to do there.

Given the small size of the prefecture's population, I had no one to talk to. There was an old man named Huang whose ancestors had been officials. His family had books, but he himself could not read. From time to time, I would borrow one or two of their books to entertain my eyes. But I was old and my eyesight fading so could not read for long. My alternative was to close my door and shut my eyes and think about past events, as if recalling dreams. I might only remember one or two out of ten incidents. My recollections vary in detail and are probably not all worth recording. I had Yuan sit next to me and write the incidents down on paper. Altogether, we recorded forty items, filling ten chapters. I titled the book *Brief Record at Longchuan.*

SOURCE: Su Zhe, *Longchuan luezhi* 龍川略誌, ed. Kong Fanli 孔繁禮, in *Quan Song biji* 全宋筆記, ed. Zhu Yi'an 朱易安 and Fu Xuancong 傅璇琮, series 1, vol. 9 (Zhengzhou: Daxiang Chubanshe, 2006), 255.

Preface to *Separate Record at Longchuan,* by Su Zhe 蘇轍

When I lived in Longchuan, I compiled the *Brief Record* [*at Longchuan*] to record a small fraction of what I experienced over the course of my life. I hadn't had time to also include what I had learned from others. But I should—given that I am almost fifty, have traveled far, and have met some of the dynasty's senior figures. Ouyang Yongshu [Ouyang Xiu, 1007–1072] and Zhang Andao [Zhang Fangping, 1007–1091] were eminences of their day. Su Zirong [Su Song, 1020–1101] and Liu Gongfu [Liu Ban, 1023–1089] were erudite and famous. I was lucky to have associated with them and heard them talk. Younger generations will never have such opportunities.

Once, when Liu Gongfu and I were on duty at the Central Drafting Office, he sighed and said, "When the last of us dies, what we said and did will be lost. If you can write some of it down, it could be passed on." I had too many things to deal with at the time, so was too lazy to make a record.

I have now lived in exile for six years, with little to fill my days. I wanted to do research on what I had heard earlier, but there were no scholar-officials to consult in this hot and desolate place. Since I am old and feeble, I must have forgotten nine out of ten things. Recollecting Gongfu's words, I feel chastened. Therefore, I have written down what I heard and compiled it into *Separate Record at Longchuan.* Altogether, it includes forty-seven episodes, filling four chapters. The twenty-second day of the seventh month of the second year of the Yuanfu reign period [1099].

SOURCE: Su Zhe, *Longchuan biezhi* 龍川別誌, ed. Kong Fanli 孔繁禮, in *Quan Song biji* 全宋筆記, ed. Zhu Yi'an 朱易安 and Fu Xuancong 傅璇琮, series 1, vol. 9 (Zhengzhou: Daxiang Chubanshe, 2006), 313.

Preface to *Family Journal at Yizhou,*
by Fan Xinzhong 范信中

In the fall of the *jiashen* year during the Chongning reign period [1104], I was sojourning in Jiankang [Jiangsu] when I heard that Mr. Shangu [Huang Tingjian, 1045–1105] was exiled to Lingbiao [south of the ridges, referring to Guangdong and Guangxi]. Regretting that I had never met him, I traveled upstream on the Yangzi River, sailed on the Pen River, and left my boat at the Dongting Lake before proceeding to Jingxiang [Hunan], then heading to Bagui [Guangxi]. I arrived in Yizhou [Guangxi] on the fourteenth day of the third month of the *yiyou* year [1105] and lodged at the Chongning Monastery.

The next day, I called on Mr. Huang at his rented house. Seeing him was truly like seeing an exiled immortal. I promptly forgot the hardships of the road and the dangers of catching tropical diseases. From that day on, I kept him company. On the seventh day of the fifth month, we both moved in to the South Tower. There we played Go, recited books, chatted at night while lying in bed, and raised our wine cups to sing loudly. He and I were inseparable.

Mr. Huang kept a journal recording guests' visits, the receipt of letters from family and friends, the weather, and daily routines and itineraries. He titled it *Family Journal of the Yiyou Year.* His calligraphy was marvelous. He once said to me, "When I return north someday, I will give this to you."

In the ninth month, Mr. Huang suddenly fell ill and passed away without any family members by his side. By myself I managed his final affairs. When his coffin was sealed at the South Tower, I was overwhelmed with grief. In the confusion, someone took the *Family Journal,* which still pains me when I think of it.

In the *guichou* year of the Shaoxing reign period [1133], an old friend unexpectedly sent me a copy of the journal. I had no idea that it had survived! Reading it was like being back in a former time. I therefore had blocks carved to print it and circulated it among interested parties. I also wanted people to see that, even though Mr. Huang was in exile and suffered hardships, he never gave in to despair. In this respect, he was different from Han Tuizhi [Han Yu] and Liu Zihou [Liu Zongyuan]. Dongpo [Su Shi] aptly described him as "driving the wind and riding on *qi*, roaming with the Creator."

On the fifteenth day in the fourth month of the *jiayin* year [1134], Fan Liao, courtesy name Xinzhong, of Shu Prefecture authored this preface.

SOURCE: Fan Xinzhong, preface to *Yizhou jiacheng* 宜州家乘, ed. Huang Baohua 黃寶華, in *Quan Song biji* 全宋筆記, ed. Zhu Yi'an 朱易安 and Fu Xuancong 傅璇琮, series 2, vol. 9 (Zhengzhou: Daxiang Chubanshe, 2006), 5.

Preface to *Records of Official Travel,* by Zhang Shinan 張世南

From the time I was a boy, I accompanied [my father] on official trips. We climbed up high into the sky, as we traveled ten thousand *li* to Shu [Sichuan]. In my prime, no year went by when I did not travel by river or lake. I learned a lot, but since I am not especially smart, I forget things quickly. In the first year of the Shaoding reign period [1228], I was in mourning for my brother. I closed my door and declined to see guests. I started to write down what I recalled and filled many scrolls before realizing it. I named my book *Records of Official Travel*. My purpose was to record the facts lest I forget. If I remember anything else, I will add it to the collection. Zhang Shinan (courtesy name Guangshu) of Boyang [Jiangxi].

SOURCE: Zhang Shinan, *Youhuan jiwen* 游宦紀聞, ed. Li Weiguo 李偉國, in *Quan Song biji* 全宋筆記, ed. Zhu Yi'an 朱易安 and Fu Xuancong 傅璇琮, series 7, vol. 8 (Zhengzhou: Daxiang Chubanshe, 2006), 31.

Notes

1. Zhu is an animal in the deer family whose tail hair was used to make writing brushes.

Further Reading

Fu Daiwie. "The Flourishing of *Biji* or Pen-Notes Texts and Its Relations to History of Knowledge in Song China (960–1279)." *Extrême-Orient, Extrême-Occident* No. 1 (2007): 103–30. doi:10.3406/oroc.2007.1071.

Hargett, James M. *Jade Mountains and Cinnabar Pools: The History of Travel Literature in Imperial China*. Seattle, WA: University of Washington Press, 2018.

Zhang, Cong Ellen. "Things Heard in the Past, Material for Future Use: A Study of Song (960–1279) *Biji* Prefaces." *East Asian Publishing and Culture* 6, no. 1 (2016): 22–53.

———. "To Be 'Erudite in Miscellaneous Knowledge': A Study of Song (960–1279) *Biji* Writing." *Asia Major* (Third Series) 25, no. 2 (2012): 43–77.

15

CHANTING ABOUT ONESELF
Poems by four Song scholars (11th–13th c.)

Song poets describe the most mundane aspects of their daily lives
as well as their lofty ambitions and unfulfilled dreams.

Poetry played a larger role in Chinese culture and society than in Western civilization for a variety of reasons. *The Classic of Poetry's* (Shijing) classification as a Confucian classic elevated the place of poetic writing and appreciation. Another important factor was the strong belief that good poetry "was the highest form of speaking to someone else, an activity appropriate to all human beings on certain occasions and in certain states of mind."[1] For these reasons, poetry remained a key component of general education for men throughout imperial Chinese history. All educated men grew up memorizing a large number of poems and were trained in the basic rules for the patterns of tones and use of imagery, then tried their hand in composing their own poems. The greatest age of Chinese poetry was the Tang dynasty. *The Complete Tang Poems* (Quan Tang shi) includes about 49,000 poems by 2,200 poets. Even more survive from the Song, as *The Complete Song Poems* (Quan Song shi) contains about 270,000 poems by close to 90,000 poets.

Good poetry was often autobiographical. Poets recorded their observations of changes in natural conditions and visits to scenic spots. Other prominent themes included drinking and banqueting, bidding farewell, missing family and friends, and life in exile. All are revealing of the poet's everyday life and professional experiences. A particular type of poem, entitled "chanting about oneself," stands out for its vivid depiction of daily and private life. In these poems, the poet often resorts to humor or self-denigration to convey his innermost feelings of contentment, disappointment, or frustration. The selections below vary greatly in their tone but address several topics of general concern to members of the scholar-official class: aging, hobbies and taste, enduring poverty, and office-holding and its alternatives.

Chanting about Myself at Forty,
by Wei Ye 魏野 (960–1020)

At rest my heart does not pound,
But I realize that my memory is growing weaker.
Chess skills retrogressing, it is hard to yield to my guests;
Out of practice on my *qin*, I have to ask my son for the right notes.
Hands lazy, the agricultural tools are left randomly.
Body falling apart, my Daoist gear reveals.
What are the uses of the brush and inkstone
Other than to polish old poems.

Mocking Myself, by Bi Zhongyou 畢仲遊
(1047–1121)

Once there were fresh, delicious crabs under my chopsticks,
Now only old filtered muddy wine in the jug.
When I get drunk today, please do not laugh at me—
The grandson of a past minister of personnel

Pitying Myself, by Bi Zhongyou 畢仲遊
(1047–1121)

I pity myself for wanting to be a scholar despite my poverty and
    ill health.
For over ten years, I have stayed up late to study,
Once a boy, now already old.
On my desk still a pile of books to be read.

Laughing at Myself, by Zheng Gangzhong 鄭剛中 (1088–1154)

Other people invest their money in fields and gardens,
Then worry about getting rich too slowly.
In my case, I borrow money to buy rare books,
Vexed that I never have enough for all the ones I want.
Since I do not put essential needs first,
How could I have jars filled with grain?
My foolishness makes me laugh and laugh,
Done laughing, I playfully pick up a book to read.

Cautioning Myself, by Lu You 陸游 (1125–1210)

Hair falling out—it gets tangled in my comb in the morning.
Deserted fields get hoed at dusk.
The arrival of cool weather lets me set aside the round fan.
As my health improves, I use my short walking stick less often.
In pursuing the Way of the sages, I have accomplished little,
And I haven't yet cut off all human ties.
Fortunately, the lonely green lamp is steadfast.
Moving closer to it, I read an unfinished book.

Amusing Myself, by Lu You 陸游 (1125–1210)

For half of my life I was stuck in officialdom and rushed about
    in society.
Only when drunk did I relax and dream of the quiet life.
Now I get to enjoy having nothing to do.
When tired of reading, I go roaming in the mountains.

SOURCE: Beijing Daxue Guwenxian Yanjiusuo, ed., *Quan Song shi* 全宋詩 (Beijing: Beijing Daxue Chubanshe, 1986–1998), 2:79.901, 18:1042.11939, 30:1692.19051, 39:2180.24825–26, 40:2207.25260–5261.

Notes

1. Stephen Owen, "Poetry in the Chinese Tradition," in *Heritage of China: Contemporary Perspectives on Chinese Civilization*, ed. Paul S. Ropp (Berkeley: University of California Press, 1990), 294–308.

Further Reading

Hawes, Colin C. *The Social Circulation of Poetry in the Mid-Northern Song: Emotional Energy and Literati Self-Representation*. Albany: State University of New York Press, 2011.

Lu You. *The Old Man Who Does as He Pleases*. Translated by Burton Watson. New York: Columbia University Press, 1973.

Owen, Stephen. "The Self's Perfect Mirror: Poetry as Autobiography." In *The Vitality of the Lyric Voice: Shih Poetry from the Late Han to the Tang*, edited by Shuen-fu Lin and Stephen Owen, 71–102. Princeton, NJ: Princeton University Press, 1986.

——. "Wit and the Private Life." In *The End of the Chinese "Middle Ages": Essays in Mid-Tang Literary Culture*, 83–106. Stanford, CA: Stanford University Press, 1996.

16

AN ENVOY'S TRIP TO THE JIN COURT
Travel diary by Lou Yue 樓鑰 (1137–1213)

*As part of an ambassadorial mission to the Jin court, the Southern
Song scholar-official Lou Yue kept a diary in which he detailed his
and his colleagues' daily activities and his keen observations of the
political and cultural landscape.*

The Song faced a political reality that the Han and Tang dynasties had
not: it had northern neighbors that it had to treat as equals, above all Liao
(907–1125), founded by the Khitans, and Jin (1115–1234), by the Jurchens.
Negotiated treaties regulated the exchange of envoys on important occasions,
including the birthdays, enthronements, and deaths of emperors and em-
presses. Envoy missions were highly structured, with protocols for gift-giving,
formal audiences, receptions and farewell parties, government lodging, and
official correspondence.

Hundreds of such missions were dispatched by the Song court to the Liao
and Jin. Official policies required that Song envoys keep daily records of their
missions. Upon their return, these accounts would be catalogued in official
archives and sometimes consulted for intelligence purposes. Those that survive confirm the usefulness of the diary format in organizing and narrating a
lengthy trip. The diarist provides detailed eyewitness reports of what he and

his companions saw and mused about on the road and their observations of natural and social conditions. When encountering places of historical and cultural significance under foreign occupation, the envoy refers to relevant incidents and personalities of the past and registers his nostalgic sentiments.

The three entries below are from Lou Yue's "Diary of a Journey to the North." In late 1169, Lou and his colleagues were dispatched to offer New Year greetings to the Jin emperor. The group left the Southern Song capital, Lin'an (Hangzhou, Zhejiang) in the tenth month of the fifth year, arrived in the Jin capital in modern Beijing more than two months later, stayed there just a few days, and got back to Lin'an after another three months' journey. Lou Yue made an entry for each day of this long mission, detailing the logistic aspects of their journey, the administrative units they passed, the lives of ordinary people they observed, and the historical sites that they passed. The three entries selected here are especially rich in information about material culture in the twelfth century, especially the logistics of crossing the Yellow River.

Diary of a Journey to the North

Third day of the twelfth month (*jiashen*), sunny. We traveled by carriage for sixty *li* and had breakfast at the Jing'an Township. Another sixty *li* later, we stopped for the night at Suzhou [Anhui]. Ever since we left Sizhou [Anhui], we have been traveling along the Bian River. At Suzhou, the river is more silted up than before, the water almost level with the riverbanks, on which carriages and horses travel. Some people have even built houses on them. The prefecture's city wall is newly built, and its outer parts are in good order. I heard that the court ordered the construction to begin in the late fifth month and be completed in forty days. All the expenses were shouldered by the local residents.

The town looks very prosperous. Wheat flour is 210 cash per catty; unhulled millet costs 120 cash per peck, hulled twice as much. Altogether, there are sixty blocks. There are several large Buddhist monasteries, all built during the peaceful times in the past. There are two magnificent restaurants. One of them, Qingping, stretches across both sides of the street. Its upstairs is protected with reed mats. People cannot be stopped from admiring its magnificence. Some old men simply treat it as a temple, touching their foreheads before prostrating to pray. I also see dead bodies lying on the street. Earlier envoys have reported that stores here smuggle and sell Song government pharmacy medicine and the Cai Wujing brand flat cake rheumatism medicine.

Two *li* from the prefectural seat is the Shrine for Erlang. The Pavilion for Dismounting One's Horse in front of the shrine was where the commander Li Xianzhong [1109–1177] executed Li Fu and Li Bao [for cowardice during the Song-Jin War of 1163–1164]. The government lodging station is close to the prefectural office complex. Li Xianzhong's troops were once stationed here. When they took Suzhou, each soldier was given only three hundred cash as a reward, which outraged them. When they were defeated by the Jin army and fled south, the wounded too weak to manage on their own were slaughtered by the enemy, who buried them in several large pits. At the center of the shrine is a well where many people committed suicide. The prefectural seat is located in Fuli County. It was also in this county that Xiang Yu [232–202 BCE] defeated Liu Bang's Han troops east of Lingbi [in 204 BCE]. So many soldiers died in that campaign that their bodies stopped the flow of the Sui River.

Thirteenth day of the twelfth month (*jiawu*), sunny. We left by carriage early in the morning and arrived at the Yellow River after traveling forty-five *li*. Last year, a breach damaged the ferry crossing, so people have had to detour dozens of *li* to board a ferry. This year, they spread some firewood and grass on the ice where the river is shallow to make a one *li*-long path. When carriages and horses moved on this temporary road, I could hear the sound of ice cracking. At places where the river is deep and dangerous, barefoot guards direct travelers to cross quickly.

In the middle of the river there is a long sandbar, which must have resulted from repeated breaches. Our entire party, including horses and carriages, boarded boats here. The ferry boats have flat bottoms and no awnings. The boatmen steered the boat from the bow and used large rectangular wood blocks as oars. When they rowed, they synchronized their movements by shouting in unison. Everyone other than the chief and associate envoys of the mission sat in the open and crossed the river in several different boats. With no wind, it was not cold at all. I could see from the boat that the ice was only about two inches thick. Where the boats passed, the water was dozens of feet deep. This is called the Ligu Ferry Crossing. It was not the usual place to cross the river. The floating bridge, the normal crossing, was several *li* away.

After we rode by horse for about three *li*, we ate in Wucheng Township, also known as Shadian. After going by carriage another forty-five *li*, we spent the night at Huazhou [Henan]. On our route, we passed by a road sandwiched between hills. There is so much dust in the air that people a few feet apart can't see each other, so it is called Little Dusty Cave. There may well be a place ahead that is worse than this. West of the road is the White Dragon Pool, with a large stone stele next to it. Apparently, the pool was created by a previous breach of the Yellow River.

Huazhou was the territory of the Shiwei people in ancient times. It was under the jurisdiction of the Wei state during the Spring and Autumn period [770–476 BCE] and the Warring States period [475–221 BCE]. Its administrative seat was located in Baima County, originally Caoyi of the Wei. When the Di (northern barbarians) conquered Wei [in 660 BCE], they set up Daigong [the prince of Shen] as the king, who at the beginning had to live for some time in a hut in Cao. Yuan Shao [d. 202] sent Yan Liang [d. 200] to the Baima River, and Guan Yu [d. 220] killed Liang to pay back Cao Cao's [155–220] kindness to him. Li Shiqi [268–203 BCE] suggested that Liu Bang [d. 195 BCE] occupy the Baima region. These events happened here. There is a Hua Tower, which was originally the state of Zheng's Linyan.

The twenty-fourth day of the twelfth month (yisi), sunny. We departed by carriage early in the morning. After traveling forty-five li, we arrived at the south city of the Ansu Commandery [Hebei]. We crossed the city on horseback and entered the north city, where we had breakfast at the lodging station. The commandery originally had its headquarters in Suicheng County of Yizhou [Hebei]. When our court established the Jingrong Army, its headquarters was moved here. Both city walls are firm. The south city's southern gate has three layers, the north gate one. This is also where the Ansu County seat is located, with its two Xiongwei battalions. The two gates of the north city each have two layers. Between the north and south cities are moats and ditches, mostly frozen. I see ice being taken into cellars [for use in warmer weather]. The town has a Xiangguang Tower and a Fushan Monastery.

After finishing breakfast, we left on horseback from the north gate. En route, we passed by a large temple. Someone said that it was a temporary imperial palace called Northern Marchmount. After going by carriage another twenty-five li, we crossed the Baigou River. We spent the night at Gucheng Township, another five li further. People here look and dress differently from Hebei. Most men shave their hair, and most women wear Jurchen-style double-bird hairpins. Our driver said, "Once you cross Baigou, all residents are northerners. It is easy to tell them apart."

SOURCE: Lou Yue, *Beixing rilu* 北行日錄, in *Quan Song wen* 全宋文, ed. Zeng Zaozhuang 曾棗莊 et al. (Shanghai: Shanghai Shiji Chuban Youxian Gongsi, Shanghai Cishu Chubanshe, Anhui Chuban Jituan, Anhui Jiaoyu Chubanshe, 2006), 265:5972.79, 265:5793.85–86, 265:5973.91–92.

Further Reading

De Weerdt, Hilde. "What Did Su Che See in the North? Publishing Laws, State Security, and Political Culture in Song China." *T'oung pao* 9, nos. 4–5 (2006): 466–94.

Hargett, James M. *Jade Mountains and Cinnabar Pools: The History of Travel Literature in Imperial China.* Seattle: University of Washington Press, 2018.

Levine, Ari Daniel. "Welcome to the Occupation: Collective Memory, Displaced Nostalgia, and Dislocated Knowledge in Southern Song Ambassadors' Travel Records of Jin-Dynasty Kaifeng." *T'oung pao* 99, nos. 4–5 (2013): 379–444.

Walton, Linda. "Diary of a Journey to the North: Lou Yue's *Beixing rilu.*" *Journal of Song-Yuan Studies* 32 (2002): 1–38.

17

WOMEN AND SUICIDE

Writing on an inn wall by Qiongnu 瓊奴 (11th c.)
and a poem by Han Ximeng 韓希孟 (mid-13th c.)

In the face of physical and mental abuse and the prospect
of violation by foreign invaders, women might choose to commit
suicide. Below are two pieces in which Song women write about
the crises they faced and their decisions to die in defense
of their honor.

Most of what we know about women in early Chinese history was recorded by men. Didactic writing instructed women to limit their activities and influence to the domestic sphere and act subservient to fathers, husbands, and sons. Biographies in the dynastic histories celebrated women from palace ladies to commoners as dutiful daughters-in-law, devoted wives and mothers, and capable household managers. Actual women's lives certainly varied greatly, but only a very small number of them, such as Ban Zhao (45–117), Cai Yan (Wenji, ca. 177–ca. 249, selection 7), Zuo Fen (ca. 255–300, selection 9), and Li Qingzhao (1084–1155), left behind self-narratives of any sort. All three of them were intelligent, scholarly, and talented writers. Their life stories therefore challenged dominant ideals about women and their places in the family and society. Ban, Cai, and Li each suffered a variety of trials and tribulations, ranging from widowhood at a young age and family misfortune to political turmoil, dynastic change, and forced relocation.

Less prominent women sometimes also wrote about similar experiences. The two pieces below offer examples of how sudden changes in family situations and foreign invasion could impact the lives of individual women. Qiongnu and Han Ximeng were from office-holding families. Both were literate and would have enjoyed a comfortable life had it not been for the unexpected domestic or political disruptions. Due to the sudden passing of her father, negligence of her brother, and annulment of her engagement, Qiongnu became a concubine and had to endure jealousy and domestic abuse from the main wife. After being captured by Mongol conquerors in the last years of the Southern Song, Han Ximeng was adamant about protecting her honor as a devoted wife and a chaste woman. She and Qiongnu turned to the last resort in life, suicide, when there seemed to be no other way out. Qiongnu survived, but Han did not. The two women not only protested against their misfortune in action, they also expressed a desire to be remembered. This wish explains the strong tone in their accounts: both intended for their writing to be widely publicized.

It should be noted that there was a long tradition of men writing in women's voices in Chinese literary history. Given that neither woman's identity is verifiable through other sources, there is the possibility that these accounts were indeed written by men, as contemporary male writers showed great interest in and concern for family relationships, downward social mobility, and female chastity.

Writing on the Inn Wall, by Qiongnu

In the past, I passed by this government lodging station with my father, who at the time was a high-ranking official. My family was rich and powerful, and everything was done as we wanted. There were parties day and night during which we sang, drank, played music, and recited poems. Since this happened on a daily basis, how could I have anticipated that someday I would suffer from hunger and cold!

Unfortunately, during the early Jiayou reign period [1056–1063], like a severe frost falling in the summer, my parents died in quick succession. Once the family's wealth was all gone, my brothers took their wives and children and went away. Left with no resources, I had no idea where to go. When I was young, I was betrothed to the Zhang family from Qinghe [Hebei]. After I fell into poverty, they quickly broke off the engagement. I realized I would never be able to marry and would have to lower myself just to survive. Unable to escape a concubine's destiny, I ended up in the household of Chief Minister of Imperial Sacrifices Zhao.

In the beginning, the entire family was happy to have me join them. Then I had the misfortune of becoming the master's favorite, which led the principal wife to turn against me. I had to endure flogging every day and was unable to leave the family. Many times I wanted to kill myself. But when I had the knife or rope right in front of me, to my surprise I couldn't bring myself to do the deed.

On my previous visit to this place, I was high-spirited and happy. Passing by the same lodging station now, I see that the building and scenery have not changed. It is as if the people I was with the first time are still around. Who could possibly know the pain and sorrow this causes me!

At night, holding a candle, I sneaked out of my room and wrote this on the wall. I hope that heroic and righteous gentlemen will see it and sympathize with the hardships I have suffered. Humbly written by Qiongnu of Taiyuan [Shanxi].

SOURCE: Liu Fu 劉斧, *Qingsuo gaoyi* 青瑣高議, ed. Li Guoqiang 李國強, *in Quan Song biji* 全宋筆記, ed. Zhu Yi'an 朱易安 and Fu Xuancong 傅璇琮, series 2, vol. 2 (Zhengzhou: Daxiang Chubanshe, 2006), 3.40.

Poem, by Han Ximeng

Han Ximeng of Baling (Hunan) was Han Qi's [1008–1075] fifth-generation granddaughter and was married to Jia Qiong, son of Minister Jia. When Yuezhou [Hunan] was taken by the Mongols, she was captured and wrote a poem on a piece of cloth torn from her clothes, hoping that interested gentlemen would circulate it to let people know that the Song had subjects who preserved their chastity. The poem reads:

I am the daughter of a good family,
And by nature eccentric and unsophisticated.
I married the son of a minister

Who served in the palace library.
I married him because of his talent and virtue;
He did not mind that I was less than good-looking.
When we first tied the knot,
We swore to love each other for as long as the sun and moon
    continue to shine.
Mandarin ducks fly in pairs;
Flounders wish to stay side by side.
How could I expect that our vows to stay together forever
Would end so abruptly?
Our love was at its zenith
When war broke out.
I did not expect that the seemingly impossible would happen:
The Mongols taking my native region.
Once the area was captured and looted,
All my relatives perished in an instant.
I was like a *yi* bird forced to fly backward by a gale,
Or a solitary phoenix gliding in the sky without her partner.
A hairpin is strong enough to break white jade;
A jar's weight can sever fresh rope.
The path leading to death is dark.
My heart is heavy, but I am undeterred.
My heart is firm, unwavering.
They can transfer me but not alter my loyalty to my family and home.
I started as a ritual vessel—
How could I be willing to serve as a chamber pot?
My determination to remain chaste can move a boulder,
But my *qi* is choked, like a fishbone stuck in a throat.
If I can't be a torch burning brightly,
I'd prefer to be the cold ash.
I'll give up my life, insignificant as a tiny moth.
Begging for mercy would be as humiliating as being trapped is
    for a tiger.
Into the water of the Qing River
I'll bury my whole body.
If Heaven has consciousness

It will surely let me to make a sincere request.
I want my spirit to become the Jingwei bird,
To carry enough stones to turn the sea into a mountain range.

Soon after finishing the poem, she drowned herself in the river.

SOURCE: Ding Chuanjing 丁傳靖, *Songren yishi huibian* 宋人軼事匯編 (Beijing: Zhonghua Shuju, 1981), 8.362–63.

Further Reading

Bossler, Beverly. *Courtesans, Concubines, and the Cult of Female Fidelity*. Cambridge, MA: Harvard University Asia Center, 2016.

Davis, Richard L. *Wind against the Mountain: The Crisis of Politics and Culture in Thirteenth-Century China*. Cambridge, MA: Council on East Asian Studies, Harvard University Press, 1996.

Ebrey, Patricia Buckley. *The Inner Quarters: Marriage and the Lives of Chinese Women in the Sung Period*. Berkeley: University of California Press, 1993.

Zhang, Cong Ellen. "The Multiple Lives of the Woman of Huaiyin in the Song (960–1279)." *Tsing Hua Journal of Chinese Studies* (New Series) 51, no. 1 (March 2021): 199–249.

18

....

WITNESSING DYNASTIC COLLAPSE
Writings by Yuan Haowen 元好問 (1190–1257)
and Wen Tianxiang 文天祥 (1236–1283)

....

*Decades apart, Yuan Haowen and Wen Tianxiang both suffered
capture by the Mongols. Both were strongly loyal to their former
sovereigns, but they chose to express their loyalty in different ways.*

China was torn apart by war many times over the centuries, but to men of the
time, the destruction wreaked by the Mongols seemed unprecedented. From
the Mongols' first campaigns into northern China against the Jurchen Jin in
the 1210s to the final destruction of the Southern Song in 1279, cities were
razed and populations slaughtered or enslaved. Even after the first wave of
violence had passed, life was difficult for many, especially in northern China.
At the local level, in particular, people had to develop new ways to preserve
their families and secure their livelihoods. For literati families, the diminished
opportunities for government service remained an especially large concern.

Two important witnesses to these events were Yuan Haowen and Wen
Tianxiang. From a scholar-official family and well educated in his youth, Yuan
passed the *jinshi* examination in 1221 on his seventh attempt but never rose
high in the Jin government. Both when he held office and when he returned
home to farm, he maintained active ties to a large network of scholars and

intellectuals. When the Jin capital, Kaifeng (Henan), fell, Yuan was among thousands of officials and imperial relatives who were captured by the Mongol troops. After enduring several years of imprisonment, Yuan spent the rest of his life in his native place in Shanxi, devoting some of his time to preserving a record of the Jin dynasty. The preface to his book, translated below, was written while he lived in captivity.

Wen Tianxiang, from Jiangxi in southern China, was born after the fall of the Jin to the Mongols. Even though he lived in the south under the Southern Song, the threat of the Mongols was a constant in the lives of his generation. At the young age of twenty-one, he earned the *jinshi* degree, taking the top place. When the Mongols intensified their attacks in 1275, Wen personally organized military resistance. The next year, he was appointed as an envoy to negotiate with the Mongols, who detained him. He managed to escape that time but was captured again by the Mongols in 1279. When pressured to surrender, he wrote a poem with the famous line, "Since ancient times, who has avoided death? Historical records [of my death] will prove my loyalty." Wen spent three years imprisoned in Dadu (Beijing) before being executed in 1283. Wen Tianxiang's iconic status as one of the greatest patriots of all time was further celebrated in modern times, when standing up to foreign invasion again became an issue.

In the postscript, translated below, to Wen Tianxiang's report on the 1276 mission to the Mongol camp he muses over such weighty topics as life and death and duty to family and country.

Preface to *Record of a Prisoner,* by Yuan Haowen

Seven months after I was born, I was adopted by my paternal uncle, lord of Longcheng. When he died at his post in the *gengwu* year of the Da'an reign period [1210], I accompanied his coffin back to our hometown in Xinzhou [Shanxi]. I was then twenty-one, and most of the elders of the Yuan family, including my grandfather, were no longer living. When I asked about my ancestors, my uncles, being young, could provide only a few facts. Since the family's genealogy and stele inscriptions were in good order, I thought it would be fine if I postponed further inquiries.

A few years later, the Mongols attacked the Central Plains. To escape the invaders, I moved about in Yangqu and Xiurong [both in Shanxi], never staying anyplace the whole year. In the *bingzi* year of the Zhenyou reign period [1216], I crossed the Yellow River into Henan. All our family belongings were lost in the chaos. I got hold of a copy of the old genealogy from the clan's Henan branch, which had details for the Song and post-Song period. Records of prior periods, however, were no longer available. My brother Yizhi once ordered me to compile "A Record of a Thousand Years of the Yuan Family." I made an outline but did not find the time to write down the many things that he wanted recorded.

In the *jiawu* year [1234, when the Mongols conquered the Jin], I was captured and detained in Liaocheng [Shandong]. My brother Yizhi was far away in Xiangyang [Hubei], meaning that we were in two different countries. My nephew Bo was captured and taken to Pingyang [Shanxi], and I had no idea whether he was alive or not. My uncle's son, Shuyi, and my grand-nephew, Boan, were too young to be entrusted with anything. I was forty-five and barely surviving; my life could end anytime. Should I drop dead on the road one day, would the world know there was once a Yuan family in Henan? Descendants of royals [Yuan Haowen was a descendant of the Northern Wei imperial clan], my grandfather's and father's generations were renowned for their excellent writing and conduct. Wouldn't it be a great misfortune if they were forgotten as nobodies? To prevent that from happening, I wrote "A Record of a Thousand Years of the Yuan Family" and entrusted it to my daughter, Yan, lest my ancestors' deeds be forgotten. As a further precaution, I personally explained everything to her.

Alas! People who admire an accomplished person from earlier times regularly ask about his appearance, words, and actions, so historians routinely include this information. Since this is true of strangers, it is natural for descendants to want to know this sort of information. For this reason, I have included some miscellaneous stories about our ancestors.

I began to read at four and learned to write poetry at eight, forty years ago. When I was eighteen, my father taught me the principles of local administration, so during the ten years when I served the government, I dedicated my life to the welfare of the people. From an early age, I set myself the goal of becoming a lofty and principled person, not wanting to fall behind my peers.

All my life, I have been close to only a few people. While I have acquired a good reputation, I have also suffered from plenty of slander. In the whole world, my only true friend is my brother Yizhi. My lifetime accomplishments are not known to the world and will be lost to my descendants if I don't do anything about it, which would be an offense against all that is holy. I have therefore appended a chronology of my life.

My grandfather, lord of Tongshan, was granted the *jinshi* degree in the second year of the Zhenglong reign period [1157]. By the end of the Dazheng reign period [1224–1232], my family had served the court for over seventy years. When the capital was besieged, I was the office manager of the Eastern Section. When I learned that the emperor was going to be taken from the capital, I asked the prime minister to prepare a copy of *The State History [of the Jin]* (Guoshi) in small characters to be taken with him. Although the minister liked the idea, there was no time to make the copy.

When Cui Li surrendered to the Mongols in 1233, the conquerors took *The Veritable Records* (Shilu) for each emperor. Those books record a century's worth of the deeds of the [Jin dynasty's] sagacious kings and virtuous ministers, information that deserves to be preserved. Within a few decades, there won't be anyone who remembers those things. I can't help with what I don't know, but how could I bear not to record what I do know! I have therefore made a compilation of my writings and entitled it *Record of a Prisoner*. All our family's descendants, from Shuyi and Boan on, should keep a copy in their homes. If there is anything they do not understand, they should ask others to explain it. Anyone who disobeys this instruction is not a descendant of the Yuan clan.

SOURCE: Li Xiusheng 李修生, ed., *Quan Yuan wen* 全元文 (Nanjing: Jiangsu Guji Chubanshe, 1999), 1:20.318–20.

Postscript to *Record of Heading South,* by Wen Tianxiang

On the nineteenth day of the second month in the second year of the Deyou reign period [1276], I was appointed prime minister of the right and military commissioner in charge of the armies of all routes. At the time, Mongol troops were approaching the capital. There was no time to make plans for offense, defense, or relocating the capital. The court officials all gathered at the office of the grand councillor of the left. Nobody knew what to do.

During one of the many exchanges of envoys, the Mongols requested someone in authority to meet with them. Many thought that if I went, I might be able to find a way to avoid disaster. Given the desperate state of affairs, I could no longer place much value on my life. I also thought that there might still be room for negotiation with the Mongols. Up until then, envoys went back and forth, none of them detained by the Mongols. Moreover, I wanted to see for myself the situation in the north. That way, after I returned, I might be able to figure out some way to save the country. I therefore resigned the prime ministership and set out the next day in the capacity of an academician.

Upon reaching the Mongol camp, I argued so vehemently with the Mongols that I shocked their leaders high and low and made them realize that they could not treat the Song dismissively. Unfortunately, Lü Shimeng disparaged me at the court and Jia Yuqing denigrated me in his report to the throne from the Yuan camps. The Mongols incarcerated me, so I was unable to return. The situation looked bleak.

Once I realized that I would not be able to get away, I rebuked the Mongol commander-in-chief to his face for his breach of faith. I also called Lü Shimeng and his nephew traitors. All I wanted was a swift death, no longer thinking there was advantage to gain. The Mongols continued to act respectfully, but they were in fact infuriated. Two high-ranking Mongols stayed with me during the day, and at night soldiers surrounded my lodge, making it impossible for me to return south.

Not long after, Jia Yuqing and others arrived in the north as supplication envoys. Mongol troops took me to the envoys but did not consider me a part of the mission. I should have killed myself then but forced myself to endure the humiliation, keeping in mind the ancient saying, "This way I can later accomplish something with my life." At Jingkou [Jiangsu], I found the opportunity to escape to Zhenzhou [Jiangsu]. There I informed the commanders of both the east and west wings of where things stood with the Mongols. I planned to gather troops for a large campaign against them, thinking it offered the only chance for reviving the Song.

Two days after my arrival, the commander-in-chief at Yangzhou [Jiangsu] ordered me to leave. I was forced to change my name, hide my tracks, and endure all sorts of hardships traveling cross country. Between the Yangzi and Huai Rivers, I had to deal with the Mongol cavalry every day. I was exhausted and hungry and had nowhere to rest, as the Mongol soldiers were intent on capturing me. Heaven was too high and the earth too vast for my cries to be heard. Later I got hold of a boat. Avoiding the small islands that the Mongol troops occupied, I reached the north bank of the Yangzi River. From there, I entered the Eastern Sea [the ocean east of Suzhou]. Passing by Siming and Tiantai, I eventually arrived at Yongjia [all in Zhejiang].

Alas! How many times was I near death on this trip! I could have died for cursing the Mongol commander and for calling Lü Shimeng and his nephew traitors. Living with the Mongol commanders for twenty days, I could have died many times for standing up to them. On leaving Jingkou, I took a knife with me to be ready for the unexpected and almost killed myself. Passing by Mongol ships stretched out over ten *li* in their search for me, I almost became food for the fish. When I was chased out of Zhenzhou, not knowing what to do next almost cost me my life.

On my way to Yangzhou, if I had run into patrolling guards while passing through the Yangzi Bridge at Guazhou, there would have been no way I could have survived. Outside of Yangzhou's city wall, I was in no position to decide whether I should go in or leave: either choice could lead to death. While I was sitting in the trenches at Guigong Embankment, several thousand Mongol cavalry troops passed its entrance, so I again almost fell into the enemy's hands, which would have been fatal. In Jiajia Village, I was almost bullied to death by patrolling soldiers. On a night journey to Gaoyou [Jiangsu], I got lost and almost perished in a muddy swamp. When dawn broke, I was hiding in a bamboo forest when dozens of patrolling guards passed by. The chances of escaping death were slim. When I arrived at Gaoyou, there was a warrant out for me issued by the military commissioner there. I barely escaped being caught and executed. My boat was very close to the boats of the patrollers as I traveled through the city moats full of dead bodies, so I almost lost my life by accidentally bumping into them.

On my way from Hailing to Gaosha [both in Jiangsu], I was often afraid that I might die for no fault of my own. Between Hai'an and Rugao [both in Jiangsu], for three hundred *li*, Mongol troops and bandits were everywhere. Any day I could have died. When I arrived at Tongzhou [Jiangsu], I would have died had I not been admitted into the city. As for sailing through huge waves in a small boat, I put death out of my mind since there was nothing much I could do about the situation.

Alas! Life and death follow each other, just like day and night. Death is what happens. But in my case, the dangers and misfortunes I endured were more than one person can bear. Just thinking about it is painful!

During this time of adversity, I sometimes composed poems to record my experiences. I wrote them down while on the road, not wanting to lose them. I compiled what I had written during my appointment as an envoy and my detention at the Mongol camps into one chapter. Work composed after I left the Mongol camps, as I passed by Wumen and Piling [Jiangsu], sailed by Guazhou, and returned to Jingkou filled another chapter. The poems recording what happened from Jingkou to Zhenzhou, Yangzhou, Gaoyou, Taizhou [Jiangsu], and Tongzhou make up another chapter. Compositions written when I was traveling from Yongjia to Sanshan [Zhejiang] by sea fill another chapter. My plan is to keep this book at home for later people to read so that they will see that I was doing everything I could.

Alas! That I have survived is fortunate, but is it for a purpose? What I wanted was to be an official. But if my lord is humiliated, even if I die defending him, I share the blame. I also wanted to be a filial son. But if I expose the body given by my parents to danger and consequently die, I am to blame. I asked for punishment from my lord and my mother, but neither approved. I admitted my crime at the graves of my ancestors, pledging that, if I could not save the country in my lifetime, I would turn into a ghost to attack the enemies after my death. That would be my duty.

Rely on Heaven's power and the blessings of the ancestors; ready the weapons; join the front ranks of the imperial troops; wipe out the humiliations suffered by the dynasty; restore the accomplishment of the forefathers. This is what "resolving not to coexist with the enemies" means. It is also known as "giving one's all and not stopping till death." This is also a matter of duty.

Alas! Someone like me could die anywhere. Had I died in the wasteland, even though I had nothing to be ashamed of, I would have had no chance to explain myself to my lord and parents. What would they have thought of me? I never expected that I would be able to return in one piece and see his majesty again. Now that I am back in my homeland, even if I die any moment, what regret would I have? What regret would I have?

In the fifth month of the same year, after the reign title was changed to Jingyan [1276], I, Wen Tianxiang of Luling [Jiangxi], wrote this postscript to my poem collection, *Record of Heading South*.

SOURCE: Zeng Zaozhuang 曾棗莊 et al., eds., *Quan Song wen* 全宋文 (Shanghai: Shanghai Shiji Chuban Youxian Gongsi, Shanghai Cishu Chubanshe, Anhui Chuban Jituan, Anhui Jiaoyu Chubanshe, 2006), 359:8315.96–98.

Further Reading

Davis, Richard L. *Wind against the Mountain: The Crisis of Politics and Culture in Thirteenth-Century China*. Cambridge, MA: Council on East Asian Studies, Harvard University Press, 1996.

Jay, Jennifer W. *A Change in Dynasties: Loyalism in Thirteenth-Century China*. Bellingham: Western Washington University Press, 1991.

Wang Jinping. *In the Wake of the Mongols: The Making of a New Social Order in North China, 1200–1600*. Cambridge, MA: Harvard University Asia Center, 2018.

West, Stephen. "Chilly Seas and East Flowing Rivers: Yüan Hao-wen's Poems of Death and Disorder, 1233–1235." *Journal of the American Oriental Society* 106, no. 1 (1986): 197–210.

19

PEACEFUL ABODES
Account of their homes by Yelü Chucai 耶律楚材
(1190–1244) and Xie Yingfang 謝應芳 (1296–1392)

*Two men who lived through dynastic transitions write of the joys
of the simple life in modest homes.*

What brings joy? How does one live a happy life? Can one be worry-free?
Over the centuries, philosophers, poets, artists, and religious leaders pon-
dered these questions. Some celebrated joy derived from spending time with
friends; others cherished solitary leisure; yet others claimed to delight in time
spent with common people. As a result, poetry and prose work touching on
the meaning of happiness is plentiful. Confucius and Zhuangzi, two of the
most outstanding early thinkers, presented very different approaches to the
topic. Influenced by the increasing emphasis on self-expression in literature
and the arts and evolving views on office-holding and its alternatives, later
writer-scholars continued their exploration, offering a large variety of under-
standings of ways to live a happy and fulfilling life.

A genre suited to writing about these issues was the *ji* (record), a type of
prose work written to mark the completion of a studio, private residence, or
government building. Whether the builder wrote it himself or turned to a
friend, the goal remained the same: to explain the origin and significance of

the building and, more importantly, to explain its builder's highest ideals and aspirations in life.

The first piece below, "Account of the Abode of Happiness amid Poverty" features a conversation between the Daoist Sanxiu and the lay Buddhist Zhanran (Yelü Chucai), during which the Buddhist enlightened the Daoist on the relationships between joy and worry, wealth and poverty, and the life of the gentleman and the ordinary person. Their references to Confucian, Daoist, and Buddhist ideas reflects the cultural and religious atmosphere in northern China in the thirteenth century. The author of the account, Yelü Chucai, was a direct descendant of the founder of the Khitan Liao dynasty. Since his grandfather's generation, his family had served the Jin state. After the Mongols took the Jin capital city, Yanjing (modern Beijing), in 1215, he became a trusted adviser to Chinggis Khan (1162–1227). He played a key role in the Mongol's institutional, economic, and cultural policies after the Mongols conquered northern China.

Xie Yingfang was a much more minor historical figure. He came of age during the later years of the Yuan dynasty and, like many literati of the era, supported himself as a teacher in his home region (Jiangsu). He was there when rebel armies rampaged through, including the one led by Zhu Yuan-zhang (1328–1398), the founder of the succeeding Ming dynasty. Throughout his long teaching and writing career, Xie Yingfang took it to be his duty to preserve Chinese culture and to reform popular thinking. He sought a life of simplicity and contentment for himself, perhaps because he had experienced so much adversity. As he remarked, "If my mind is at peace, how can I fail to be happy?" Although a Confucian scholar, in these essays Xie evoked key Daoist ideas. His references to the tortoise, the cosmic scheme of things, life as duckweed, being useless and living a safe life, and dying a natural death were taken from the *Zhuangzi*. This Confucian-Daoist fusion was not uncommon among Chinese scholars of his and other periods.

Account of the Abode of Happiness amid Poverty, by Yelü Chucai

The Daoist Sanxiu rented a place near the market in Yanjing and named his abode Happiness amid Poverty. I, the lay Buddhist Zhanran, visited him and asked, "Could you enlighten me on your happiness?" Sanxiu replied, "Clad in plain clothes and dining on coarse rice, I follow my innate feelings.

Sometimes I entertain myself with music. Other times I find contentment in reading. I chant the Way of the sages and follow the teachings of Confucius. Accordingly, I don't socialize with people or receive guests, which has freed me of worry and doubt. Before I had not understood that gaining and losing generate each other, the way prosperity and ruin do. Realizing this is the source of my happiness." When I asked if anything troubled him, he said, "Since I submit to the will of Heaven and am content with my lot, what do I have to worry about?"

I responded, "I've heard that whether a gentleman is poor and humble or rich and powerful, he has both worries and joys, never just one. The reason a gentleman studies the Way is not for his own sake. Rather, his goal is for his ruler to act like Yao and Shun and the people to benefit like the subjects of Yao and Shun. He would feel ashamed if there is a single man or woman in the world who has not benefited from a Yao and Shun–type king. For this reason, when a gentleman realizes his ambition and gets a position high enough to practice the Way and wealth sufficient to help others—wouldn't this bring him happiness? Insisting on being humble and cautious when one could make a difference is like using rotten ropes to guide a six-horse carriage. Shouldn't that be a source of worry?

"Likewise, a person who is poor and lowly can retreat from society and focus on cultivating his integrity. The fact that he is not in danger of inviting trouble due to his riches or high position should bring him joy. But he should be troubled by the vulgar state of popular customs, the impending decline of the Way of the sages, and the fact that no one in the whole world truly understands him. Your happiness is apparent. Don't you also have the concerns I've mentioned?" Sanxiu stared at me without replying.

I smiled and said, "I understand what you're thinking. You think that when a person is rich and powerful, he should hide his happiness and only display his worries, while when a person has no such advantages, he should hide his worries and draw attention to his joys. But why should one act this way? I am afraid that in my case, those who do not know me will think that I act proud when I am doing well and appear dejected when I'm not." Sanxiu said, "Your words are an example of the saying, 'Others have their thoughts, but I can see through them.' I'd like to base my account on what you have said."

Composed on the day of winter solstice in the *bingzi* year [1216] by the lay Buddhist Zhanran, Yelü (Yici) Chucai, courtesy name Jinqing, of Qishui [Shaanxi].

SOURCE: Li Xiusheng 李修生, ed., *Quan Yuan wen* 全元文 (Nanjing: Jiangsu Guji Chubanshe, 1999), 1:12.234.

Account of the Tortoise Nest, by Xie Yingfang

In the spring of the *bingshen* year in the Zhizheng reign period [1356], I cleared a plot of land on Lake Ge [Jiangsu], where I built a house next to the residence of my old village friend, Mr. Liu. The house was small and barely big enough for me, my wife, and children. I therefore named it Tortoise Nest.

A guest once asked, "When do tortoises ever have nests?" I replied, "Haven't you heard? A thousand-year-old tortoise nests under a lotus leaf. It uses the leaf as its nest because it does not require any effort on its part. My situation is similar. I got the land from a villager, which cost me nothing. Not only did my neighbors help build the house for free, but also all the materials were donated by local friends. I made no contribution. Now, hiding inside it, I am as quiet as a tortoise hiding in its cave. This is why I have named my house Tortoise Nest.

"The completion of my house was followed by beautiful spring days when everything was quiet and peaceful, so I invited my fellow villagers to celebrate. Carrying jugs of wine, we crossed ramie fields and stretches of mulberry, peach, and plum trees. Everyone had a good time dancing, singing, and cheering. Joining in the fun, I felt as happy as a tortoise dragging its tail in the mud. Although this joy was experienced outside my nest, it was building the nest that made it possible. My only regret is that, unlike the tortoise, I cannot possibly achieve immortality by preserving my vital energy through breathing exercises. The truth is that I would be more than happy if I manage to survive this adverse time and die a natural death. As for understanding turns of fate, solving the country's large problems, and offering strategies to usher in great peace and cultural flowering, those tasks are for the other divine animals. I am content with the happiness derived from living in a small nest. Sharing the same sky with pots and jars, I do not know the differences between the pleasures of the large and small beings."

My guest said, "The way you describe it, your life sounds very satisfying. From now on, I want to live the way you do and enjoy the same pleasures. What do you think?" I said, "Sure," and my guest left in a good mood. I therefore recorded my conversation with him to commemorate the building of my Tortoise Nest.

Follow-Up Account of the Tortoise Nest, by Xie Yingfang

In the early eighth month of the same year [1356], the heavenly soldiers [Zhu Yuanzhang's rebel army] arrived from the west. They set everything on fire and ate the flesh of those who died. My Tortoise Nest and ancestral estate were both burned to the ground. I put my wife and children on a boat and headed east. We first passed Hengshan, then fled Wuxi [both in Jiangsu]. For a month, we repeatedly faced danger. We had to be very careful and dared not make a sound, yet our emotions were such that we could not help but turn our heads toward the direction of our hometown.

In midautumn of the next year, we reached Loujiang [Jiangsu], near the ocean. Living on the boat, we felt like floating waterweeds as we endured the winds and rain and the morning and evening tides. After a while, we left the boat and rented a place to live. Over the course of the next four years, we moved five times. When we heard that no one in our native place had survived, we all realized just how lucky we were to be alive. Even though we were poor, we did not mind it. In fact, we considered our life to be happy.

What brings me joy is that my cramped quarters and lack of work allow me to focus on reading the classics by the ancient sages and thus broaden my thinking. To have no regrets and worries is what I call clear understanding. Yet, in the larger cosmic scheme of things, my life is like duckweed. How is this different from a tortoise seeking a nest under a lotus leaf? This is why I give the name Tortoise Nest to every place we move to. Even though I live in tiny quarters, my mind has all the space it needs because I do not consider the building I live in as my home. Rather, I take the whole space between Heaven and Earth as my nest. For this reason, whether my dwelling is a grandiose palace or a crude hut makes no difference to me. What I know is that this nest has lasted for thousands of years since the time of creation. I and myriad other beings have occupied it and do not have to limit ourselves with fences and borders. Seen this way, why mourn losing the old nest?

It is of course true that many kinds of beings live in nests. Why have I repeatedly compared my house to a tortoise nest, rather than another kind? I have done so because tortoises are one of the four *ling*, spiritually efficacious animals. *Ling* beings can come to ruin when they choose to be useful in the world. Since the world does not use me, my life is safe. Alas, whether I am employed or my life is preserved is up to the Creator: it is not something that I the tortoise can decide. As long as I believe that my Heaven and Earth nest will protect me, it is enough to stay calm. If my mind is at peace, how can I fail to be happy? Worrying that those who do not understand my thinking will consider it preposterous to give a name to a nonextant nest, I am taking the trouble to explain myself yet again.

SOURCE: Li Xiusheng 李修生, ed., *Quan Yuan wen* 全元文 (Nanjing: Jiangsu Guji Chubanshe, 1999), 43:1349.235–37.

Further Reading

Bol, Peter. "Neo-Confucianism and Local Society, Twelfth to Sixteenth Century: A Case Study." In *The Sung-Yuan-Ming Transition in Chinese History*, edited by Paul Jakov Smith and Richard von Glahn, 241–83. Cambridge, MA: Harvard University Asia Center, 2003.

Dardess, John W. *Conquerors and Confucians: Aspects of Political Change in Late Yuan China*. New York: Columbia University Press, 1973.

de Rachewiltz, Igor. "Yeh-Lü Ch'u-Tsai: Buddhist Idealist and Confucian Statesman." In *Confucian Personalities*, edited by Arthur Wright and Denis Twitchett, 186–216. Stanford, CA: Stanford University Press, 1962.

Tsai Wei-chieh. "Ethnic Riots and Violence in the Mongol Empire: A Comparative Perspective." *Mongolian Studies* 33 (2011): 83–107.

20

A FEMALE DOCTOR'S
LIFE AND WORK
Preface and postfaces to a book
by Tan Yunxian 談允賢 (1461–1556)

*This is the story of Tan Yunxian, one of the most famous female
doctors in imperial China. She and her relatives narrate the story
of her professional career as well as her legacy in her family and
within the medical profession.*

Chinese medicine drew not only on a series of canonical works, beginning
with *The Yellow Emperor's Classic of Internal Medicine* (Huangdi neijing), but
also on great practitioners and pharmacologists, such as Zhang Zhongjing
(ca. 150s–215), Hua Tuo (d. 208), Sun Simiao (d. 682), and Li Shizhen (1518–
1593). Some established themselves through formal education with a master;
others continued a family profession or were self-taught. Almost all of these
esteemed medical specialists were men, but historical sources do occasionally
mention elite women becoming interested in medicine after witnessing loved
ones suffering from illnesses or observing incompetent doctors. By the Ming
period, there is more evidence of women practicing medicine professionally
and playing an active role in the transmission of medical knowledge.

Perhaps the best known of these women doctors is Tan Yunxian. Born into a family with a long tradition of practicing medicine in southeastern China, Tan received her medical education from her paternal grandmother. It was not until she fell ill, however, that she began to put her knowledge to actual use. Over time, not only did she acquire a reputation for her skills in her native place of Wuxi (Jiangsu), but she also compiled her own casebook, *Miscellaneous Record of a Female Doctor* (Nüyi zayan). This book provides detailed descriptions of her patients' symptoms as well as her diagnoses. Tan concluded that many of her patients' illnesses could be traced back to physical exertion and mental stress that resulted from problematic family relationships, especially those between in-laws and husband and wife. Mainly using herbs and acupuncture, Tan treated women unwilling to see male doctors. Tan lived well into her nineties, so she must have treated a great number of patients. Tan's experience offers a concrete example of a strong grandmother-granddaughter relationship and the impact of women's education on women's lives.

The first selection below is Tan's narrative of her education and professional experience. This is followed by a postscript to *Miscellaneous Record*, in which her younger brother expresses his admiration for his sister's intelligence and accomplishments. The third piece was composed by Tan's grandnephew on the occasion of the reprinting of her book.

Preface to *Miscellaneous Record of a Female Doctor,* by Tan Yunxian

The Tans have been known for their scholarship in Wuxi for generations. My great-grandfather (known by his honorary titles of the gentleman litterateur and investigating censor of Nanjing and the Huguang Circuit) married into fellow native Huang Yuxian's family, a clan with a long tradition of practicing medicine. My grandfather (whose titles were grand master for governance and director in the Ministry of Justice of Nanjing) acquired a reputation as a good doctor. The next generation (my uncles, who held the ranks of secretary and gentleman for managing affairs at the Ministry of Personnel, and my father, prefect of Laizhou [Shandong] with the rank of lesser grand master of the palace) all earned the *jinshi* degree. As a result, the family stopped practicing medicine.

When my father was serving in the Ministry of Justice, he brought my grandparents to his post in order to take care of them. I was a little girl at the time. Once when I was with my father, for amusement he asked me to chant some five- and seven-character poems and recite from *Instructions for Women* (Nüjiao) and *The Classic of Filial Piety* (Xiaojing). Pleased with my performance, my grandfather said, "My granddaughter is very intelligent and should not be restricted to learning only women's work. Let her study medicine with us." I remembered what he said but did not fully understand how kind those words were. After that, I began to study *The Classic of Difficult Cases* (Nanjing), *Rhymed Formula on the Pulse* (Maijing), and other books, keeping at it day and night. When I was taking a break, I would ask my grandmother to explain the gist of those works and felt that all my questions were quickly resolved. At the time, I already knew how useful her instruction was but had not yet tried to use anything I had learned.

When I grew up and married [into the Yang family], I frequently suffered from *qi*- and blood-related illnesses. Before the doctor came, I would examine myself, then compare my diagnosis with the doctor's. When I got my prescription, I would handpick certain herbs to determine whether or not they suited me. Later I gave birth to three daughters and one son while ill but did not take anyone else's prescriptions. I simply asked for advice from my grandmother, then tried to come up with my own prescriptions. Even though I was gaining experience in making medical decisions, I still was not sure whether medical treatments were effective.

When my grandmother was dying, she left me all the prescription manuals and herb-processing tools, saying, "Study these diligently. Then I can die at peace." I accepted those items on my knees. Then excessive grief left me so sick for over seven months that my mother secretly made preparations for my death. In my stupor, I dreamed that my grandmother told me, "You will not die from this illness. The cure is in a certain chapter of a certain book. If you follow the treatment, you'll soon recover. You'll live to seventy-three and be able to carry forward my techniques to save people. Do not worry!" Waking from the dream in a state of alarm, I forced myself to get up and find the prescription to begin my treatment. I fully recovered soon thereafter. Only then did I have proof that medicine works.

Women I knew who did not want to see male doctors came to me in an endless stream. My treatment often proved extremely effective. The years have gone by quickly, and I reached fifty this year. In terms of the life span my grandmother predicted, two-thirds has now passed. I cannot help but feel sad that life is as brief as a glimpse of a colt flashing past a crack in a wall. How many years do I have left? I have therefore carefully recorded what I have learned from my grandmother and my own experience and organized it as cases. Titled *Miscellaneous Record of a Female Doctor*, it adds to the works of practitioners. As I am a woman, it is inappropriate to go outside to see to its publication, so I have told my son, Lian, to copy it and have it carved on blocks for printing in the hope that it may help other doctors. I beg readers' indulgence and ask that they not laugh at me.

Written by Yang Tan Yunxian on the sixteenth day in the third month of the *gengwu* year, the fifth year of the Zhengde reign period [1510].

Postscript to *Miscellaneous Record of a Female Doctor,* by Tan Yifeng

The entries in *Miscellaneous Record* were all cases treated by my sister, Child Nurturess Yang [Tan Yunxian]. My sister was more intelligent than her brothers. When young, she was the favorite of our grandmother, who made sure she had everything she needed. Their conversations were about nothing but medical treatment. My sister was able to remember everything and wrote down the most important points. When she reached adulthood, she further investigated thoroughly the secret and most important prescriptions of the various schools, combining and using them in her practice. For this reason, she always achieved outstanding results. When local women fell ill, they considered it fortunate to have her treat them.

As she grew older, she worried that her knowledge would be lost, so she wrote this book. Alas! The ancients said that a good doctor's contribution can equal that of a good minister. This saying conveys how difficult it is to save lives. Looking back, not many of a generation's ministers deserve to be called good. Similarly, how many good doctors were there in the past, or even in more recent generations! Not to mention female doctors! This book will surely find people who recognize its value. I am too ignorant to understand its subtle and profound insight. Besides, words are unreliable and incapable of conveying the most significant knowledge. Even so, how could I take words lightly? I have therefore written this postscript.

Respectfully composed by unworthy younger brother (*juren* 1503) Tan Yifeng on the first day of the fourth month in the *xinwei* year of the Zhengde reign period [1511].

Postscript to Reprint of *Miscellaneous Record of a Female Doctor*, by Tan Xiu

My great-aunt Madame Yang was a famous woman doctor in our county and lived to age ninety-six. She cured countless people throughout her life. As boy, I witnessed her treating sick women quickly and effectively. For this reason, doesn't she deserve to be called the female Bian Que [5th c. BCE]? I heard that the descendants of one who saves many lives will flourish. Yet her son, Lian, died young; her grandson, Qiao, also lost his life after being implicated in a crime, bringing her family line to an end. Was what I learned from history unreliable? I sigh deeply for her.

Recently, I have had a lot of free time, so I got to go over the records left by my forebears. Among the documents I found were the writings of my grandfather, the lord of Dayi, which contained a postscript to *Miscellaneous Record of a Female Doctor*. I thought that if I could circulate this work, then my great-aunt's name would become immortal. However, despite my best efforts, I failed to acquire a copy. A guest, Guo Hanjiang, brought me a copy and said, "I heard that you are compiling your ancestors' work. Please take this to add to your collection." I bowed and accepted his kindness. Opening the volume and reading it carefully, I realized that all the records were from the *gengwu* year in the Zhengde reign period [1510]. After that, as my great-aunt grew older, her skills became even more miraculous. Is this why she stopped making records? Or did she record more cases that haven't survived?

This work had been carved onto woodblocks and published. Our local leading figures, Mrs. Shao Wenzhuang and Ru Shaotian, wishing to promote the famous and principled, not only supported the publication project but also authored postscripts, in which they showed full understanding of the origin and effectiveness of Madame Yang's work and celebrated her contributions. Those woodblocks are no longer extant, which is very unfortunate. With her family line cut off, her legacy could easily be lost. I therefore have made a hand-copy and have seen it into print. This way, even if the good that Madame

Yang did in saving people did not bring a reward in terms of descendants, at least her name will be passed down and she will achieve immortality that way.

Postscript respectfully authored by grand-nephew, Tan Xiu, on the third day of the third month in the *yiyou* year of the Wanli reign period [1585].

SOURCE: Tan Yunxian 談允賢, Nüyi zayan *ping'an yishi* 《女醫雜言》 評按譯釋, ed. Wang Jian 汪劍 (Beijing: Zhongguo Zhongyiyzo Chubanshe, 2016), preface and postscripts.

Further Reading

Furth, Charlotte. *A Flourishing Yin: Gender in China's Medical History, 960–1665.* Berkeley: University of California Press, 1999.

Leung, Angela Ki Che. "Recent Trends in the Study of Medicine for Women in Imperial China." In *Medicine for Women in Imperial China*, edited by Angela Ki Che Leung, 1–18. Leiden: Brill, 2006.

Wilms, Sabine. "Ten Times More Difficult to Treat: Female Bodies in Medical Texts from Early Imperial China." *Nan Nü* 7, no. 2 (2005): 182–215.

Yates, Robin D. S. "Medicine for Women in Early China: A Preliminary Survey." In *Medicine for Women in Imperial China*, edited by Angela Ki Che Leung, 19–73. Leiden: Brill, 2006.

21

AN ECCENTRIC CONSIDERS SUICIDE
Self-authored funerary biography by Xu Wei 徐渭
(1521–1593)

In this self-authored funerary biography, Xu Wei, a talented
writer, artist, and one of the most eccentric personalities in Chinese
history, narrates his life, family, and career.

The second half of the Ming was a time of great social and cultural change.
The market economy flourished. The influence of Wang Yangming's philosophy expanded beyond the literati elite. Ming individualism fostered unprecedented creativity in literary production and artistic expression, making the
period a great age of painting and calligraphy. Popular culture, in the form
of vernacular literature and theatrical performance, attracted both literati
and nonliterati participation. In the second half of the sixteenth century,
the Ming fought four major military campaigns along its borders, giving
military officials new power in politics and society. The same era was infa-
mous for corruption and bitter factionalism at the court. For decades, two
notorious figures, the grand secretariat Yan Song (1480–1567) and eunuch
Wei Zhongxian (1568–1627), dominated politics and destroyed the morale
of its civil servants.

All these developments were intertwined in Xu Wei's life and career. A native of Zhejiang, Xu passed the lowest level of the examinations at twenty but failed eight times at the provincial level. For some time, he made a living by serving as a private secretary to Yan Song's protégé Hu Zongxian (1512–1565), attempting to curb piracy along the southeast coast. When Yan and Hu lost power, Xu Wei was imprisoned for several years. In contrast to his lack of success in government, Xu's literary and artistic accomplishments were stunning. In his own assessment, he was above all a first-rate calligrapher. This was followed by his achievements in poetry, prose and play writing, and painting.

Xu was also known for his eccentric personality and family drama. A few examples should suffice. The first time Xu married, he "married into" his wife's family instead of bringing his wife into the Xu household. He killed his second wife during a mental breakdown. He attempted suicide multiple times using extremely violent methods, including driving a spike into his own ear. At the age of forty-five, he self-authored the funerary biography translated below, explaining his decision to die. He did not succeed, however, and in fact lived to seventy-three.

Self-Authored Funerary Biography

I, Xu Wei, am a native of Shanyin [Zhejiang]. I became familiar with the writing of the ancients as a boy and studied even harder when I was older. Later I became interested in the Way, so I went to study the teachings of the Wang [Yangming, 1472–1528] school under Ji Ben [1485–1563]. Realizing its links to Chan Buddhism, I went on to study with Chan masters. Years passed before people thought I was making any progress, and in the end, I understood neither writing nor philosophy. Since I was a person of no status who was, moreover, lazy and blunt, I feared that friends in high positions saw me as overly self-confident. I also spent time with people who casually violated respectability—even going nude in public. Since many disliked the way I behaved, in the end, my arrogance and impudence assured that I did not get anywhere.

At age nine, I was able to compose examination essays, but then neglected to continue practicing for over a decade, which I later regretted. Being impractical and in search of broad learning, I divided my effort among many schools of classics and history and wanted to investigate thoroughly even the most insignificant matter. Once I started pondering something, I would forget to eat or sleep; when reading, I would leave books everywhere. For this reason, I am approaching forty-five and have been a government school student for twenty-six years. Half of that time, I was on a stipend at the county school. I have taken the lowest level of the civil service examinations eight times and failed every time. People all made fun of me, but I did not let it bother me. For ten years, I rented a place in an out-of-the-way alley and made do with the bare necessities.

Then the junior guardian Hu Zongxian recruited me to serve as an aide with responsibility for drafting official documents. I took the post but several times resigned and left. Once, when Mr. Hu wrote to ask me to return, I did not even get up from my bed when the messenger arrived. Everyone thought that I was being obtuse and worried about my situation, but I remained unconcerned. After that, Mr. Hu acted even more deferential, treating me as an equal. In the end, I worked for him for two years, during which time he bestowed on me hundreds of ounces of silver and treated me with great respect. Everyone was impressed by my success, but for my part, I felt deep unease.

Then, all of a sudden, I wanted to kill myself. People thought that a scholar with integrity like me had no reason to die. They did not know that many scholars with lofty character from the past who aided powerful men ended up dead. In my case, I wanted to commit suicide, so it was different from being executed. As a person, when a matter has nothing to do with moral obligation, I am usually relaxed and choose not to be bound by the Confucian principle of righteousness. But if a matter violates righteousness and carries the risk of bringing me shame and a bad reputation, I am willing to sacrifice my life in order to act on principle. For this reason, my relatives cannot stop me from killing myself. Nor do my friends understand why I want to do it.

I am especially terrible at earning a living, to the extent that on the day I die, I will not have enough money to cover the costs of my funeral. My belongings include several thousand volumes of books, two chime stones, plus some inkstones, swords, and paintings, as well as a number of my own works of prose and poetry. I have asked a fellow townsman to sell the swords and paintings for me and have written to urge him to proceed so that the funds from the sale will be available for my burial. My unfinished drafts were also taken by a friend.

I once said that, of all the books I have studied, I have gained the most from *The Śūraṅgama Sūtra, Zhuangzi, Liezi,* and *The Yellow Emperor's Classic of Internal Medicine* (Huangdi neijing). If I had had more time to expound on them, I would have been able to demonstrate all the errors of the commentators and show posterity their original meaning. I am profoundly fascinated by the "Basic Question" chapter in *Internal Medicine* and confident of my reading of it.

I was planning to arrange a marriage for my son this year. That way, I could entrust my mother's welfare to the new couple so that I could tour all the celebrated mountains, get out of the house, and escape distractions. These wishes are all impossible to realize now. I don't hide my mistakes, and I consider it shameful to claim I know what I don't know. Describing me that way is not far from the mark.

My original courtesy name was Wenqing, but I later changed it to Wenchang. I was born on the fourth day of the second month of the *xinsi* year in the Zhengde reign period [1521] to a concubine of my father, the associate prefect of Kuizhoufu [Sichuan]. My father died when I was a hundred days old. I was raised by my legal mother, Madame Miao, for fourteen years. After she died, I lived with my eldest brother, Huai, for six years. In the *gengzi* year of the Jiangjing reign period [1540], I enrolled in the county school and took the first level of the civil service examination without success.

I married into the Pan family as their son-in-law. My father-in-law was the recorder of Yangjiang in Guangdong. We accompanied him there and lived south of the Ridges [Guangdong] for two years. Two years after we returned, my eldest brother, Huai, died during the summer. That winter, I lost the family property in a lawsuit. In the winter of the next year, my father-in-law died. The next fall, I rented a place and began to teach students. Ten years later in the winter, I became an aide at Mr. Hu's office. Altogether, I worked under him for five years. I died four years later on a certain day in a certain month in the *yichou* year of the Jiangjing reign period [1565].

I have two sons. The older, born to Madame Pan, is Mei; the younger, Du, by my successor wife, is only four. Information about my ancestors is included in the funerary biography for my father, so I won't repeat it here. I am buried in Mount Muzha of Shanyin. Since I don't know the date of my funeral, I'll skip that information too. The inscription reads:

Cui Zhu [d. 546 BCE] allowed Yan Ying [d. 500 BCE] to express his
  loyalty;
Geng Liang's [289–340] illness saved his life.
They should have lived;

Their deaths would have destroyed their trust in each other.
Zhong Jing [n.d.] imprisoned Ban Gu [32–92];
Wang Yun [137–192] arrested Cai Yong [133–192].
It was fine for them to die;
What would have justified a different outcome?
I ridicule myself for jumping into the water because of my fear
of drowning,
But sympathize with Ma Rong [79–166] for attempting suicide
following his demotion.
When his life was in danger, Confucius [551–479 BCE] escaped
by hiding his identity;
Jizi [n.d.] faked lunacy after King Zhou [d. 1046 BCE] [of the Shang]
rejected his advice.
Again and again, I recite "The People of Our Race,"
Feeling ashamed that I am not as wise as Zhong Shanfu [Western
Zhou].

SOURCE: Xu Wei, *Xu Wenchang sanji* 徐文長三集, in *Xu Wei ji* 徐渭集 (Beijing: Zhonghua Shuju, 1999), 26.638–40.

Further Reading

He Yuming. "Difficulties of Performance: The Musical Career of Xu Wei's 'The Mad Drummer.'" *Harvard Journal of Asiatic Studies* 68, no. 2 (December 2008): 77–114.

Kwa, Shiamin. *Strange Eventual Histories: Identity, Performance, and Xu Wei's "Four Cries of a Gibbon."* Cambridge, MA: Harvard University Asia Center, 2012.

Ryor, Kathleen. "Regulating the Qi and the Xin: Xu Wei (1521–1593) and His Military Patrons." *Archives of Asian Art* 54 (2004): 23–33.

22

....

LIFE IN THE EXAMINATION HELL

Preface to a set of examination essays
by Ai Nanying 艾南英 (1583–1646)

....

*In the preface to a collection of his examination essays, the
Ming scholar Ai Nanying recounts the trials and tribulations of
examination preparation.*

During the last thousand years of imperial history, scholar-officials (*shidafu*)
were the most prominent elite group. Members of this class varied in their
geographic and family backgrounds as well as political and intellectual inclinations. What they shared was participation in the civil service examinations.
Instituted at the end of the sixth century as a way to counteract the influences
of the great families and military nobility, the examination system was expanded and institutionalized in subsequent dynasties as the major method of
recruiting men for government service. Successful candidates earned degrees
and eligibility for office-holding, and they and their families gained social
prestige, tax exemptions, and gentry status in local society. The civil service
examinations continued to attract the most ambitious and intelligent men
from well-off families until the system was abolished in 1905.

The specific policies and procedures of the examinations were changed
many times, but much also stayed the same: preparation took many years;

candidates had to be qualified in their native regions to be able to take the exams in the capital; and the *jinshi* (Advanced Scholar) degree enjoyed the most esteem due to its requirement that candidates demonstrate proficiency in the classics and literary and analytical abilities.

Over time, the examinations became increasingly competitive, especially at the local and provincial levels. By the twelfth and thirteen centuries, hundreds of thousands of students were contending for a few hundred spots. While some lucky candidates passed on their first try—a tiny number in their late teens—most took the examinations multiple times well into their thirties or even beyond. For these repeat takers, examination participation became a career in itself.

The narrative below, by Ai Nanying, provides us with the perspective of a seasoned candidate. Ai was an accomplished writer and literary critic in the late Ming, but he failed to earn the *jinshi* degree despite multiple attempts, giving him a great deal to say about the hardships of examination preparation. His anxieties and frustrations were condensed into one sentence that he repeated several times: "Alas! In terms of experiencing the miseries of examination preparation, no one has suffered more than I have." It is interesting to note that Ai was not at all against the examinations as an institution and encouraged his son to take the exams. Moreover, he thought that his unsuccessful examination essays might be of interest to future candidates. His preface to that collection tells his story in a way that helps us understand a key element in the life experience of literati in late imperial China.

Preface to *A Collection of Examination Essays*

I passed the county-level exam for youths at seventeen, when Mr. Li Yangbai was the magistrate, and enrolled in the county school at Dongxiang [Jiangxi] the next spring, which was the *gengzi* year of the Wanli reign period [1600]. By the *yiwei* year of the Wanli reign period [1619], I had been a student for twenty years, had taken the provincial examinations seven times, and for fourteen years had enjoyed a stipend provided by the county government. I had the good fortune of being selected as an examination candidate by two county magistrates, three prefects, and six education commissioners. Over the years, I have accumulated several volumes of examination essays. After discarding the inadequate ones, I assembled and published those that were worth preserving. I have done this not only because I worried that, if they were lost, I would have nothing for future reference, but also because these essays were the product of hard work, misery, terror, and physical duress. Besides, they remind me to be grateful to those who understood me. I hereby write this preface to express these thoughts.

Alas! In terms of experiencing the miseries of examination preparation, no one has suffered more than I have. Old policies stipulated that students were tested at the prefectural and county schools each season, called the "Seasonal Exams." When the censors arrived, they would inspect one-tenth of the exams, called "Observing the Common Practice." Because neither procedure impacted my status as a student and because I was habitually lazy, I never participated in either exam. The education commissioner's exam, however, was crucial to maintaining my candidacy status. Its annual licensing exam affected a student's promotion or demotion. Unless one was ill or in mourning, no one would miss it. The qualifying examination took place every three years; through it, the county recommended its talents to the prefecture, the prefecture to the education commissioner, and the commissioner to the Provincial Examinations. Those who did not make it might still be recommended to participate in two forms of special exams. There is no other path for advancement. If Confucius and Mencius lived in my time, they would not have had any other way to distinguish themselves. All the essays included in this collection were written for these two types of exams.

On the day of the examination, the drum at the government office would be struck three times. Even if it was freezing, all the students would stand outside the door. The education commissioner would sit in the hall wearing red robes. Surrounded by lit candles and stoves, he would be warm and comfortable. The students would have to loosen their clothes and bare their feet, holding their brushes and inkstone in their left hand and socks in their right. The prefectural and county officials would call their names, following which the students would line up in the hallway and proceed to stand in front of the commissioner. Each candidate would be searched by two soldiers, who would go thoroughly from the student's hair to his feet. With our bodies almost naked, the process would take a long time. Even the strongest would shiver from the bitter cold, with their lower bodies numb. If the weather was extremely hot, the education commissioner would sit in a cool place while sipping tea and fanning himself. The students would gather in groups, standing in the dust. The law stipulated that they could not use fans. They also wore heavy cotton robes. By the time they were allowed to sit down, several hundred people would be gathered together, enduring the steaming hot weather and body odor. All sweated profusely but were not permitted to have drinks of water. Even though tea service was provided, no one dared to ask for it, because if one stopped for water, his exam would be marked with a red stamp, arousing suspicions of cheating. Even if his writing was good, it would be downgraded a level. This was how much examination candidates suffered from the weather.

When we were seated, the questions were read out aloud by a teacher to accommodate the nearsighted. They were also written out on a board for a clerk to hold and show around the hall. This was for the benefit of those who were hard of hearing. Now, questions are no longer read aloud, only written out for students of each school. When several schools were tested in the same location on the same day, several clerks would hold different boards. Since I was nearsighted and couldn't see things even a few feet away, I had to ask the students sitting next to me what the questions were, keeping my voice down. All this time, the commissioner watched from a terrace, with four soldiers proctoring the entire examination hall. Students did not dare to look up or around, stretch, or talk to their neighbors. If anyone did, his writing would be stamped with a red mark as evidence of violations. Even if his essay was excellent, it would be downgraded one level. For this reason, everyone huddled up at their desks, even hesitating to go to the toilet. This was how much our bodies are constrained during the examinations.

The desks and chairs in the examination hall were procured by the clerks, who misappropriated the majority of the funds for such equipment. Since everything was prepared in a rush, the desks and chairs were often too small to allow even a stretch of the leg. Moreover, the material was thin and the gaps too wide. If one sat down too heavily, one could fall over. There were often a dozen or so students in the same section. The examiner, worrying that they might switch places, linked all their chairs with bamboo sticks. Subsequently, if one of the students moved even slightly, everyone else would feel it. As a result, one could not have a peaceful moment the whole day, causing their writing to be crooked. Furthermore, a few commissioners from Fujian forbade candidates from bringing in any personal items, not even inkstones, which were provided by the clerks. The clerks only prepared blue stones that were hard and slippery and did not absorb ink easily. A minor thing like dealing with the stone was already exhausting. If unfortunately you happened to sit under a leaking roof or near the eaves when it was pouring outside, you had to cover your exams with your clothes and finish as soon as possible. This was how much examination candidates suffered from the clerks' irresponsible behavior.

When it came to grading, what usually happened was that the one commissioner read thousands of students' papers, which varied in terms of style and substance. So did the commissioner's taste and preferences. He was expected to select the best talents, which terrified even the most knowledgeable students, but I have enjoyed more than my share of good luck. When the assessment process was over, the commissioner again appeared in the hall in his red official robe. Prefectural and county officials waited outside the door while the instructors stood below the stairs. The students, keeping their heads low, walked to the commissioner's desk, where they knelt and listened to his instructions quietly. Based on their grades, they would leave through the door located on the west corner of the corridor. Their sorry state at the time was beyond their ability to describe even to their wives and children. This was the extent to which they were constrained by the rules of composition and rhetoric. Alas! In terms of experiencing the miseries of examination preparation, no one has suffered more than I have.

At the level of the provincial examination, students endured the same body searches, anticheating measures, disheveled appearance, exposure day and night, and hot weather and dust as they did at the annual and qualifying examinations. The only exception was that candidates enjoyed slightly more freedom when it came to food and lodging. More than one person could serve as grader. Because they served as graders in their spare time from drafting documents and adjudicating cases, they were not as attentive as the commissioner, whose main duty was evaluating essays. I took and failed the provincial examination seven times, during which I changed my approach to try to please the graders and made use of every bit of my talent and intelligence. At first, I wrote in the style of Qin and Han philosophers and historians, which was considered by the examiners as uncultivated. Later I changed to the styles of the esteemed scholars Wang Ao [1450–1524] and Tang Shunzhi [1507–1560] of the Chenghua [1465–1487] and Hongzhi [1488–1505] reign periods, but that was criticized as outdated. Recently, I based my essays on the *Gongyang* and *Guliang* commentaries on *The Spring and Autumn Annals* (Chunqiu), *The Classic of Filial Piety* (Xiaojing), and the works of Han Yu [768–824], Ouyang Xiu [1007–1072], Su Shi [1037–1101], and Zeng Gong [1019–1083], but the examiners were not impressed.

Following each examination, the successful candidates, even though their writing was empty, inferior, unsophisticated, or shallow, would be treated as equals with the prefectural and county officials. Yet I have studied for over twenty years and thoroughly examined the works of Qian Fu [1461–1504], Wang Ao, and the great scholars of the Hongzhi, Zhengde [1506–1521], Jiajing [1522–1566], and Longqing [1567–1572] reign periods. I have studied everything from the Six Classics, the ancient philosophers and histories, and the works of Zhou Dunyi [1017–1073], Cheng Hao [1032–1085] and Cheng Yi [1033–1101], Zhang Zai [1020–1077], and Zhu Xi [1130–1200], to the Hundred Schools, the Yin-Yang School and military treaties, calendars, geographical books, Buddhism, and Daoism. Yet, I do not get to be equals with those who wrote empty, inferior, unsophisticated, and shallow words. Every time I think of this, I want to abandon my examination pursuit and focus on writing books that explain the rise and fall of the past and present as a way to distinguish myself. Then I admit that I can't live the life of an independent scholar. Alas! In terms of experiencing the miseries of examination preparation, no one has suffered more than I have.

Accomplished gentlemen of the past all drew lessons from the progress they made and the hard work they put in. Ancient sages, such as Yu the Great, heard helpful advice, accepted it with gratitude, then recounted their challenges and difficulties. Hence the saying, "When in comfort, one can remember past hardships; when stable, one can think about earlier difficulties." I have not accomplished anything. My examination essays are unsophisticated and of low quality, so hardly worth keeping. But they were the result of hard work, misery, terror, and physical duress. In addition, the scholars that I have benefited from are all today's men of fame and achievement. I have had the honor of becoming their disciple based on my participation in the examinations. There is a saying: "Someone who really knows you is worth more than someone who can do you favors." If someone clothes me in silk, feeds me fine food, and entertains me with gardens and music, yet on reading my work doesn't understand that it is based on the ideas of the sages and offers insight into morality and human nature from the past and present, then I would not exchange my current situation for the comfortable life that he could offer.

Besides, I have been stuck as an examination candidate for quite some time and have no way to pay back those who have appreciated me, especially the few who have passed away. Nor have I achieved anything to face my mentor when I die. I am publishing these essays because they were the result of hard work, misery, terror, and physical duress and reflect my gratitude for those who understood me. It is not my intention to criticize the problems with the examinations. Since the world judges people based on their successes and failures, I would not want to contaminate people's mind this way. Publishing this collection might appear a way of bragging about myself or exposing the examiners' strengths and weaknesses. Yet if I hide them, I would not be able to forget their names. My son, Tao'er, could read when he was five. I am going to group the essays and give them to him, telling him, "This is what a certain grader and magistrate dismissed." This way, I'll be able to remember that name. Tao'er will read the essays, avoid making the same mistakes, and master the trick of following popular trends. This way, he won't be as obtuse as his father.

SOURCE: Ai Nanying, *Tianyongzi ji* 天傭子集 (Guangxu *yimao* edition, 1879), 2a–9a, accessed May 17, 2021, https://ctext.org/library.pl?if=gb&file =105689&page=214.

Further Reading

Chaffee, John W. *The Thorny Gates of Learning in Sung China, a Social History of Examinations.* Cambridge: Cambridge University Press, 1985.

De Weerdt, Hilde. *Competition over Content: Negotiating Standards for the Civil Service Examinations in Imperial China.* Cambridge, MA: Harvard East Asia Center, 2007.

Elman, Benjamin. *A Cultural History of Civil Examinations in Late Imperial China.* Berkeley: University of California Press, 2000.

Ho, Ping-ti. *The Ladder of Success in Imperial China: Aspects of Social Mobility, 1368–1911.* New York: Columbia University Press, 1962.

23

....

A ROYAL CONSORT'S SONG
Music for the zither by Madame Zhong 鐘氏
(fl. 1570–1620)

....

The lyrics and music of this song were written and published by the consort of a Ming prince. Addressing the boy she raised as his heir, she narrates her life experiences over a span of thirty years, presenting herself as a chaste widow, committed daughter-in-law, loving mother, and competent regent for the child.

The sons of Ming emperors were made kings and sent out of the capital to palace establishments in major provincial cities, their titles and palaces to be passed down to their eldest sons. Over time the number of kings steadily grew, and together they constituted a hereditary aristocracy supported in considerable style. Their younger sons and later descendants received lesser titles and smaller incomes, but all members of the imperial clan were given state stipends. The women who married kings and princes received corresponding titles as queens or princesses.

One woman who married the eldest son of a king is known to history because she wrote both the music and lyrics for a long poem that narrates the story of her life. Although the late Ming saw a significant increase in publication of women's writings, there are few surviving poetic works as long or detailed as this. The author, Madame Zhong, had not been married long when her husband predeceased his father, the king, but fortunately there were posthumous sons, so her position in the family was secure, and she would eventually serve as regent for the child heir after his grandfather died. The song was published sometime after 1620 in a collection of musical scores that she compiled, a woodblock printed copy of which has survived.

The music, notated in a special kind of tablature, is written to be played on the *qin*, a seven-stringed zither. Among the over three hundred premodern *qin* songs that are extant, this song is the only one known to have been written and published by a woman. Like many other *qin* songs of this period, this song is divided into multiple stanzas, each with a number and title that was not supposed to be sung. Her choice to write her story in the form of a *qin* song adds to the author's moral image. Not only were music and morality closely linked in Confucian theory, but also the *qin* in particular was valued for its connection to the ancient sage-kings. Both men and women in literati society enjoyed performing and listening to *qin* music.

In Madame Zhong's own preface, she explains that she hopes later generations will learn of her hardships and virtues through the song. The content of the lyrics is centered on her contribution to the kingdom and the family, presenting her as an exemplary woman who fulfilled her social roles despite adversity of many kinds. In fact, Madame Zhong was already known as a moral exemplar before the publication of the song. As she recounts, a memorial arch commemorating her as a chaste woman was constructed by imperial decree.

Sincere Words on Enduring Hardship

1. I TELL MY STORY TO PASS IT ON

I was born in Dong Village and selected to enter the king's household.
Then with the gracious approval of the emperor,
My title was changed to make me an official consort—
The one and only in the inner palace.
Colorful banners shine on the phoenix carriage,
The golden edict glows with its dragon patterns.
I was overwhelmed by all the blessings from Heaven.

The wealth and noble rank, the splendor and esteem.
Yet who would have foreseen
The thousands and thousands of hardships to come?
Fatherless children, let me tell you the story.

2. SERVING MY FAMILY

I remember at that time, the mother queen Cheng was elderly
And the father king had long been ill.
My restless mother-in-law, Her Majesty,
Worried that the king would not recover.
I served them day and night, dashing about to help.
All the state affairs fell upon the crown prince.
I feared his health wouldn't bear the toil—
Were that to happen, whom could I depend on?
When once in a while he suffered a minor ailment, my heart would
     tremble with terror.
I had to taste all his medicine
And see that he improved,
Only then did I feel relieved.
With concerns and sorrows, one after another,
It was hard to express my fear,
Hard to express my pain.

3. ASSISTING THE PRINCE IN CULTIVATING EXCELLENT VIRTUE

Everyone praised the prince for his benevolence and wisdom,
Like the renowned kings in history.
Still, he exhausted himself to assist in governance
And stayed close to the worthy and talented.
He took pleasure in kindness
And his effective governance extended far.

4. ATTEMPTS TO PRAY FOR AN HEIR

Sadly, I once gave birth to a baby who failed to grow up.
Thinking there were not enough proper palace ladies,
I requested that a concubine be taken in to assist,
Hoping she might produce heirs for the kingdom.
But I noticed the prince was restrained around the concubine,
His chamber tightly closed to her.
So to my lord I said, "Please be lenient if she has displeased you,"
And to the concubine, "Be more attentive, and serve him well."
Incense burning, I fasted and bathed to pray,
And personally recited Buddhist and Daoist scriptures often.
All I wished was for the prince to be blessed with a boy,
It did not matter who would bear him.
I tried my utmost in those days to make sure the family line would continue.

5. DOUBLED DISASTERS OF THE STATE

Yet Heaven showed no mercy—
Misfortunes fell upon us one after another.
We lost Queen Cheng, and then Lady Xu.
The eulogy was sent, the funeral granted.
I followed every ritual and observed the mourning protocols.
My filial affection for them was of a high order,
So was my effort and hardship.
Who would have known that in only three years, all my effort would prove
    in vain.
When my husband became bedridden,
The best doctors were gathered, but none could cure him.
Anxiously we waited for the stars to send a sign,
As I prayed to Heaven in tears. How I wished
My life could be shortened in exchange for extending his.
Despite my utmost sincerity, the deities did not respond.
The heavens fell, the sun no longer shone.
In a court with no master, panic spread all over.
Outsiders constantly took advantage of us.

Who could be trusted with the kingdom's affairs?
My dress was soaked by streams of bloody tears.

6. PRESERVING CHASTITY AND FULFILLING FILIAL DUTIES

In ancient times there were many virtuous women,
Their names and stories recorded in the histories.
If I were to follow my husband to the netherworld,
It'd be as easy as tossing a weightless Mount Tai.
I am always surrounded by numerous palace maids,
For they fear that I might follow him at any time.
I have contemplated this over and over again,
Taking all into consideration, from the beginning to the end.
In ancient times there were both heroic deaths
And survivors with the purest virtues.
Plus the father king is old; who else would look after him?
If death is not feared, why should life be held dear?
Still I must live to care for the old and worship the spirits.

7. MY HEARTFELT STATEMENT TO OFFICIALS

With matters of significance piling up,
I stood alone, frail and helpless,
Fearing that state affairs might go wrong.
Watching officials all come to send condolences,
I carried out the rituals one after another.
I had no choice but to speak to them
From behind a screen, weeping and wailing.
Alas, the father king was old and sick,
The miserable widow all on her own.
To rely on the powerful was the only way
For a vulnerable kingdom to survive.
Despite all my efforts, I had no options.
I was just managing to sustain myself, balancing on the edge.
Heaven gave me life,
Why must it then drive me to extremes!

8. REPORTING THE HAPPY NEWS OF PREGNANCY

With the funeral completed, the bequests had to be distributed fairly
To all the beauties of the inner palace.
I asked some close servants to unlock the delicate cabinets.
Then I noticed five ladies, pale as if sick.
Doctors were summoned to check: it was true that all were pregnant!
I decorated them with red fabric and flowers.
With joyous drum and flute music leading their way,
I reported the great news to the father king.
Congratulatory memorials were presented to our majestic emperor
From government departments, counties, and prefectures.
I prayed to Heaven and the gods for the birth of the royal offspring.

9. BIRTH OF THE POSTHUMOUS CHILDREN

Auspicious vapors and colorful clouds cluster,
Casting lights on the ornate palace rooftop.
The first one, a baby girl, left me heavy-hearted.
But thanks to the ancestors' blessing,
A few boys were born in the same year.
Since you were your mothers' firstborns
Your births were difficult and dangerous.
Luckily all turned out well—we're grateful for the mercy of Heaven.
Requesting titles for you
I exhausted my energy in writing up petitions.

10. NURTURING THE FATHERLESS NEWBORNS

All were born in the leap month of the year of the Tiger.
Your fast-growing teeth and glib tongues are signs of extraordinariness.
All the time I held you in my arms, caressing your skin.
Watching you play, I shared in the happiness.
I carried you on my back, I held you with my hands,
I'd hold you in my mouth if I could.
I constantly asked the nannies to be careful.
Inside and outside the palace, young and old,

I treated everyone with kindness and leniency
In exchange for their care and compassion.
I was concerned whenever one baby got indigestion, or another had a
    cold—
Which made me feel as if I were submersed in cold water.
I exhausted myself to care for you,
Not to mention supplying rich cradles and pearl-encrusted nappies, and
    a nursery supplied with silver fixtures and golden fittings.

11. REQUESTING NAMES FOR THE CHILDREN ACCORDING TO REGULATIONS

Following the regulations of our great dynasty—
The brilliance of which is on a par with the stars and the sun—
The three orphaned boys' names were registered at the age of five.
We were so fortunate to receive the imperial grace,
Thanks to the support of the Ministry of Rites.
The widowed consorts had endured hardships
But finally got to celebrate the growth of the king's family tree.
With a radiant glow arising from the jade certificate,
The palace and the court are joyful,
And the whole kingdom bursts into cheers.
These were not simply requests for names:
They were in fact crucial to the titles conferred later.
When I think back to the beginning,
I see everything was due to the successful title request.

12. COMMANDED BY IMPERIAL DECREE TO MANAGE THE STATE

The father king was worried about his age,
And the children were too young to understand the gravity
    of state affairs.
Following the precedent of the Tang dynasty,
Imperial permission was granted—
The king placed all of the state affairs under my command.
"The tax and revenue shall not be appropriated.
The ritual ceremonies shall not be interfered with by the powerful."

He urged me to raise the sons for the throne.
The earnest words of His Majesty laid stress on you boys.
I, a helpless widow, could hardly carry out the heavy tasks,
But how could I fail to accept them respectfully?
Adhering to morality and keeping calm,
I took on the hard work under Father's order.

13. EDUCATING THE CHILDREN

You were born of noble rank and raised in wealth,
But should never develop haughty or prodigal habits.
Watch your behavior, and make no error.
Be serious about the canons, and take pleasure in the rites.
Draw near to the righteous, and expel the wicked.
Compete to listen to and take good advice.
Observe the familial rules: be filial, loving, and reverent.
Carry on the heritage of your predecessors,
So that my sufferings and endless longing will not have been in vain.

14. MY JOYS AND WORRIES REGARDING
MY FATHER-IN-LAW'S OLD AGE

The father king had reached his seventies and was planning his
    retirement.
Moved by Heaven's generosity,
I raised my glass with the boys to toast his longevity,
Colorful decorations filling the eyes.
Happy for his long life,
Yet fearful too.
For the radiance of a setting sun doesn't last long.
Afraid that the maids might be neglectful and indolent,
I asked after him three times a day
And checked on him at night in the others' stead.
The water-clock and bells resonated with my worries.
How I wished you could instantly grow up and mature
To serve your grandfather and manage the kingdom—
Other than that, I had nothing more to ask for.

15. HUMBLY GRANTED A MONUMENT BY IMPERIAL DECREE

It was my duty to serve my father-in-law;
It was my responsibility to raise the children.
I willingly took on the hard work,
With no intention of making my name known.
To my surprise, following the imperial decree
To encourage and exalt virtues, the local commentators,
Officials of the ministries, and scholars of national academies
Reported on my loyal, filial, and motherly deeds.
Recommendations were sent from local governors and inspectors
To the emperor, who ordered a memorial arch to be built for me.
"Gentle and vigilant, moderate and chaste,"
The language is exalted yet sincere.
The imperial announcement shines with magnificence,
And was quoted in the local gazetteer.
I am abashed by the honor.
Deeply I am abashed by the honor.

16. SERVING MY FATHER-IN-LAW IN MY HUSBAND'S STEAD

How sad, the husband prince passed away early,
Leaving the father king behind, old and sick.
I looked after him in my husband's place,
Day and night, attentive to his care.
I tasted his medicine and personally served him fine meals—
If only I had elixirs to extend his life!
How sad, father-in-law, that I will never see you at the dining table again.
Then making the offerings properly, I was all alone;
Managing the burial properly, I was all alone.
Rituals and ceremonies were arranged in a hurry.
Upset that I was unable to hold his coffin-ropes, my tears fell in vain.
As I sent the children off with the procession, my heart could not rest.
My body stayed in the palace, but my spirit followed the funeral
    procession.
Husband, if you meet your father there, you will know
The countless hardships I have endured.

17. ACCUMULATING VIRTUE AND DOING GOOD

Everyone shares feelings of compassion.
I find the custom of cremating the palace maids inhumane.
It is said that kindness should reach even the dried bones,
So I ordered graves built for them on grounds selected by divination.
More unfortunate are the old and poor with no family;
I provided them all with shelter and food.
I ordered the whole kingdom to worship Bodhisattva Guanyin.
On vermilion cliffs, amid purple bamboos,
Her manifestations were seen and heard.
I had many temples built, prayers made often,
Incense was burned on Mount Wudang,
Incense was burned on Mount Tai.
All of these were my sincere wish for the sons and the kingdom.
I performed many acts to gain spiritual merit
And worshipped the deities with the highest reverence.

18. EXALTING THE UPRIGHT AND EXPELLING THE EVIL

"Throughout hundreds of generations,
The one teacher of all monarchs is none other than Confucius."
These were the earnest words from the king
When he entrusted me with the boys.
How could I endure the sight of Confucius's shrine in disrepair?
I urged immediate repair.
Sir Liu repaid the state with his devotion to three reigns.
His loyalty as a servitor was impeccable.
So I saw that his temples and sacrificial rituals were properly maintained.
Who would have expected that there would be such malicious people
Who bully a widow and orphans. A crisis arose
With false charges from the outside and disorders inside the household.
Empowered by Heaven and blessed by the gods,
I put the defiant in prison and the wicked to death.
Since I purged evil and upheld justice,
The kingdom was at peace.

19. INHERITING THE TITLE OF KING

We celebrated the great turnaround in the fortune of the kingdom.
We were grateful for the unexpected imperial favor written on a
    silken edict.
The palace residents leaped with joy.
Springtime returned to the halls and gardens.
Inheriting the kingdom at a young age,
Bestowed with a golden signet and red ribbons,
The heir looked solemn and majestic in the king's regalia.
Benevolent and talented, studious and filial,
He was exceptionally intelligent since childhood.
His manifold beauty comparable to the sages,
He seemed an offspring of the phoenix and the unicorn.
In the past we received the emperor's instructions,
But it was not until this moment that my heart was finally comforted.

20. GRANTED HIGHER TITLES BY SPECIAL DECREE

Posthumous titles were conferred according to the norms.
Procedures had to be followed in the various departments,
The same for every kingdom, as in the past.
The emperor was moved by the sincerity of the king,
Who had begged many times for the emperor's favor,
Thus I was honored to receive the queen's crown.
This will not be a precedent for the future—the edict said it clearly,
Nor had this ever happened to other kingdoms in the past.
Miraculously, we were granted this exceptional grace.
How did I deserve the honor and glory?
The emperor's decree brought glory to the family,
Granting the deceased prince the title of King Zhao.
My filial son showed deep reverence for his parents.
Since he developed such a kingly heart, all my effort paid off.

21. SELECTING A GOOD MATE

His sagacious virtues were evident from a young age.
So a gentle lady would make him a good match.
I asked for permission to select one from among ten thousand.
She was as decent and beautiful as a precious jade.
The golden screens glowed along with the fair lady.
She looked reserved and retiring, steadfast and serene,
A befitting person to entrust with a household.
With the wedding carriages lined up, bystanders vied for a look.
The incense was burned, ceremonial prayers recited.
Their shadows overlapped on the palace stairs,
Like two birds singing with each other in harmony.
Good for your household, good for your descendants.
Generation after generation, on and on.

22. TRACING BACK TO THE ORIGIN AND
PASSING DOWN THE LESSONS

I remember when I received my lord's favor,
We were a good match like a pair of harmonious zithers,
A happy couple that treated each other with respect.
He taught me to read and write,
To know about the past and the present.
Yet against all expectations, misfortunes fell upon the kingdom.
I kept quiet on all the sufferings—
To whom could I pour them out?
Through the music of the *qin* zither I express my heart,
My voice shaking, tears streaming down.
The bitterness is stronger than the bile of a bear.
May Your Majesty always keep this in mind with compassion,
And exert yourself to practice benevolence.
May your children and grandchildren
Thousands and thousands of years later
Know there was once a widow who endured hardships.

Translated by Zeyuan Wu

SOURCE: Zhongguo Yishu Yanjiu Yuan and Beijing Guqin Yanjiu Hui, comp. *Qinqu jicheng* 琴曲集成, vol. 9 (Beijing: Zhonghua Shuju, 2010), 1–95.

Further Reading

Fong, Grace S. *Herself an Author: Gender, Agency, and Writing in Late Imperial China.* Honolulu: University of Hawaii Press, 2008.

Van Gulik, Robert H. *The Lore of the Chinese Lute: An Essay in the Ideology of the Ch'in.* 3rd ed. Bangkok: Orchid, 2011.

Wang, Richard G. *The Ming Prince and Daoism: Institutional Patronage of an Elite.* New York: Oxford University Press, 2012.

Wu, Zeyuan. "Becoming Sages: *Qin* Song and Self-Cultivation in Late Imperial China." PhD diss., Ohio State University, 2020.

24

....

ENVIRONMENTAL CATASTROPHES
Harrowing reports by Chen Qide 陳其德 (fl. 1640s)
and Pu Songling 蒲松齡 (1640–1715)

....

*Spanning the late Ming and early Qing, the two accounts
below describe the hardship experienced in the authors' home
regions as a result of extreme weather.*

During the seventeenth century, much of Eurasia experienced a "little ice age."
Climate change, especially a drop in temperature, brought environmental
stress, often leading to famine, insect infestations, epidemics, and violence.
Disorder of this sort contributed to the collapse of the Ming dynasty, as desperate farmers formed gangs and ravaged the countryside, soldiers deserted
and joined them, and the Ming government lacked the resources to alleviate
the situation. The Manchus' Qing dynasty restored order, but they could
not do anything about the weather, which continued to make life difficult
in various places at certain times. Among the abundant sources that survive
from this period are detailed accounts of what particular places experienced
as disaster struck.

The first of the two accounts below was written by Chen Qide in 1641,
near the end of the Ming dynasty. Although one book of moral advice by
him survives, little else is known about him beyond what he reports in this

essay. He was from Tongxiang County in Zhejiang, not far from Hangzhou, generally a part of the country that did not have to worry about drought. As he reports, however, in the early seventeenth century, the region faced crisis after crisis. He wrote a follow-up account the next year, reporting that things had only gotten worse with further spread of disease and death.

The second account was written in the early eighteenth century by Pu Songling, who lived in northern China (Shandong) and offers evidence that even during the relatively peaceful years of the Kangxi reign (1661–1722), severe weather could lead to social problems of many sorts. Pu today is known primarily for the fictional stories that he wrote, but he was a widely read scholar with broad interests.

Although it would seem that both authors are reporting what they had learned firsthand, they adopt the style of the historian, trying to write objectively about the general situation in their area, and do not mention what they or their families personally experienced. Perhaps to make their case as forcefully as possible, neither stresses the impact of these calamities on those closest to them.

Record of Disasters, by Chen Qide

I was born too late to see the glories of the founding Hongwu [1368–1398] and Yongle [1403–1424] reigns, nor did I manage to see the dazzling brilliance of the reigns of Chenghua [1465–1487] and Hongzhi [1488–1505]. But I do remember the early years of the Wanli period [1573–1620], the time of my youth, when prosperity was widespread, commoners lived abundantly, and the cost of a peck of rice never exceeded 0.3 or 0.4 tael of silver. At that time, anyone who sought to trade using millet was turned down with a haughty sneer. Wheat and beans were fed to the cattle and pigs. Every household consumed fresh fish and fine meat.

People thought that such a situation would go on forever. However, as people grew indulgent, Heaven turned against the miscreants. Within the flash of an eye, in the *wuzi* year [1588], rain fell in a continuous downpour. Far and near, all the land turned into swamps. The next year, there was a drought that extended over a thousand *li*. For two months, the rivers didn't have even a spoonful of water to keep the grass alive. During this time, one picul of rice could be sold for 1.6 taels of silver. Within a month of this great surge in the price of rice, people had stripped the uncultivated land of plants and the trees of bark. In the wilderness, there was no more green grass, nor did trees have their bark untouched. People wandered off, and everywhere corpses were lying in the roads.

Between the end of this crisis and the early years of the Tianqi reign period [1621], although the price of rice was constantly fluctuating, conditions did not reach those of severe famine. However, the vicious clique of Wei Zhong-xian [1568–1627] tyrannically oppressed the gentry scholars. They turned the nation's loyal and righteous heroes into angry ghosts. Heaven was angry above, and the people were resentful below. Although the new emperor was brilliant and determined and exterminated Wei and his followers, the country could not recover from the devastation caused by the Wei clique. There were still many bandits and thieves, and the troubles within and without lasted more than twenty years.

In the thirteenth year of the Chongzhen reign [1640], heavy downpours lasted for almost a month. The water rose two feet higher than it had in the Wanli period [1588]. Whatever direction one looked, everything was covered with water. Boats were tied to bedposts; fish and shrimp frolicked in wells and sinks. Those with multistory houses used the top floors as a refuge. Those who had no upper story either lived on their rooftops or climbed up towers, afraid that they would not live through the day.

At first the price of rice was only a little more than one tael per picul, then it went up to more than two taels. After the floods retreated, the farmers of the Wuxing region searched for good young seedlings, competing for these rare commodities. Even during the last ten days of the seventh month, one could still see the boats departing one after the other.

The next year, the fourteenth of the Chongzhen reign [1641], the drought demon brought disaster. The rivers all dried up. The price of rice suddenly jumped from two taels to three taels per picul. Finally, in my village, a single peck was selling for 0.4 tael. Although there were twice as many wheat shoots than the previous year, there were not enough of them to fill people up. Some ate the bran of wheat and rice; others made wild grass and tree bark their main dishes, with bran as side dishes. Even the wealthy families all ate porridge mixed with noodles. Those who ate two meals a day claimed that they were full, but most of the people had only one. Husbands deserted their wives, and fathers deserted their children, as each person put himself or herself first. Consumer goods piled up in the markets and could be purchased for half-price. As for luxuries and toys, people did not even bother to ask the prices! Alas, people had reached the most extreme limit of desperation. Not only was it impossible to get a loan, but also there was no place to pawn one's possessions. Though one called upon Heaven for help, there was no response. Though one begged at gates, no relief was obtained. Given these circumstances, those who cried bitterly for help in the morning by evening might be so weak they could only crawl. Once they fell, it was like they had sunk into a churning wave, making survival impossible. There were stories of those who still had morsels of food in their mouths although they had been lying dead for some time. No benevolent person could fail to weep on seeing these scenes of extreme suffering.

Next, those who had the luck to survive and managed to get their crops planted were struck by locusts, which swarmed over the fields and destroyed the young sprouts. Then the rivers dried up. The pumps on the wells could bring up no water, or just a dribble, too little to nourish those withered shoots.

Then came the epidemics. Five or six out of every ten families fell victim to disease. Some of the dead could be buried in wooden coffins; many, however, were wrapped in reeds and had only flies attending their funerals. Uncounted dead were thrown into the rivers. The price of daily necessities increased several-fold; even the price of young chickens and ducklings was four or five times higher than usual. If they could not afford the several dozen cash necessary to buy bean curd, a family of eight might have nothing to eat. Moreover, since feeding pigs had gotten so expensive, even middle-income families could no longer afford to raise them. Those with two sows had already moved them into their cooking pots.

Previously, one tael of silver could get a whole pig. But now even the price of a pig's head was about 0.8 to 0.9 tael. In the past, the racket of chickens and dogs could be heard throughout one's neighborhood; now to hear a single cock crow was as rare as the cry of a crane at Huating, even if one carefully listened in a busy marketplace all morning long.

Whereas previously famines were confined to one prefecture or one province, this time the famine not only struck in Zhejiang; it also spread nearby to Nanjing and as far as Shandong, Henan, and Hubei. The suffering was especially severe in Nanjing, where people who were not killed by armed men died of starvation or, if not that, of disease. How could people cope with so much? Was the Creator destroying the people because they had multiplied so rapidly? Or had people so wasted the gifts of Heaven that Heaven hated to see such waste and therefore punished them?

Suffering leads people to aspire to goodness. Yet when they have enough food and clothing, they get indulgent, which gives rise to evil desires. If people could just remember that the cost of rice may at times equal that of pearls and the cost of firewood that of cassia, then they may be able to attain the great Dao, not to mention being able to find ways to support themselves.

I fear that later generations will not always keep these events in mind and stay vigilant. Therefore, I have written these earnest words to let people know what happened. Please do not look on this as useless words.

Written in the fourteenth year of the Chongzhen reign period [1641], on the fifteenth of the seventh month, the day of the Ghost Festival, by retired scholar Songtao.

SOURCE: *Tongxiang xianzhi* 桐鄉縣誌 (Guangxu ed.), 20.8a–9a.

First Account of Disasters in the Forty-Third Year of the Kangxi Reign Period, by Pu Songling

In the fourth month in the *guiwei* year, the forty-third year in the Kangxi reign period [1704], red rain fell. It was a lean year for both wheat and barley. On the twenty-fourth day of the fifth month, wind and rain lasted a whole day. From then on, rain did not stop for a long time, so much so that clear water flowed between the ridges of the fields. As a result, farmers were not able to weed and weeds became rampant and competed with the crops. It was not until the nineteenth day of the sixth month that it stopped raining and fully cleared up.

By then, the standing water in low places reached people's shin bones, and even after many sunny days, the water still had not dried up. Having been exposed to the burning sun, the water in the fields was close to boiling, killing all the seedlings. There was not much standing water on the high fields, but stink bugs ran rampant there and were extremely malodorous. They mounted in large numbers on the seedlings and bamboo shoots and would fly out when one broke the leaves and stems of those plants. By midday, they would hide underground. Seedlings bitten by the stink bugs all died or decayed and smelled bad. Even oxen and horses refused to feed on them. Because they came in large numbers and were good at hibernating, stink bugs could survive freezing conditions. Before the wheat crop leafed out, they were everywhere and impossible to chase away or eliminate, wreaking nonstop havoc.

The only crop stink bugs did not like was beans, so they were spared at first. But before the bean crop bloomed, when the need for precipitation was the greatest, not one drop of rain fell. The local people had no way to keep their hopes up. By harvest time, when people went to gather the beans in the morning, they saw blooms, blighted pods, and some beans amid the shimmering dew. One *mu* of land yielded only two pecks of beans. There seemed no logic to the actions of Heaven.

Because there had been a drought, the soil was not moist even half a foot down, so planting wheat had to be delayed. There was a light rain on the fifteenth day of the eighth month, but the amount was not enough to make plowing possible. Some farmers became impatient, digging up the surface and sowing some of their land instead of leaving it completely untended. It rained twice as much on the twenty-seventh. By then the weather had turned cold, so no one dared to delay any longer. When they plowed their fields, the moisture had barely reached the plowshares. They plowed and then flattened the field, covering up the seeds with a layer of damp soil, then another layer of dry soil [to preserve moisture]. Five days later, the land became too dry to plow.

The seedlings that were sowed the earliest sprouted, with some dying and more opening up, but they were as thin as a thread. Most of the seeds sowed later did not germinate. If you bent over to look closely, you could probably see one or two sprouts. The seeds that were planted around the mid-eighth month looked neat, but because the ridges had not been maintained [due to the flooding], the soil was poor. The hope was to rejuvenate the fields with next year's precipitation. Yet, it did not snow at all the whole winter. When it became slightly warmer, yellow dust blew so hard one couldn't see the road.

Because of the lack of timely rainfall, hunger became common everywhere in the six prefectures. Grain prices skyrocketed. By the end of the twelfth month, one peck of wheat or sorghum cost seven hundred cash and beans and millet cost five hundred cash. Also, sellers were strict with the type of payments they would accept. Earlier, the government announced that it would allow people to use all the different types of currency in circulation in the market but that when the newly minted coins arrived, other varieties would not be permitted anymore. Vendors, frightened by this policy, would accept only official coins. But most of the government-issued coins had been split into two by private casters, only a few left whole. New official coins did not arrive for a long time. Prices continued to rise to the point that even a thousand cash was not enough to buy one pint of rice. Many in Jiaozhou and

Laizhou [both in Shandong] starved to death with money in their hands, ready to buy food. Not until local officials threatened vendors with heavy penalties if they did not accept unofficially issued money did a variety of currency circulate again.

There was a husks-and-sweepings market in the county seat that stretched for one *li* where everything would be sold out by dusk. On the empty ground that was used to husk grain, one bag of swept-up leftovers [grain mixed with husks and dirt] cost fifty to sixty cash; a bag of mixed millet with sweepings cost twice as much. Beggars passed by households nonstop and couldn't even get food made of sweepings and blighted grain. When there is an abundant harvest, large merchants are the wealthy; when there is a hunger, the frugal farmers are the wealthy; during a famine, the diligent are the wealthy. At this time, if a family had a thousand piculs of grain and thousands of rows of cabbages and chives, their wealth was seen as equal to a high nobleman's. The court diverted five hundred thousand piculs of government grain and sent over a hundred Manchu officials to manage relief work. But Zizhou was not considered a disaster area so did not receive any relief grain. Still, imperial grace did reach Zizhou, as the residents were exempted from the spring and fall taxes. This was the work of Heaven and Earth; even the thunder and lightning deities do not get to choose where it rains.

After New Year's day, it snowed on the twenty-seventh day of the first month, then again on the twenty-third of the second month. When the snow melted, the wheat seeds that had not germinated all sprouted and grew well. Those who did not plant wheat the previous fall went north to search for seeds for spring planting. Every day, they went to look for wheat seeds, which by now sold for fifteen hundred cash per peck. They nonetheless carried the seeds home from faraway places and planted them all.

After that, the rain stopped and the fall wheat crop died from drought. The spring wheat was killed by stink bugs. Zhuangwan wheat for high land died from extreme heat. Only the autumn drought-resistant wheat grew to be four inches tall and bore some tiny ears of wheat. Even a family owning several *mu* of wheat fields, in order to survive, had to have the men go out to beg and the women harvest the wheat, carry it home, dry it in the yard, then husk it. By then, grain prices surged, to a thousand cash per peck. Those selling their sons or wives hired thugs as brokers and had to pay them commissions.

In the early spring, people peeled off and consumed the bark of all the elm trees. Looking from afar, one saw a host of beautiful trees, poplar, willow,

Chinese scholar trees, with all their leaves and branches gone, leaving only bald trunks. Families guarded the edible wild herbs grown on their property. If one approached a village known for vulgar social customs, one saw hooligans with baskets on their backs, roaming around in groups of tens, even hundreds, just like ants and monkeys. People did not dare to shout at them but only looked askance.

By now, all the six prefectures had suffered from crop failure, with Zizhou having had it twice. All the six prefectures suffered from drought as well, but Zizhou also suffered from stink bugs. All the six prefectures suffered from famine, but Zizhou also suffered from banditry. Banditry began in the winter, to the point where no village was left undisturbed in an entire township and not one day was peaceful. If a family had more than one peck of grain, one string of cash, or one set of clothes in their possession, they would not dare to close their eyes. If they momentarily let their guard down, they might be robbed and killed any minute. Therefore, there were families who were rich in the morning and by dusk were begging for food. The number of bandits grew, reaching to groups of dozens, even of forty or fifty people in a band. They burned villages, killed people, and raped women, not stopping at anything. People did not dare to report them or fight back. The reason was that if there was a robbery, local officials could pretend not to know of it, but if human lives were lost, they would learn of it. When bandits murdered local residents, officials would not investigate. But if local residents killed robbers, they could face legal consequences. Robbery was not subject to the death penalty, but murder was. For this reason, villagers stood guard all night, but they would take out the arrowheads and bullets when they shot arrows or blunderbusses at the robbers, aiming only to scare them away.

By then, there was no green grass left in sight in Zizhou. But there was wheat south, west, and north of its borders. So the people one saw carrying their belongings and young children and wandering about as vagrants were all from Zizhou. Only four families stayed in a village of more than twenty households. Then, as banditry grew more rampant, they became afraid of being left alone and moved away too. So an entire village became abandoned. At the time, of every ten people in Zizhou, two died, three fled, three stayed, and two turned to banditry.

By the end of the fifth month, it still had not rained. Those who had stayed had gradually fled, leaving only robbers. The robbers stuck like lice; even if the thing is poor, as long as it is alive, they cling to it. People who died on the road were left unburied and were devoured by vultures or dogs. People grew thin, and scavenging animals grew fat. The prefectural seat was filled with the displaced; the entire region was completely lifeless. Kindhearted people in the suburbs had pits dug several feet deep to bury the corpses. Once one was filled, another would be dug. Altogether, over ten were dug, which was still not enough to hold all the bodies. Those who sold human flesh would transport the meat to the markets on donkey-drawn carts early in the morning. The price was one-tenth that of mutton. Others marinated the meat, carried it in a container to the market, and sold it by making a sound by clicking copper coins. The price was similar to that for crows and sparrows. Those who got to be buried in pits at least enjoyed a decent interment.

Those not yet dead, exposed to filth and sleeping by the roadsides at night, lost all sense of shame as death approached. Those who survived lost their ability to react emotionally. Some families that left home would keep going even when one of them died on the road. As a result, many corpses lay next to thoroughfares with no one mourning them. Children were deserted on the grass. Some were taken in by those who had sympathy for them. As time went on, human life became ever cheaper. A young girl could be traded for as little as one peck of grain.

Fortunately, it rained on the ninth day of the sixth month. When people plowed, they saw about three inches of dry soil, yet everywhere one looked, farmers were working in the fields. Even though sowing took place late, there were no stink bugs underground. Because there was no vegetation aboveground, they did not have anything to feed on and no humid soil for them to burrow into. As a result, all the adult and juvenile stink bugs were scorched to death. It was as if Heaven said, "The stink bugs have harmed the people of Zizhou, but it took three years of drought to wipe them out." All the counties suffered from the drought, but Zizhou was the only one that suffered from stink bugs.

SOURCE: *Pu Songling ji* 蒲松齡集 (Beijing: Zhonghua Shuju, 1962), 2.47–49.

Further Reading

Elvin, Mark, and Ts'ui-jung Liu, eds. *Sediments of Time: Environment and Society in Chinese History*. Cambridge: Cambridge University Press, 1998.

Fong, Grace S. "Reclaiming Subjectivity in a Time of Loss: Ye Shaoyuan (1589–1648) and Autobiographical Writing in the Ming-Qing Transition." *Ming Studies* 59 (2009): 21–41. doi:10.1179/175975909X466426.

Wakeman, Frederic. "China and the Seventeenth-Century Crisis." *Late Imperial China* 7 (1986): 1–26.

Will, Pierre-Etienne. "Coming of Age in Shanghai during the Ming-Qing Transition: Yao Tinglin's (1628–after 1697) *Record of the Successive Years*." *Gujin lunheng* 44 (2000): 15–38.

25

A CON MAN POSING AS AN OFFICIAL

Legal Confession of Luo Fenpeng 羅奮鵬 (b. 1726)

A man making a living as an itinerant scribe began impersonating an official and calling on people from his hometown to ask for loans. After being caught, he made a full confession.

The eighteenth century, perhaps especially the Qianlong reign period (1736–1796), is remembered as an age of peace and prosperity, when the population was increasing and taxes were kept low. Yet one does not need to dig too far below the surface to find evidence of political conflict and social tension. The Qianlong emperor orchestrated a massive censoring of books, wanting anything that referred to northern non-Han in insulting ways either rewritten or destroyed. Banditry, rebellion, and ethnic conflict disrupted the peace from time to time. Nonviolent crimes like fraud and theft, which rarely appear in the historical records of earlier periods, are well documented because of the survival of the Qing archives, full of reports of even routine legal cases. Such records provide glimpses of the lives of people close to the margins.

Below is the legal confession of a swindler named Luo Fenpeng. He must have been a man of talent, since successful deception requires astute understanding of other people: Who can be most easily tricked? How might one gain their trust? What are they willing to spend money on? What would make them suspicious? If impersonation is involved, one must also have acting skills to play the part convincingly. Thus, it is likely that Luo Fenpeng, who managed to trick a long series of people out of money, was in fact a person of considerable ability. In the end, however, he was caught. Impersonating an official was considered a political crime by the Qing government (and by the Ming before it), a threat to the government, punishable by death even when the guilty person had no political motives and committed the offenses primarily as an easy way to get money, not that different from theft.

In his confession, Luo describes leaving his home in Jiangxi and traveling rather long distances, west into Hunan and Hubei, then east into Jiangsu, at first supporting himself by the legal if not very well-paid job of scribe. Not surprisingly, he does not tell us anything about his inner feelings. We do not learn why, unlike so many other men with enough education to serve as teachers, he did not stay in his home region and accept his modest circumstances. Perhaps he had a bad case of wanderlust. Nor do we learn what went through his mind when he decided to turn to swindling people by impersonating an official. Perhaps he got a thrill from discovering that he was good at tricking people. He remained wary, however, and more than once moved on.

Confessions secured in legal cases must of course be read with the occasion in mind. The accused person has to admit facts known from other evidence but doesn't want to come across as a truly evil person. Even though Luo was literate and could have written out a confession himself, this was probably put together by a legal clerk from his oral responses to questions.

Confession

I am from Luling County in Ji'an Prefecture [Jiangxi]. I was originally surnamed Luo, and my name is Fenpeng; Li Rongzong is an assumed name. This year, I am thirty-eight. My father is Luo Junzheng, and my younger brother is Luo Yunpeng. I have taken a wife surnamed Li, who gave birth to a son, Xunguan, only eight years old. In the twenty-fourth year of Qianlong [1759], I left home and went from Hunan to Hubei, working as a scribe along the way to get by. I did not falsely pretend to have official rank. In the twenty-fifth and twenty-sixth year of Qianlong [1760 and 1761], I went to various places in Henan, selling calligraphy, and committed no acts of banditry or swindling.

In the eleventh month of the twenty-sixth year of Qianlong, I heard that the emperor was touring the south, and I wanted to go and see. After the twentieth, I arrived at Yangzhou and first stayed at the Jiangxi native Shan Zixian's needle shop on Coppersmith Street. As I saw that Yangzhou was bustling, I conceived the idea of pretending to be an official in order to swindle. So I invented the name Ouyang Zhang and said I was a vice prefect by purchase. Then, I met Li Huancai, who had a tailor shop on Peppertree Alley and was also from Jiangxi. I told him that I was Ouyang Zhang of Anfu [also in Jiangxi, and close to Luo's home] and that because of a boating accident when crossing the Yellow River, my baggage had been swept away and lost. He believed it and borrowed sixteen taels on my behalf. I also borrowed a total of eighty taels from Shu Wen and Zeng Er, who were on a Ji'an tribute boat. I had clothing made, hired servants, and, wearing a crystal-buttoned official's hat, used the name Ouyang Zhang and went to visit the Nanchang government student Lu Xuan. I met him several times and also went to visit the Yangzhou subprefectural magistrate Xie Tao. He, too, is from Ji'an, and I thought he would give me some traveling money, but he had gone off on business, and I never got to see him. There was also the Zhenjiang Transport Command company commander Ouyang Weiguo, escorting [grain boats] to Yangzhou, and his brother Ouyang Zhiping and the fellow provincial lumber merchant Xiong Wenjin. I went to see all of them. Ouyang Weiguo had already departed, and I did not swindle any money from him.

As I had stayed at Yangzhou for a long time and feared discovery, on the nineteenth of the second month, I threw the hat button away and, taking the remaining two or three taels, fled across the [Yangzi] River. On the twenty-third, I reached Suzhou and, on the second of the third month, reached Hangzhou, where I amused myself for a few days on West Lake. As my traveling money was exhausted, I again thought of swindling, whereupon I bought a dark blue rank button at a stall. Fearing that someone from Yangzhou would come searching, I dared not keep using the name Ouyang Zhang and changed my name to Li Chunguan. Saying I was a Ji'an native and a prefect by purchase, I went to visit the Hangzhou prefect Zeng Yueli, who was also from Jiangxi, but was not received. There was also the Chuzhou brigade commander Zeng Jieji, at Hangzhou on a horse-buying mission. He was a Jiangxi native, and I went to visit him, hoping he would give me some traveling expenses, but I did not meet him either. I had no money to spend, so I worked as a scribe to make a living.

Later, I traveled on foot to Jiangning. Seeing that there were many Jiangxi lumber merchants there, I again wore the blue-buttoned hat and, using the name Li Chunguan, went to visit them. I wrote some calligraphy samples and gave them to the lumber merchants Chen Lüxiang and Huang Canxian, earning more than thirty taels.

In the fifth month, I set out from Jiangning, going north of the [Yangzi] River to the Shouzhou area [Anhui] and, as before, getting through the days by working as a scribe. On the twentieth of the first month of this year, I arrived at Nine Temple Mountain in Tongshan County, Hubei, and stayed at Jiuyi Temple. The Daoist priest, Liu Jingting, was also a Jiangxi native, and he invited me to eat. But I had no money to donate. Recalling that there was a fellow provincial, Li Xuan, [who] had served as county magistrate of Yuanrang [Hunan], I wrongfully used his name to write the calligraphy for two door tablets. Moreover, I wrote the words, "Rewarding the regular metropolitan graduate, Board of Revenue office director, and grand master for governance of Shaowu Prefecture, Fujian, who accompanied the imperial carriage on a southern tour, imperially favored with conferral of a court necklace, satchel, and advancement by one class." I meant only to show off to him. Unexpectedly, when I went to stay at an inn outside the Tongshan County walls on the twenty-third, someone surnamed Yu was gambling for high stakes there with some others; they were arrested by constables, and I was taken with them for questioning. In the heat of the moment, I put on my official's cap and said I was Li Xuan and was awaiting an appointment as prefect. The Tongshan magistrate questioned me for a while and handed me over to underlings to keep in custody for further investigation. I seized an opportunity to escape. On the sixth of the second month, I reached the Shankou area in Wuning County and spent the night at the home of one Hong Nanyang. On the seventh, the dismissed stipend student Ye Guangjia, seeing that I wore a rank button, took me to his home. I lied that I had served as prefect of Zhangzhou, Fujian. Because his relative Nie Xianmo was in the midst of a lawsuit over the compilation of a clan genealogy, Ye Guangjia promised me eighty taels if I would intercede with the district magistrate on his behalf. We went to the district seat together. Considering my own false position, I dared not go to meet the district magistrate and seized an opportunity to flee. I reached the Shatian area but on the fourteenth was caught by magistrate's runners from the two counties of Wuning and Tongshan and brought to this court. I did not receive money from either Ye Guangjia or Nie Xianmo and except for [what I have related in this confession] have not done anything illegal. Even in my home of Luling, I merely made a living by instructing the young.

Translated by Mark McNicholas, in *True Crimes in Eighteenth-Century China: Twenty Case Histories*, ed. Robert E. Hegel (Seattle: University of Washington Press, 2009), 219–21, modified.

SOURCE: Guoli Gugong Bowuyuan 國立故宮博物館 (National Palace Museum), ed., *Gongzhongdang Qianlongchao zouzhe* 宮中檔乾隆朝奏折 (Secret palace memorials of the Qianlong reign) (Taipei: Guoli Gugong Bowuyuan, 1982–89), 17:243–46.

Further Reading

Bodde, Derk, and Clarence Morris. *Law in Imperial China: Exemplified by 190 Ch'ing Dynasty Cases.* Cambridge, MA: Harvard University Press, 1967.

Hegel, Robert E., ed. *True Crimes in Eighteenth-Century China: Twenty Case Histories.* Seattle: University of Washington Press, 2009.

McKnight, Brian E., and James T. C. Liu, trans. *The Enlightened Judgments Ch'ing-ming Chi: The Sung Dynasty Collection.* Albany: State University of New York Press, 1999.

McNicholas, Mark. "Poverty Tales and Statutory Politics in Mid-Qing Fraud Cases." In Robert E. Hegel and Catherine N. Carlitz, eds. *Writing and Law in Late Imperial China: Crime, Conflict, and Judgment.* Seattle: University of Washington Press.

26

A PRIVATE SECRETARY'S ITINERANT LIFE
Year-by-year autobiography by Wang Huizu 汪輝祖
(1730–1807)

*After serving many years as a private secretary and a few years
as an official, Wang Huizu wrote a book-length autobiography,
something relatively rare in the Chinese tradition of writing about
oneself. Drawing on journals or notebooks he kept over the years,
he relates many important turning points in his life.*

As more and more men took the civil service examinations, the number
of those who repeatedly failed steadily increased. While some came from
landowning families able to support them while they continued to study
and take exams, most of those who persisted had to find other means of
support. Working as a tutor or teacher was common, and by the Qing period,
a better-paying alternative was to become a private secretary or adviser to a
magistrate, prefect, or other regional official. The demands placed on local
officials meant that they needed more assistance than the government provided, so on their own they hired men able to handle paperwork, especially

if they also had expertise in the legal code or taxation policies. These private secretaries/advisers should be distinguished from clerks, who were also literate and handled paperwork but were not considered in the same social class as the local official they served. Clerks usually stayed in one jurisdiction their whole careers and often came from families of clerks. Private secretaries, by contrast, were considered literati, had personal ties to the official they served, and might follow him from one post to another.

The eighteenth-century legal adviser/private secretary we know the most about is Wang Huizu, author of a lengthy autobiography. He came from Shaoxing Prefecture in Zhejiang, well-known for producing private secretaries. He began working as one himself at age twenty-three in the office of his father-in-law. Within a few years, he began studying the legal code, eventually serving as a legal adviser. For his autobiography, he adopted the year-by-year style, a format that lets the author draw attention to experiences and people that shaped his values and choices at different stages of his life.

As Wang Huizu's autobiography shows, the life of a private secretary/legal adviser was an itinerant one. While working, he lived at the government yamen (the walled office complex), leaving his family in his hometown. To make it possible to visit them occasionally, he accepted assignments only in Jiangsu and Zhejiang. There was also time between assignments, as local officials generally held their posts for only two or three years at a stretch, allowing Wang Huizu to return home for months at a time before accepting a new position, sometimes with his previous patron, sometimes with someone else. He records all of these moves in his autobiography.

Wang Huizu did eventually gain the *jinshi*, but not until he was forty-six, and even then it took another decade before he got a regular appointment as a magistrate. In time, he achieved a considerable reputation for his books of advice on local administration. He was also known for his devotion to his widowed mothers (his father's legal wife and the concubine who bore him). Of the five children in their care, only one was a boy, and in his telling they poured their hopes into him. Widows like them, who refused to remarry, were celebrated in the Ming and Qing periods as moral heroes. Wang Huizu made repeated efforts to ensure that his mothers' story of widow chastity was recognized.

The passages from his autobiography included here were selected to show what he saw as formative experiences. They constitute only a small fraction of his full autobiography and go only through age fifty-six, his final year as a private secretary. He records the births, deaths, and marriages of the twelve children born to his first wife, concubine, and successor wife, but these have been omitted here. Also omitted are all but one of the many legal cases he relates at length.

Reveries from a Sick Bed

THE EIGHTH YEAR OF THE YONGZHENG REIGN [1730]

I was born into the Wang family on the fourteenth day of the twelfth month, between three and five in the morning, in the eastern room of the Reverence for Friendship Hall, which is in the central lane of Great Righteousness Village. From the time my ancestor Wang Dalun moved to Xiaoshan County [Shaoxing Prefecture, Zhejiang] from Yin [Ningbo, Zhejiang] until the time of my great-grandfather Bizheng sixteen generations had passed.

My great-grandmother, Madame Shen, had three sons, of whom my grandfather Zhihan was the youngest. My grandmother (who was the daughter of my great-grandmother's brother) had two sons, the elder of whom was my father, Kai, the jail warden of Qi County in Henan's Weihui Prefecture. Thus, counting from the ancestor who moved to Xiaoshan, I was a nineteenth-generation grandson.

At the time of my birth, my father had gone to the capital [Beijing] to await selection for a post. His principal wife, Madame Fang, was recuperating from a chronic illness. My birth mother, Madame Xu, got up four days after my birth to take care of the kitchen work, causing a hemorrhage from which she never recovered fully. All my life I have felt bad about this.

THE NINTH YEAR OF THE YONGZHENG REIGN [1731], MY SECOND YEAR

Father was still in the capital. Wang [王 different Wang character] Tanren of Shanyin [in Zhejiang] and he were the closest of friends. When Mr. Wang had a daughter in the sixth month of the previous year, they made plans to marry their two children. The matter was settled when I was born, without the participation of a go-between.

THE TENTH YEAR OF THE YONGZHENG REIGN [1732], MY THIRD YEAR

Father was appointed jailer of Qi County in Weihui Prefecture, Henan.

THE ELEVENTH YEAR OF THE YONGZHENG REIGN [1733], MY FOURTH YEAR...

THE TWELFTH YEAR OF THE YONGZHENG REIGN [1734], MY FIFTH YEAR

This year I started going to an outside teacher.

On the twenty-ninth day of the fifth month, Father's principal wife, Madame Fang, died. Concerning her, Mother Xu once told me, "When you were born, I was still young. Because I worked very hard in the daytime, Madame Fang was afraid I would get exhausted and not be able to nurse you. Therefore, in the evening, she would take you in her arms. If you cried, she would bring you to me to nurse; after that was done, she would carry you back to her room and personally attend to changing your wet clothes. When she was dying, she took your hand and told your two elder sisters to take good care of you. Her great love for you is something you should always remember." When I was in my forties, I reported this conversation to my two sisters, and thinking back on our mother's love, we cried together.

In the eleventh month, Grandfather brought in a new principal wife for Father, Madame Wang [王 different Wang character].

THE THIRTEENTH YEAR OF THE YONGZHENG REIGN [1735], MY SIXTH YEAR

Mother Wang and Mother Xu joined Father in Qi County [Henan], bringing me with them. They invited Teacher Jingshan to come to the office to give lessons.

THE FIRST YEAR OF THE QIANLONG REIGN [1736], MY SEVENTH YEAR

Grandfather came to Qi and gave me the name "Huizu" [bringing luster to the ancestors]. When I was born, Grandfather was already fifty-nine; just to have a grandson made him extremely happy. He gave me the baby name "Scraps" because scraps were cheap and plentiful but useful in farming. At five, when I began studying with a teacher, I was given the name "Ao" [turtle]. When Grandfather saw that I could make out the meaning of characters and could read books, he settled on my present name. . . .

THE SECOND YEAR OF THE QIANLONG REIGN [1737], MY EIGHTH YEAR

I studied at the official compound. One day, two pieces of pottery fell to the ground, and the thin one broke. Father, showing me the whole one, said, "If you can be as thick as this one, then you'll remain even and complete throughout your whole life. Remember this when you are a man: be thick like satin to endure many years' use, or be like cocoon paper, from which several layers can be removed. However, don't be like bamboo paper, or you'll rip apart in one touch."

THE THIRD YEAR OF THE QIANLONG REIGN [1738], MY NINTH YEAR

I studied in the official compound.

THE FOURTH YEAR OF THE QIANLONG REIGN [1739], MY TENTH YEAR

In the first month, because Grandfather was old and my uncle was not able to care for him, Father quit his post on the excuse of illness. In the third month, we left Qi and departed for Jining [Shandong]. Mother Wang was pregnant and rode with Mother Xu in a very uncomfortable single-axle covered wagon, as we did not have enough money to rent a large carriage. We arrived home in the fifth month. Soon my younger brother Rongzu was born, but in the seventh month he died.

At this stage of my life, Grandfather cherished me and took me along whenever he went to watch a play. On our return, he would ask me the names of the characters and whether or not they were worthy people, always pleased if I could answer. One day we saw the play *A Record of Embroidered Jackets*. Grandfather said, "In the play, Zheng Yuanhe strove to capture the first place in the palace examinations in order to become a man of character." I remarked, "Although he made number one, in the end he did not become a man of character." Because of this incident, Grandfather told my relatives, "This boy knows enough to become a man of character," a comment I have never forgotten.

One day a neighboring student got a low grade on the yearly test. When people ridiculed him, I joined in. This made Grandfather angry, and he slapped me. "This man has the rank of 'flourishing talent' [qualified to take the provincial examinations], while you do not yet have any rank. How can you make fun of others so lightly?" I knelt and apologized, and Grandfather added, "I expect you someday to be a 'flourishing talent' and to be wearing an official robe when you bow at my grave."

In the tenth month, my second elder sister married into the Sun family. I sneaked out and climbed on a boat to watch the decorated carriage. Losing my footing, I fell into the water at the base of the boat. Before long I was rescued, but Grandfather gave me a painful beating.

On the twentieth day of the eleventh month, Grandfather died. This year I was still studying with Teacher Jingshan.

THE FIFTH YEAR OF THE QIANLONG REIGN [1740], MY ELEVENTH YEAR

On New Year's Day, I joined a game of kickball. Father stopped me and scolded me. He gave me a volume of *Editor Chen's "Four-Six" Style Works* (Chen jiantao siliu) and ordered that I read half a section every day. I was not allowed to come downstairs until I had finished my assignment. The fact that later, when I served as private secretary, I was known for my ability to write in the balanced style probably can be traced back to this incident.

This year Teacher Zheng Youting was invited to take charge of the school, and I studied with him.

Father had started his career as a merchant. He bought over a hundred *mu* of land and entered office through purchase. His younger brother, who lived in our village, was corrupted by associating with gamblers and, when deeply in debt, sold almost everything we owned. On Father's return, he was advised that if he sued, he would be able to get back his fields. Father could not bear to bring an accusation against his brother, so from this time on, our resources were never enough. After arranging for Grandfather's tomb, Father made plans to go to Guangdong to try to make a living there.

Before he left, on the evening of the fifteenth of the eighth month, we took an excursion to visit Mother Wang's family in Kuaiji [Zhejiang]. As our boat trip began, the rain was coming down so hard it looked like silk. I slept, using Father's left leg as a pillow. After we had gone twenty *li* or more, he woke me, gazed out through the awning, then turned to me and said, "Son, do you know why I'm making this trip?" When I could not answer, he continued, "I don't want to have to depend on others in my old age. Fortunately, I am still healthy. But unless I plan now for our livelihood, what will we live on?" I began to cry, and Father also cried, neither of us able to stop. He made an effort to control himself and picked up some books at random and asked me to read aloud from them. "Son, what do you seek through your reading?" he asked. "To become an official," I answered. "You are wrong. To become an official is one of the reasons we study, but you shouldn't aim at it. Being an official does not necessarily mean that you're a man of character. If you aim, instead, to become a man of character, then, even if you don't become an official, you'll at least be a good person. On the other hand, if you are lucky and do become an official, you'll be a good official and certainly won't incur the hatred of the common people and thus bring calamity on your descendants. Remember what I've said."

Later he picked up *The Analects*, turning to the sections "Study," "Filial Piety and Brotherly Love," and a few others. He discussed them with me until midnight, after which we slept. When we reached Kuaiji, he gave me a copy of *The Concise Official Histories* (Gangjian zhengshi) and told me to become familiar with it by the time I was grown up. Then he sent me home and left for Guangdong. Those were the last instructions I was to receive from him.

THE SIXTH YEAR OF THE QIANLONG REIGN [1741], MY TWELFTH YEAR

I studied with Teacher Zheng Youting.

Father had died the year before on the fifteenth of the twelfth month in a hostel by the Southern Ocean. In the fourth month, his body arrived. Neither of my two mothers remarried, managing by economizing. After they spun and wove, if they still had time, they would earn money by making imitation paper money to be burned for the dead. From morning to night, they never rested. They often instructed me with tears in their eyes, "Son, if you don't study, you won't be able to become a man of character, and your father won't have an heir. We two would be better off dead." They then supervised me even more strictly.

THE SEVENTH YEAR OF THE QIANLONG REIGN [1742], MY THIRTEENTH YEAR

I studied with the Teacher Zheng Youting.

In this period, our family was in decline. A number of close kinsmen who fell in with gamblers suspected that my two mothers had private savings from Father's official service. My father's younger brother demanded money from my two mothers, and when he did not get it, he beat me. To deal with the situation, my two mothers had to borrow money all around. Once someone even snatched me out of Mother Xu's hands. Often we were urged to move to avoid these greedy people, but my mothers absolutely refused to leave because Grandmother was still alive and the ancestral temple was there. My mothers often had no food, and it even reached the point where they each had only one single layer of clothing. But Grandmother and I never lacked anything in the way of food or clothing.

THE EIGHTH YEAR OF THE QIANLONG REIGN [1743], MY FOURTEENTH YEAR

I studied with Teacher Zheng Youting. There were four fellow students, but he was strict only with me. Every time I wrote an essay, he would make me revise it three or four times, not giving me a moment's rest from morning to night. Discouraged, I privately asked my sister's husband, Sun Huichou, why the teacher treated me this way. He reported that the teacher said, "This boy has real potential, but unfortunately he is not concentrating on his studies. I discipline him to make him apply himself. If I relax my vigilance, then as long as he lives he will fall short." Teacher Zheng's words became a part of me, and I have never forgotten them. But because my two mothers were not able to pay his salary, at the end of the year he left to teach elsewhere.

THE NINTH YEAR OF THE QIANLONG REIGN [1744],
MY FIFTEENTH YEAR

A kinsman, Wang Huanruo, invited Teacher Xu Guanzhou of Shangyu [Zhe-jiang] to come to his house to start a school. I attended it, going in the morning and returning in the evening, Mother Xu personally taking care of my needs. The teacher was about seventy and had a young son. Since I reminded him of his own son, he taught me with extreme care and gave me the courtesy name "Huanzeng" [illuminating what came before]. He once advised me, "If you don't exert yourself to study, you won't be able to establish yourself, and your mothers won't have a bright future." He must have known about my family difficulties. Our house was separated from the school by a river. I still am moved when I remember how every time I left school he would watch me until I crossed the bridge.

Teacher Zheng was always careful in correcting essays. He considered it his duty to encourage students, and he often praised me. Therefore, after a year with him, my writing became smooth and pleasant. Probably I would not have acquired a foundation in writing if it were not for Teacher Zheng, nor an interest in studying if it were not for Teacher Xu. Instruction from these two teachers was thus a kind of "mutual reinforcement."

This year my father-in-law-to-be, Wang Tanren, held office in Huai'an's Shanyang County [Jiangsu] as jail warden. Someone spread the rumor that I followed my uncle's bent for gambling and was a troublemaker. Men currying his favor whispered, "Since there was no go-between, the engagement can be broken if you wish." A few times, the members of my father-in-law's family almost believed it. When my future wife heard that the marriage might fall through, she cried day and night. Her mother told her father (my future father-in-law) to show sympathy for his daughter.

THE TENTH YEAR OF THE QIANLONG REIGN [1745],
MY SIXTEENTH YEAR

After Teacher Xu left because of poor health, it was beyond our means for me to study with another teacher. Depending on my two mothers, I spent my days and nights in a small upstairs chamber. Under my mothers' watchful eyes, I did not dare take a step outside the gate.

Looking through my late father's books, I came across *The Annotated Book of Rewards and Punishments* (Taishang ganying pian zhu). I trembled when I read it. From that time on, on getting up in the morning, I would chant it once devoutly. Thanks to this work, for the rest of my life I was cautious in my behavior.

THE ELEVENTH YEAR OF QIANLONG [1746], MY SEVENTEENTH YEAR

With the help of my two mothers, I studied for the county examination for youths. When I asked permission to take it, my mothers refused on the grounds that my studies were not yet complete and we were too poor. When I begged, they asked if I expected to pass. I exaggerated my skills and said that I did, to which they replied, "If you have a chance of passing, how can we refuse to let you go?"

In the sixth month, I arrived at the county seat. I saw that most of the men to be examined wore silk gowns, and I began to long for one. Someone offered me money to have a gown made, and I wrote an essay for him. After the examination results were announced, all eighteen of my kinsmen were invited to take the second exam, but not me. This disappointed my two mothers. When they learned that I had taken money from someone, they angrily demanded, "Have you no willpower? It seems you don't mind risking your reputation for the sake of a little financial gain." They hit me and sent me to return the money. Bitterly regretting what had happened, I studied day and night.

In the eighth month, at the prefectural exam, none of the eighteen kinsmen succeeded, yet I passed. In the ninth month, the superintendent of education Chen Qiuyai of Jiangning [Jiangsu] gave the next set of tests. I placed sixth and was admitted to the county school [making him qualified to take the provincial examinations]. There I studied essay writing with Teacher Mao Zailu of Shanyin [Zhejiang].

THE TWELFTH YEAR OF THE QIANLONG REIGN [1747], MY EIGHTEENTH YEAR

Mother Wang's brother invited me to teach the seven boys in his family for a salary of twelve strings of cash. I gave three strings to Teacher Zhang Baisi of Shanyin and studied essay writing with him. I also took the provincial examination for the first time. . . . When the lists of successful candidates were posted, I learned I had not succeeded.

THE THIRTEENTH YEAR OF THE QIANLONG REIGN [1748], MY NINETEENTH YEAR

In the second month, my father-in-law-to-be, thinking I could not spend all my time in solitary study, invited me to his office to study with Xu Xuzhou, a provincial graduate of Shanyang [Jiangsu]. I stayed there until the eleventh month, when I returned. . . .

On hearing that my uncle was going to move elsewhere with his family, my grandmother wanted to go with him. My two mothers, weeping, tried to stop her, until finally she agreed to stay.

THE FOURTEENTH YEAR OF THE QIANLONG REIGN [1749], MY TWENTIETH YEAR

I was still working for my father-in-law and studying essay writing with Teacher Zhang Baisi. In the eleventh month, Madame Wang joined our family as my wife.

THE FIFTEENTH YEAR OF THE QIANLONG REIGN [1750], MY TWENTY-FIRST YEAR

. . . On the first of the fifth month, at night, I felt dizzy and fell while walking by the pond in the back garden, landing in waist-deep water. When the sun came up, a servant was able to help me get out, but I had still not regained consciousness. After I regained consciousness, I got sick, so I returned home. In the eighth month, I took the exams unsuccessfully.

THE SIXTEENTH YEAR OF THE QIANLONG REIGN [1751], MY TWENTY-SECOND YEAR . . .

THE SEVENTEENTH YEAR OF THE QIANLONG REIGN [1752], MY TWENTY-THIRD YEAR

. . . This year my father-in-law was appointed magistrate of Jinshan in Songjiang [Jiangsu]. On the fifteenth of the third month, I moved to Jinshan and began my career as a private secretary. Since I did not want to make this my lifework, I continued my studies on the side. My salary was only three taels a month.

THE EIGHTEENTH YEAR OF THE QIANLONG REIGN [1753], MY TWENTY-FOURTH YEAR

I was employed at Jinshan.... When my father-in-law was appointed magistrate of Wujin in Changzhou [Jiangsu], I accompanied him there.

In the seventh month, when I returned home to take the provincial examination, Grandmother was sick, and after I took the examination, I also became ill. Because my father-in-law had summoned me to return to work, I had to leave, yet I did not like leaving Grandmother in her condition. Learning that I was about to leave, she asked me when I would come back. "If I pass the examination," I replied, "I will come back probably on the twenty-second or twenty-third of the ninth month. Otherwise, I will be back at the end of the twelfth month." "You will pass the examination," she assured me, "but the time has not come yet. I can't wait for you, and you can't wait for me. You go ahead, and don't worry about me."

Mother Wang sobbed, "Our son is sick. What am I to do?" Grandmother replied, "Don't worry. He will have good luck, a long life, and lots of children and grandchildren."...

Soon thereafter I left. On the second of the tenth month, Grandmother died. I did not return home, so my two mothers presided over the funeral. It was not until fifteen years after Grandmother's death that I passed the provincial examination, and another seven years before I passed the metropolitan one. Now that I am sixty-plus years old, I realize how prophetic her words were.

THE NINETEENTH YEAR OF THE QIANLONG REIGN [1754], MY TWENTY-FIFTH YEAR

In the fourth month, my father-in-law's mother died. While waiting for his replacement in Wujin, he recommended me to a Yangzhou [Jiangsu] salt merchant, Mr. Cheng, to handle his paperwork at a salary of 160 taels per year. This pleased me until I heard that he was very haughty and reclined on couches or leaned against tables, facing south like a ruler, with attendants sitting nearby to explain matters. Not thinking I could tolerate such treatment, I told my father-in-law to decline the offer. In less than two months, Hu Wenbo of Haiyang, the prefect of Changzhou, invited me to be his secretary since he had been a subordinate of my father-in-law's. The annual salary would be twenty-four taels, and I accepted. Those who heard of this were surprised, but I explained that though the pay is low, the prefect will treat me with courtesy. My father-in-law considered me proud but shared my feelings.

THE TWENTIETH YEAR OF THE QIANLONG REIGN [1755], MY TWENTY-SIXTH YEAR

In the second month, I took up work in Changzhou. When I had time, I studied legal principles with Luo Bingwen of Zhuji [Zhejiang]. In the ninth month, when Mr. Hu was promoted to fiscal intendant of Jiangsu, I declined to go with him. He said to me, "I won't keep you in a low position for long," and tried hard to get me to change my mind, offering an additional eight taels per month. After he raised my salary five times, I went with him to Changshu. Mr. Hu was an upright person and treated me with more courtesy than his other secretaries. Whenever there was an important issue, he could call me in and discuss it with me and often adopted my recommendation....

This year my fourth sister married Shen Yougao of Shanyin [Shanxi]. In Shaoxing [Zhejiang], the fall harvest fell far short, so the next year in the spring and summer, rice sold for three hundred cash a peck, and beggars and bodies filled the roads.

THE TWENTY-FIRST YEAR OF THE QIANLONG REIGN [1756], MY TWENTY-SEVENTH YEAR

Mr. Hu became fiscal intendant of Linqing [Shandong], but not wanting to go so far away, I declined on the ground of illness and instead took up work with Mr. Wei Tingkui, the magistrate of Wuxi [Jiangsu]. There I assisted Mr. Qin on legal matters. Mr. Qin was a legal expert, familiar with the code....

In the fifth month, Mr. Wei's mother died, so I returned home and took the provincial examinations, for which the quota had been expanded by ten. In the ninth month, I learned I had failed. Mr. Hu sent an invitation asking me to return to Changshu to work for him as a secretary.... In the tenth month, I accompanied him to Qingjiangpu [Jiangsu]. While I worked as a secretary, it was my practice to go home to see my family at the end of every year. But this year I passed the New Year on the road. Since it was my duty as a secretary to work for my master when he was busy, I had no time to see my mothers.

THE TWENTY-SECOND YEAR OF THE QIANLONG REIGN [1757], MY TWENTY-EIGHTH YEAR

I stayed on with Mr. Hu. In the fourth month, an assignment was over, and I went with him to Jiangning [Jiangsu] to prepare a report. While in the region of the Qinhuai River, I was able to tour around the famous sites of Jinling [Nanjing], not returning to Changshu [Jiangsu] till the seventh month.... Early in the twelfth month, we arrived at Changzhou to inspect grain transport at Suzhou [both Jiangsu]. The commander of the grain transport division, Yao Qirui, offended Mr. Hu, who wanted to immediately impeach him. I argued against it because it was an error of speech. Because of this disagreement, on the fifth, I resigned and went home.

THE TWENTY-THIRD YEAR OF THE QIANLONG REIGN [1758], MY TWENTY-NINTH YEAR

... On the eighth of the first month, Mr. Hu sent a relative with a letter to my house to apologize. After he pleaded with me two or three times, I returned with him to Changshu....

At the end of the year, Mr. Hu wanted me to stay with him over the New Year holiday; even as late as the twenty-sixth of the twelfth month, he had not let me go home. Because of this, I wrote a poem on the wall.... At dawn on the following day, when he read my poem, he felt very sorry and immediately sent a fast boat to take me home. I arrived on New Year's Eve....

My third sister married Chen Jingsheng of our city....

THE TWENTY-FOURTH YEAR OF THE QIANLONG REIGN [1759], MY THIRTIETH YEAR

In the first month, I took my wife's maid, Yang, as a concubine. I then returned to work for Mr. Hu....

On the eighth of the eighth month, the day I entered the examination hall, it rained so heavily that water flowed over my bench. Almost unable to finish my examination, I felt that I had failed to live up to my teacher's instructions. On the twelfth day, during the second test, I got sick and could neither eat nor drink. After exerting myself to finish the third test, I hurried back home.

My illness became so bad I could not get up; I even needed other people to help me turn half-around and could eat no more than a few chestnuts. Several times I neared death, and my family even prepared a coffin for me. The doctors could not figure out what kind of illness I had, and I was sure recovery was impossible.

On the evening of the eighth day of the ninth month, Mother Wang dreamed of a group of people sitting in the middle of a hall, facing south. Servants lined the hall on the east and west sides. In the right corner were Grandfather and Father, in attendance on the people who faced south. There was loud talk, but she could not make out what was being said. Those standing on the east and west sides of the hall were tall and thin and wore hats, and some had mustaches. They bowed to those facing south and said, "We should save Scraps!" Some people who had been crying then left the hall. My father and grandfather, appearing very happy, went forward and kowtowed to those facing south.

When Mother Wang told me of her dream the next morning, she said, "There is no need to worry about your illness worsening, because your ancestors have protected you." That afternoon, Xu Yiting came to examine my pulse. He told Mother, "He has no disease. The reason for his present weakness is water vapor, which entered his body when it rained heavily during his examination. This prevented the food and drink that he consumed from circulating. I suggest a heavy dose of cinnamon bark as a cure."

As soon as I drank the dose, I fell asleep. When I woke up, I urinated voluminously, and then could turn over. After the second dose, I could sit up. Not long afterward, I recovered, and on the first day of the tenth month, I went back to work for Mr. Hu.

In my family, everyone from my great-grandfather down to my three uncles and nine cousins had been healthy and strong except me. Because I was weak and sickly, my two mothers were worried that I would not live long. Yet from the tenth month of this year to the second month of the following year, my uncles and cousins all passed away, except for one uncle who lived elsewhere. By contrast, after this sickness I gradually grew strong and healthy and seldom got sick. This probably was due to the chastity and devotion of my two widowed mothers. But the saving of "Scraps" was due to the spiritual protection of my ancestors.

Because I had debts, had been ill, and did not want to borrow any more, I needed a better salary. However, I could not bargain over my pay with Mr. Hu, with whom I had been associated for so long. Thus, at the end of the year, I decided to resign my post and accept the invitation of Zheng Yuxian, magistrate of Changzhou County [Jiangsu]. . . .

THE TWENTY-FIFTH YEAR OF THE QIANLONG REIGN [1760], MY THIRTY-FIRST YEAR

I worked at Changzhou County. . . .
I resigned from Changzhou and returned home. . . .

THE TWENTY-SIXTH YEAR OF THE QIANLONG REIGN [1761], MY THIRTY-SECOND YEAR

Teacher Sun filled the vacancy as magistrate of Xiushui County in Zhejiang, and I became his adviser. . . .

THE TWENTY-SEVENTH YEAR OF THE QIANLONG REIGN [1762], MY THIRTY-THIRD YEAR

I still worked in Xiushui. On the seventeenth of the third month, Mother Xu, my birth mother, passed away.

In the past, each time I had taken the provincial examination, she had said, "Our family has had no degree holder for generations. If you make a career of being a private secretary, your preparation for the degree will interrupt your work as a secretary, and you will probably make a great many mistakes. On the other hand, if you concentrate on your job and study for the degree only on the side, you probably won't have enough energy to accomplish anything."

After I had recovered from that serious illness three years earlier, Mother had advised me not to take the examinations again. On the fourteenth day of the third month of that year, I hurried back to my office. When I returned home this time, she was critically ill. On the morning of the seventeenth, she suddenly said, "If by any chance I don't live to the ninth month, you will be delayed in the examinations." From this I realized that she actually was very eager to see me pass. What she had said earlier was just her way of being kind to me. After that, I was determined to study hard and keep attempting the examinations.

THE TWENTY-EIGHTH YEAR OF THE QIANLONG REIGN [1763], MY THIRTY-FOURTH YEAR

Sometime earlier a commoner named Jiang of Xiaofeng County [Zhejiang] was robbed while traveling by boat, and we were ordered to catch the culprit. Then during the New Year recess when I was on my way home, a runaway soldier called Big Sheng was arrested for collecting a gang and committing violence. On questioning, he proved to be the robber. Mr. Liu asked me to return to investigate and draft the confession. It turned out that there was almost no law that this man had not violated—conspiracy to gather a gang to commit robbery, injuring the owner, stealing his goods, and so on. Moreover, the thief had a blue cotton quilt, which the victim recognized.

That night I asked Mr. Liu to question the man again while I listened to each item of the confession from outside the courtroom. The suspect did not appear nervous, and his confession came out smoothly, as though he was reciting something from memory. Moreover, the eight members of the gang used exactly the same words, arousing my suspicions. The next night, I asked Mr. Liu to purposely change the charges and question the suspects separately. This time some confessed and others did not, and the eight each gave different versions, some of them even protesting that injustice had been done. At that point, we stopped the hearing and bought or borrowed twenty new and old quilts like the one recognized by the victim in his accusation to the magistrate. I secretly marked the one the victim had originally identified. Mr. Liu continued the investigation in the courtroom, and this time the suspects could not pick out the quilt. Moreover, on close questioning, they would not confess.

The explanation for all of this turned out to be that when Big Sheng first came to court, he knew that as a violent deserter he would face certain death, so when he was questioned about the robbery, he made a false confession, and his followers all went along with him. In reality, they were being sacrificed for his sake. Some of them had offenses of their own, but these did not merit death. Subsequently, we let them go....

From this time on, I was increasingly unwilling to rely on draft confessions.

Whenever the offense merited a punishment of exile or heavier, I always personally listened to the judicial examination from outside the room....

It was this year that I petitioned the governor to honor my mothers as chaste widows. In the twelfth month, I received his permission to send a memorial to the emperor requesting this honor.

THE TWENTY-NINTH YEAR OF THE QIANLONG REIGN [1764], MY THIRTY-FIFTH YEAR

I still worked in Pinghu [Zhejiang]. In the twelfth month, I received an order from the Board of Rites stating that the emperor had approved the honoring of my two mothers as chaste widows.

THE THIRTIETH YEAR OF THE QIANLONG REIGN [1765], MY THIRTY-SIXTH YEAR

In the first month, I received a communication from the Board of Rites granting me permission to erect a memorial to my two widowed mothers. I recorded their merits so that whoever might read of them would praise them.

In the second month, I returned to work in Pinghu. Zou Yingyuan, from Jinkui, the prefect of Jiaxing [Jiangsu], had a great deal of respect for me and spoke of me to Mr. Liu, saying, "When Secretary Wang handles legal cases, he gives the accused some leeway, and his judgments are fair and impartial. Someday he will hold an official position and command a large salary." This led to the other secretaries envying me and trying to get me fired. I did not get along well with them and felt isolated. Fortunately, I had Mr. Liu's confidence, and after it became well-known that Mr. Zou had praised me so highly, my coworkers stopped bothering me....

THE THIRTY-FIRST YEAR OF THE QIANLONG REIGN [1766], MY THIRTY-SEVENTH YEAR

I still worked in Pinghu....

In the twelfth month, Mr. Liu was promoted to the post of prefect of Jiujiang [Jiangxi]. Zou Yingyuan, who had been transferred from his position as prefect of Hangzhou to prefect of Taiwan, offered me a salary of sixteen hundred taels to work with him in Taiwan. I asked Mother Wang for permission, but she advised me not to go.... Soon I accepted the invitation of Li Xueli in Renhe [Zhejiang].

THE THIRTY-SECOND YEAR OF THE QIANLONG REIGN [1767], MY THIRTY-EIGHTH YEAR

In the first month, I returned to Pinghu. In the second month, Mr. Liu had imperial business, and I went to Renhe. In the tenth month, Mr. Li was dismissed due to anonymous letters accusing him of wrongdoing. I was then asked by Mr. Jiang Zhiduo to work for him in Wucheng [Zhejiang]....

THE THIRTY-THIRD YEAR OF THE QIANLONG REIGN [1768], MY THIRTY-NINTH YEAR

I worked at Wucheng. In the fourth month, I built the memorial arch for my two mothers on the north bank of Jukui Bridge in Great Righteousness Village. As I was preparing to buy the piece of land for the arch, Mother Wang said, "We don't have an inch of land to grow food for our meals. Why not save these hundreds of taels for food?" I replied, "This is an event that immortalizes you, and besides, it will only be ten *mu*. Being an unfilial son, I haven't been able to provide adequately for you and Mother Xu. But through your virtuous protection, we will be able to survive even though we haven't any land."

When the memorial arch was completed, I accompanied Mother Wang to thank the god of the earth. She performed the kowtow, touching her head to the ground numerous times. When she stood up, her forehead was swollen and red. On my asking why she had done it, she said, "Your mother and I have been unfortunate, living much of our lives in widowhood. Such was our destiny. Now you have been so good as to request imperial permission to build this arch in our honor. When I prayed I told the gods of your virtuous behavior and kindness toward us and asked them to allow you to pass the examinations this next time. Now I can close my eyes and die in peace."

We both wept for several hours. As I was returning to my office, she told me, "You should make a point of studying hard for the upcoming examinations."...

In the seventh month, I took the provincial examination.... After I had finished, I heard that Mr. Hu, the Guangdong provincial treasurer, had been transferred to Jiangsu and that my old friend, Teacher Sun, had accompanied him. I went to Mr. Hu's office to see Mr. Sun. When he read my essays, he praised me and said that I was sure to win first place. After I had returned to Wucheng on the eighth of the ninth month, I saw the roster of successful candidates. I had taken third place.

I went to Hangzhou to see Zeng Dongzhuang of Xiangyin, the Xiangshan magistrate who had been one of the examiners. He told me, "It was well into the night of the sixteenth of the eighth month before I finished reading your examination papers. I then put them on the right side of the table and was resting my eyes when suddenly a piece of tile dropped onto the table against your papers. The tile was not even as thick as a finger and was covered with moss. I immediately reexamined your papers, then put them in a case. When I went to sleep, I heard a noise coming from the table. The piece of tile had disappeared, and your papers had come out of the case and were lying on the tabletop again. The next morning, I recommended you to the two chief examiners. However, they said that the first candidate had already been selected. On the tenth day, Lu Ershan put you in third place, as he wanted to have you as his disciple." He then asked me how I had merited such heavenly intercession, and I answered that it must have been my ancestors who had helped me.

Later I met the top candidate in the examination, and together we went to call on the two chief examiners.... I learned that the poems of my second test and the essays on government from my third test had been submitted to the emperor and that all the court officials had been greatly surprised at the story; no one could understand where the flying tile had come from, in the deep of night, with all of the doors and windows closed. Everyone said it was a reward for my two mothers who preserved their chastity despite difficult circumstances.

Twenty-three men passed the Zhejiang examinations that year. As we were trying to set a date for the celebration banquet, I said, "There's no need to set aside a separate date for the party. The twentieth of the twelfth month is my mother's birthday. Please come to my home to drink a cup of wine in her honor."

Seventeen were able to come. After they had left, Mother Wang said, "Today is the first time in twenty years that I have been able to relax my brow. I now feel that I have not failed your father. When I didn't approve of your going to Taiwan, I worried that you might have difficulty getting a job with a good salary. But if you had gone, you wouldn't have been able to pass the examination this year. Thus, everything has worked out well in the end."

Over the course of twenty-one years, I had tried nine times to pass but only succeeded after Mother Wang prayed for me. It is indeed amazing that, although Heaven is high, it hears even the lowest....

THE THIRTY-FOURTH YEAR OF THE QIANLONG REIGN [1769], MY FORTIETH YEAR

In the first month, I set out to take the metropolitan examination [in the capital]....

THE THIRTY-FIFTH YEAR OF THE QIANLONG REIGN [1770], MY FORTY-FIRST YEAR

... On the fourteenth of the fourth month, a messenger came from home and told me that my wife was critically ill. When I arrived home on the fifteenth, I found she had died two days earlier. She had fallen ill on the eighth but before that had made a shirt for me. I wrote four poems ... and made a drawing to mark the event. Mr. Pan Tingyun of Qiantang, a secretary in the Grand Secretariat, wrote my wife's biography and also painted a picture on the same subject as mine. Many of my colleagues wrote poems on both of the pictures.

After the funeral, I continued my work in Qiantang....

On the twenty-third of the seventh month, there was a great storm and a tidal wave. The sea flowed over West Prosperity Lake up to Song Family Village [Zhejiang], a distance of over eighty *li*.... Ten thousand people died, their bodies clogging the waterways.... My house had two feet of water in it, which didn't retreat until the next day.

In the tenth month, I married my successor wife, Madame Cao, the daughter of Mr. Cao Yunqi, a tribute student from my hometown. At the end of the year, I resigned my position to get ready for the metropolitan examination.

THE THIRTY-SIXTH YEAR OF THE QIANLONG REIGN [1771], MY FORTY-SECOND YEAR

In the first month, I went to take the metropolitan examination....

In the ninth month, I conducted a burial ceremony for my father and my mothers at the foot of Mount Xiu in Shanyin County [Zhejiang]. I also purchased a plot of land at the foot of Hangwu Mountain and buried the coffins of two grand-uncles and their wives and the wife of my father's cousin and performed the sacrifices to them. . . .

Many years earlier, Mother Xu had told me that her family lived in Yincheng [Ningbo, Zhejiang] and that her house was close to a stone bridge. I had often asked friends to make inquiries, but no one had found it. This time I went there myself for four days and visited each bridge. I met a man named Xu, but he did not recognize my uncle's name. It was with great disappointment that I returned home.

At the end of the year, I quit my job to begin preparing for the metropolitan examinations once more. . . .

THE THIRTY-SEVENTH YEAR OF THE QIANLONG REIGN [1772], MY FORTY-THIRD YEAR

In the first month, I went to take the metropolitan examination with Jiang Gao. When the results were released, I saw that Jiang Gao had passed but I had failed yet again. . . .

THE THIRTY-EIGHTH YEAR OF THE QIANLONG REIGN [1773], MY FORTY-FOURTH YEAR

I was still at Haining [Zhejiang]. . . .

THE THIRTY-NINTH YEAR OF THE QIANLONG REIGN [1774], MY FORTY-FIFTH YEAR

I was still at Haining. . . . In the seventh month, my uncle died and was buried at Hangwu Mountain. . . .

THE FORTIETH YEAR OF THE QIANLONG REIGN [1775], MY FORTY-SIXTH YEAR

In the first month, I went to take the metropolitan examination. . . . When the results were posted on the ninth day of the fourth month, I found that I had passed in the forty-sixth place. . . .

On the twenty-first, I took the palace examination. Four days later, I learned that I had passed as the twenty-eighth person in the second group and had become a *jinshi*. The next day, I was presented with pieces of blue brocade and white silk at the main entrance of the Forbidden City; the day after, a party was given by the Board of Rites. On the second of the next month, the successful candidates exchanged their rough clothes for official robes in a ceremony at the Directorate of Education. On the eighth, I took the court examination, and six days later, I was received by the emperor and informed that I was a candidate for office.

Two days later, on the sixteenth, I received a letter from home informing me of Mother Wang's death on the twenty-sixth of the third month. I memorialized for permission to go into mourning. The next day, the examiners and fellow graduates, knowing my mother was a chaste and filial person, encouraged me to put on mourning and accept their condolences, so I stayed a few days more and began the mourning rituals. To compose my late mother's biography, I asked Mr. Zhou Huang of Haishan to write the tomb record and Mr. Shao Eryun to write the funerary biography. . . .

On the seventh day of the sixth month, I left the capital, taking the road to Tai'an [Shandong]. On the fifteenth, I reached Wangjiaying [Jiangsu], where I crossed the river and hired a boat [to travel down the Grand Canal], traveling fast by starlight. On the second of the seventh month, I reached home. . . . In the eleventh month, having returned home, I managed my mother's joint-burial on the slopes of Xiu Mountain, then went to Haining. At year's end, Liu Xianpu of Pinghu extended the previous agreement, so I resigned working for Mr. Zhan. . . .

THE FORTY-FIRST YEAR OF THE QIANLONG REIGN [1776], MY FORTY-SEVENTH YEAR

I worked in Pinghu. I brought my son Jifang along and began to guide him in his studies. . . .

THE FORTY-SECOND YEAR OF THE QIANLONG REIGN [1777], MY FORTY-EIGHTH YEAR

I still worked in Pinghu. . . .

THE FORTY-THIRD YEAR OF THE QIANLONG REIGN [1778],
MY FORTY-NINTH YEAR

I was still working in Pinghu. . . .

THE FORTY-FOURTH YEAR OF THE QIANLONG REIGN [1779],
MY FIFTIETH YEAR

I still worked in Pinghu. . . .

In the *bingshen* year [1776], I had entered on a project dear to my two mothers, collecting stories of outstanding examples of chastity and filial piety among the people of Shaoxing [Zhejiang]. Now the work was completed. . . . I presented it to the lieutenant governor, who ordered it recorded and the names of the virtuous people, 305 in number, placed on a large plaque for public display at their respective county offices.

THE FORTY-FIFTH YEAR OF THE QIANLONG REIGN [1780],
MY FIFTY-FIRST YEAR

I worked in Wucheng. . . . In the sixth month, Mr. Xu had to leave office to mourn a parent, so I returned home. . . . In the ninth month, Wang Qingchuan, of Longyou, came to Zhejiang. He was a kinsman of Teacher Wang Xingyuan. Magistrate Xing had been a subordinate of his uncle Wang Yuanting. It happened that Teacher Wang Xingyuan came to inspect the Zhejiang schools, and he asked Magistrate Xing to let me work for his kinsman Wang Qingchuan. In the tenth month, I moved with him to Longyou [Zhejiang]. . . .

THE FORTY-SIXTH YEAR OF THE QIANLONG REIGN [1781],
MY FIFTY-SECOND YEAR

I worked in Longyou. . . . In the first month, Wang Qingchuan went to Hangzhou [for a legal case]. . . .

THE FORTY-SEVENTH YEAR OF THE QIANLONG REIGN [1782], *MY FIFTY-THIRD YEAR*

I went to Hangzhou. . . . Wang Qingchuan was transferred to Gui'an [Zhejiang]. . . .

This year, because of the Longyou case, I spent a lot of time in the provincial capital [Hangzhou]. It happened that Teacher Wang Xingyuan was there as an examiner, and we would often visit. If a few days went by without a visit, he would send someone to get me, and we would spend the rest of the day together, our conversations ranging widely. I learned a great deal from him about the principles of cultivating oneself, which I took to heart. He thought I was someone he could talk to and didn't get tired of admonishing me, so my understanding of moral cultivation greatly benefited.

THE FIRST YEAR OF THE QIANLONG REIGN [1783], MY FIFTY-FOURTH YEAR

I worked at Gui'an [for Magistrate Wang Qingchuan]. It had become customary in Gui'an for people to frequently file complaints and accusations against one another, more out of their quarrelsome nature than out of a desire to seek justice, causing many innocent people to be unjustly implicated. Once I fully grasped the situation, the magistrate and I took the following steps to rectify it. Written charges were to be kept secure within the inner office of the yamen. The principals in each case and any necessary witnesses were to be summoned to the yamen and questioned right away. Many accusations turned out to be false, in which case the plaintiff would be punished for defaming an innocent person.

An element of the Gui'an population thrived on gambling, fraud, misappropriation of the water conservation funds, shady brokerage agencies, and the like. The officials and clerks made lots of money by taking bribes from these people. I tried to get the magistrate to crack down on such practices and thereby aroused the ire of many of the clerks and officials. . . .

THE FIRST YEAR OF THE QIANLONG REIGN [1784], MY FIFTY-FIFTH YEAR

I continued to work at Gui'an. . . .

THE FIRST YEAR OF THE QIANLONG REIGN [1785], MY FIFTY-SIXTH YEAR

I still worked at Gui'an.

In the fourth month, an edict came down from the Hunan governor Lu Yao instructing officials who were only sons of elderly parents to go home to take care of them. As Magistrate Wang's mother was seventy-one years old and he had no brothers, he complied with the order and resigned his post to take care of his mother. Consequently, in the eighth month, I left office and returned home.

Since the *renshen* year [1752], I had worked for thirty-four years as a private secretary, spending nine years in Jiangsu and twenty-five years in Zhejiang. I chose whom to serve under and had sixteen good superiors. By nature unable to compromise, I could not put up with official injustice and had sometimes resigned my post over a point of principle. Fortunately, most of my superiors respected me, and we got along well the whole time.

Among the private secretaries I knew, there were upright, self-respecting individuals and mean, petty men who were concerned only with lining their own pockets. Even though I worked with many secretaries, I seldom was able to develop friendships with them based on a genuine meeting of minds. Often they would try to sabotage my projects. . . .

When I began my career as a private secretary, the annual salary for a legal secretary was not over 260 taels; that for a financial secretary, not more than 220 taels. These were considered good incomes in those days. Mr. Dong of Songjiang would not accept a salary under 300 taels, so was called Dong Three Hundred. After the *renwu* year [1762], the salaries of private secretaries improved; by the *jiachen* and *yisi* years [1784, 1785] some were getting as much as 800 taels. But the efficiency and integrity of private secretaries could not compare with what it had been in the old days.

A good government official should understand people and know the customs of the place where he serves. His private secretaries and advisers should help him achieve these goals. . . . If a private secretary intends to serve the magistrate well, he takes the magistrate's responsibilities as his own, concerning himself with local affairs and the people's welfare. In this way, he makes his superior look good, and the people consider the magistrate wise and virtuous. If a private secretary can do this, he may be considered to have fulfilled his role. A secretary who does not concern himself directly with the general well-being of the populace and merely handles issues and problems as they arise, who keeps his mind on how he will be evaluated and fails to coordinate with the other secretaries, may still be a moderately efficient secretary. The worst kind of private secretaries are ones who have no sense of shame or propriety, take every opportunity to enrich themselves, and blame the magistrate when things go wrong.

Over the course of twenty years, I saw many private secretaries of the last sort. With their profits from bribery and extortion, they would act like big shots for a while, but invariably their evil ways would bring their downfall. They would fall ill or die young, their children would die tragically, or their families would suffer separations. It chills the heart to see how the net of Heaven extends everywhere.

At this time, as a *jinshi* degree holder from the *yiwei* year [1775], I petitioned for official appointment.... I went to Hangzhou, where Liu Xianpu, recently promoted to prefect of Nanning [Guangxi], invited me to stay with him. He said to me, "When I first became friends with you, none of the people in my yamen, high or low, really liked you, because you were so aloof and stern. I was the only one who admired you and was able to learn from you. When you are with someone who understands you, you can talk all day without growing tired. When you are with someone you don't like, you would not say a word to him. I would like now to tell you that in my opinion you are better suited to being a private secretary/adviser than an official. The ways of the official and the private secretary are quite different. An official cannot speak his mind as openly as a private secretary; he must take account of the situation and the interpersonal relations in his yamen." Such was his sincere advice.

This year I wrote *Precepts for Local Administrative Officials* (Zuozhi yaoyan) in two chapters. Bao Yiwen published it in part 12 of *Collected Works of the Know-Your-Deficiencies Studio* (Zhibuzu zhai congshu).

SOURCE: Wang Huizu, *Bingtan menghen lu* 病榻夢痕錄 (Nanchang: Jiangxi Renmin Chubanshe, 2012), 4–42.

Further Reading

Chang, Wejen. "Legal Education in Ch'ing China." In *Education and Society in Late Imperial China, 1600–1900*, edited by Benjamin A. Elman and Alexander Woodside, 292–339. Berkeley: University of California Press, 1994.

Chen, Li. "Legal Specialists and Judicial Administration in Late Imperial China, 1651–1911." *Late Imperial China* 33, no. 1 (2012): 1–54. doi:10.1353/late.2012.0000.

Ch'ü, T'ung-tsu. *Local Government in China Under the Ch'ing*. Cambridge, MA: Harvard University Press, 1962.

Sommer, Matthew Harvey. "The Uses of Chastity: Sex, Law, and the Property of Widows in Qing China." *Late Imperial China* 17, no. 2 (1996), 77–130.

27

TRIBUTES TO CLOSE RELATIVES
Appreciations written by a woman for her husband and
a man for his elder sister (18th and 19th c.)

Xu Yezhao 徐葉昭 *(b. 1729) recounts her marriage and her
husband's recognition and appreciation of her talent. It is paired
with the reminiscences of a nineteenth-century man, Wang Zheng
王拯 (1815–1873), about the years he lived with his sister and
studied under her supervision.*

In Confucian family ethics, the hierarchical ties of father and son, husband
and wife, and elder and younger brother were seen as of central importance
and something that one could write about. Men could circulate what they
wrote about their love for their parents and their advice for their sons, but
other family relationships were much less often the subject of essays or
other writing. Wang Huizu, in his autobiography (selection 26), writes at
great length about his mothers but says very little about his wife or sisters.
This makes the writings about other relationships that do survive worth
close reading.

In the first piece below, the woman poet Xu Yezhao discusses her relationship with her husband. By her period, in literati circles, literate women

were not rare, and several thousand Ming and Qing women left behind collected works. These female authors were often supported by family members, formed their own mentor-disciple relationships, and enjoyed long-term and long-distance friendships among themselves. Xu's collected work includes poems and biographies for family members, which reveal much about her family life, including intimate details about her interactions with her father, husband, aunts, sisters-in-law, and even maids. The selection below was written in the form of a preface to poems dedicated to her husband and focuses on the various unconventional aspects of her marriage and her husband's recognition of her talent. Note especially how he directly approached her father, proposing that he marry into her family.

Brother-sister relationships were also rarely celebrated in writing, perhaps in part because sisters usually left home in their late teens to marry. This makes the essay written by Wang Zheng to accompany a portrait he had commissioned for his elder sister of special interest. Wang was from Guangxi in southwestern China and an important figure of the influential Tongcheng School, known for its prose writing and advocacy of Neo-Confucianism. Orphaned at a young age, Wang was raised by his sister, went on to earn the *jinshi* degree, and served in multiple government positions. This short memoir is a passionate declaration of his emotional attachment to his sister, almost a mother figure to him. From it, we also gain a glimpse of the sister herself: a strong but unnamed childless widow who poured her energy into her younger brother and earned his profound gratitude.

Preface to Poems Dedicated to My Husband, Mr. Xu, by Xu Yezhao

Good husband and obedient wife; husband leading and wife following: these are the correct principles of the Three Relationships and Five Virtues. Therefore, in the past, in choosing wives for their sons, families cared about nothing but the prospective bride's virtues. Nowadays, the criteria are different, with a woman judged according to wealth, status, talent, looks, and virtue. Of the five, some people talk about female virtue but do not know what it means. If a woman does not have much talent, she can still be entrusted with small household matters. As for learning, the conventional wisdom is that it is useless, so it is not sought. A pleasing appearance is of course desired. When it comes to status, a family's long history and good reputation are not as important as its current prominence. If a woman is from a rich family and the groom's family can benefit from the marriage, the match is then much desired. Contemporary thinking is roughly like this. An occasional man of refined taste may value a woman with literary ability, but no one cares as much about talent as he does about looks.

My husband, Mr. Xu, is the exception. Since his tastes and preferences are out of fashion, people consider him clueless, but he thinks he's got it right. Ah! How amazing! My husband is a student in the Haining [Zhejiang] County School. His given name is Yaozi, courtesy name Shixi, and studio name Heting. His writing is wide-ranging and rich, his conduct loyal and honest. Additionally, he loves a woman of talent and virtue. Although he married into my family with his father's permission, he did not select me as his wife through a matchmaker. After his first wife's death, he planned to remarry but found no one to his satisfaction after looking all over. He happened to visit the Zhuji [Zhejiang] County School, where my late father taught. Someone told him, "The daughter of the instructor at the school is both virtuous and a talented writer." Upon hearing this, Mr. Xu went home to ask for his father's permission. He then called on my father and brother, asking them in person to let us marry.

My late father said, "Matchmakers often exaggerate, but I am now telling you the truth. My daughter's talent and virtue are inadequate. In terms of other considerations in marriage alliances, you know that I am old and my rank is low. I have set aside no funds for my daughter's dowry, so she wouldn't even be able to prepare the simplest clothes and jewelry. Besides, her looks are ordinary. All considered, she is not a good catch at all." This pleased Mr. Xu, who responded, "She has everything I want. Others wouldn't understand." The two families then employed the service of a matchmaker and completed the marriage arrangements. The next spring, he married into my family.

Alas, the ancients esteemed such behavior. What the world favors today is different. My husband is certainly no match for the ancients, but compared to his contemporaries, isn't he an exemplary person? I feel bad that my talent and virtue are not up to what I owe him for appreciating me. Ashamed, I am at a loss on what to do, aware of my limitations. After thinking it over, the only plan I came up with to pay him back for understanding me is to recount the origin of our marriage in this preface. Although it is hardly adequate, I can't remain silent about how much I fall short of him.

SOURCE: Xu Yezhao 徐葉昭, *Zhisizhai xuewen gao* 職思齋學文稿, 1.47a–48a, accessed May 28, 2021, https://digital.library.mcgill.ca/mingqing/search/details-poem.php?poemID=44141&language=ch.

Preface to *Portrait of My Sister Pounding Clothes to Clean Them While Supervising My Study*, by Wang Zheng

I had *Portrait of My Sister Pounding Clothes to Clean Them While Supervising My Study* made while I was an official in the capital. When I was leaving for the capital, my older sister could not join me because she was taking care of her elderly mother-in-law. Now that her mother-in-law has passed away, she is temporarily living with my second older sister's family [in Guangzhou, Guangdong] and not inclined to travel long distances. Ever since I was appointed to the capital, I have been wanting to return to the south. This wish has not been satisfied due to all sorts of hardships and trivial matters.

I went to live with my sister when I was seven, right after my mother's passing. Having just lost her husband and posthumous son, she lived all alone. Behind the main residence, there was a small garden a few dozen feet long. Beautiful trees provided plenty of shade for the two-room house. This was where my sister and I resided. At ten, I went to school, leaving home in the morning and returning at dusk. At night, my sister always lit a lamp and had me study next to her while she kept busy with needlework. On extremely hot days in the summer, I was allowed to skip night study. But she would wake me up at daybreak and have me take a small table outside to study under the trees in the garden. At the base of the trees were two large stones: one was for Sister to pound and wash clothes, the other for me to sit on and read.

When the sun rose, she would send me off to school. For this reason, when I was young, every morning when I arrived at school, I did better than other boys at reciting the books taught to us the day before. Sometimes when I was tired from studying in the evening, I would play around a little. My sister would soberly describe to me how hardworking our mother had been and her death from exhaustion. She then told me, "If you don't study diligently, you'll make mother worried in the underworld!" Her words filled me with sadness and anxiety. After I begged her with tears in my eyes not to say such things again, she relented.

Alas! How unfilial I am! I am already thirty. I still remember reading aloud

TRIBUTES TO CLOSE RELATIVES *211*

by her side when I was fifteen or sixteen. Poor and distressed, I was anxious and dared not to slacken even the slightest. After I left my sister's house at twenty, I no longer read aloud and gradually abandoned my study. Determined never to forget my sister's guidance, I had this portrait painted to remind me of her and enable me to read next to her every day. That should prevent me from sinking ever deeper into laziness and ending up achieving nothing in this life. The painter of the portrait is Chen Shuo, who earned the *jinshi* degree in the same year as I did and is a good friend of mine, which is why I turned to him for the painting.

SOURCE: Wang Zheng 王拯, *Longbi shanfang wenji* 龍壁山房文集 (Guangxu *xinsi* ed., 1881), 5.18a–19a, accessed May 18, 2021, https://ctext.org/library.pl?if =gb&file=95606&page=36.

Further Reading

Huang, Martin. *Intimate Memory: Gender and Mourning in Late Imperial China.* Albany: State University of New York Press, 2018.

Idema, Wilt L. "The Biographical and the Autobiographical in Bo Shaojun's *One Hundred Poems Lamenting My Husband.*" In *Beyond Exemplar Tales: Women's Biography in Chinese History*, edited by Joan Judge and Hu Ying, 230–45. Berkeley: University of California Press, 2011.

Lu, Weijing. "Personal Writings on Female Relatives in the Qing Collected Works." In *Overt and Covert Treasures: Essays on the Sources for Chinese Women's History*, edited by Clara Wing-ching Ho, 403–26. Hong Kong: Chinese University Press, 2010.

Widmer, Ellen. "Women as Biographers in Mid-Qing Jiangnan." In *Beyond Exemplar Tales: Women's Biography in Chinese History*, edited by Joan Judge and Hu Ying, 246–61. Berkeley: University of California Press, 2011.

28

....

A TEENAGER CAPTURED
BY THE NIAN REBELS
Record of a fifteen-week ordeal by Liu Tang 柳堂
(1844–1929)

....

After he was ransomed and returned home, a teenager captured
by the Nian rebels in 1858 wrote about what he went through and
what he learned about the people holding him captive.

In the mid-nineteenth century, violence disrupted the lives of ordinary people in many parts of the country. From the point of view of the Qing state, the most threatening were the antidynastic rebels who called for the overthrow of the Manchus. The most successful of them were the Taiping rebels, who gained control of key sections of central China and governed from a capital in Nanjing for more than a decade. For ordinary people, however, it did not so much matter who appropriated their goods or forced them from their homes—other sorts of outlaws were just as much of a scourge.

The account below was written by a young man, just seventeen *sui* (fifteen years old by Western reckoning), living in Henan, who had been captured by the group known to history as the Nian rebels or Nian army. The author does not use the term "Nian," however. At first he calls them "the Anhui bandits," and afterward generally refers to them as "the bandits" or "outlaws." He refers to their military units as "banners," the same term used by the Manchus for their military units, most likely adopting the term they used themselves. These bands had plagued the region between the Huai and the Yellow River for decades, but with the diversion of military forces to fight the Taipings after 1852, they gained even greater ability to dominate the region. The new armies raised to defeat the Taipings were eventually used to blockade the Nian and cut them off from their supplies of food and manpower, finally eliminating them in 1868.

The author, Liu Tang, was from a family of enough means to give him the sort of education that would prepare him for the civil service examinations. Until his capture, he had led a rather sheltered life. Liu Tang wrote about his experiences shortly after being ransomed and returned to his family, perhaps in response to questions about what he had learned, as he tries to give names and explain the bandits' organization. He did not publish his account until several decades later, in his collected works. By then, after several decades of taking the civil service examinations while working as a teacher, he had managed to gain the *jinshi* and become an official. He does not seem to have rewritten his original account, but he did add a few notes sometime after writing up the original account (some translated here, some not). The account as we have it is focused on what happened to him, the people he met, and his own feelings and thoughts. From a modern perspective, his sympathy for his captors seems to share something of what has been termed the "Stockholm syndrome," in which hostages bond with their captors, a psychological reaction to their dependency on them for survival. He himself puts his reaction to his captors in a more Confucian context, agreeing with Mencius that one cannot expect people without enough food to remain peaceful.

A Record of Hardship Endured

On the twenty-fifth day of the tenth month of the eighth year of the Xian-feng reign [1858], the Anhui bandits reached our area, which until then had been at peace, the people unfamiliar with war. They thought that the bandits would only kill officials and rob the provincial granaries, so they did not flee to the cities.

With father away in Baidukou on business, mother took the family to her brother's house in Chenggang for protection. As soon as father heard what had happened, he left his business and joined us. He told most of the family to hide in the rushes by the bay and took my brother and me with him, heading west. Just as we were leaving the village, we met some outlaws who let us pass once we gave them our money. Arriving at the West Guandi Temple, we encountered several more bandits, but were able to get away by giving them our coats. A little farther along the way, once again we came upon a band of bandits. As we no longer had either money or coats, we were forced to accompany them. We spent the night at the Zhu Family Village in Nanguang Barracks in Lütan [Henan]. Seeing fires in our hometown, we looked at each other and wept. That night seemed to last a year.

The banner chief, Yao Fengchun, was from Jia Family Walled Village in Mengcheng County [Anhui], which is about 120 *li* from Bozhou [Anhui]. Listening to his speech, we could tell he came from a peasant family. They were first harassed by bandits, then by government troops. Since his family was poor and his parents were old, he felt he had no choice but to become a rebel. When he saw his men burning houses and raping women, he stopped them immediately, which made him a rarity among the bandit leaders. He approached Father with the request that one of his sons remain with them. Father wept but said nothing. I knew what was going through his mind: on the one hand, he did not want me to join the outlaws because I was a good student and his favorite son; on the other hand, my older brother was already married, and if he were to go with the bandits and did not return, how could Father face my sister-in-law Zhangshi? Father wept all night but still could not make up his mind. With tears in my eyes, I came to him and said, "I am willing to go with them." When Father heard this, he wept and looked at my brother, who also broke down and cried. The outlaws were getting ready to leave, and so I climbed into one of their carts and headed out with them toward the south. That was early on the morning of the twenty-sixth.

Later on, the banner chief came and told me, "I have escorted your father and brother to Nantuqiao. Your family and home are safe." In fact, he had ordered them to start a fire in front of the gate to the house, leaving the inside untouched. When other outlaw groups saw the fire, they believed that gang members had already sacked the place and left thinking there was no more booty to be had.

That night, we camped south of Zhoukou [Henan]. It was already cold at that time of year, and I did not have an overcoat. One of the outlaws entered, bringing with him an unpadded black cloth riding jacket, a blue cotton coat, and white silk-covered cotton trousers. The banner chief urged me to put them on. The cotton coat was too long and dragged on the ground, and the trousers were like a woman's, hardly an elegant outfit. But I put them on, turning the trousers inside out. In view of the bitter cold weather, I had no choice but to accept these clothes.

> Note: In the eighty days I spent with the outlaws, I never had anything like a quilt. These clothes were the only things I had to wear during the day and use to keep warm at night. One day when it was very cold, the bandit's mother took pity on me and gave me a red rug. The bandits had two horses, which the boy from Cao County [western Shandong] supplied with fodder by cutting grass. I would make a mat of grass to sleep on, sometimes thick, sometimes thin. When it was time to sleep, I unfastened my clothes and laid out my bedding, using my inner garment under me and my upper garment over me, using one sleeve as a pillow, the other to cover my face. This was called "sleeping like an immortal." The bandits had a saying: "If you master sleeping like an immortal, your whole life you will be able to endure any hardship." In addition, you don't feel the cold.

The village was small, but a large number of people had been crowded into it. The only well had dried up. The outlaws had nothing to make tea in, so they took a pottery jar, cut off its top, and put some water from a pit into it and put it on the fire. It took half the night to reach a boil. They added some sugar, which they had gotten from Zhoukou. I took some of this brew to drink. As it was both foul smelling and sweet, I could barely get it down.

Most of the village families had grain, but flour was scarce. The bandits therefore took dry wheat grain, put it on the millstone, ground it down into flour, added water to it, and cooked it. As soon as it was taken off the stove, the cake would fall apart. Even though it was only half-cooked, the bandits fought over it.

> Note: I could see that it was a life of hunger and deprivation that had driven these unfortunate men to become bandits. I sensed that in their homes they lacked even this crude cuisine.

For my part, I would not even swallow this food and choked on my tears.

Note: The banner chief, aware that I had not eaten, gave me three pieces of bean curd, which he had brought from the market town.

When the outlaws saw a pig walking along, they caught hold of it, cut off its four legs, skinned them, and put them into the pot to boil in the stinking water from the pit. As soon as the meat lost its bloody color, they consumed it with the pig still squealing.

Once night fell and all was quiet, I went out and squatted beneath a large willow tree pretending to defecate, planning to escape. At just that moment, however, I happened to observe another person trying to make a break for it from another bandit camp. The bandits chased and caught him, then chopped off his head and burned his body. I quietly returned to camp and did not dare even think about escaping after that.

On the twenty-seventh, we camped near Huaidian. We did not move for almost half a day because the neighboring villages put up a resistance. On the twenty-eighth, we arrived at the thirteen forts at Jiuli, on the west bank of the Fei River. The bandit chief ordered every banner unit to send two horsemen and three foot soldiers to encircle the thirteen forts. He also ordered that, first of all, the carts should be brought across the river. This presented problems, as there were no bridges and the banks were quite steep. Thus, the carts had to be unloaded. I got down from the cart and pushed one of the empty carts to the river bank. The banner chief knew I was not good at riding horseback and would have trouble fording the river. To the side was a path [plank bridge?] made by people from the forts, so he motioned for me to go that way. I lost my footing and fell into the water. By the time I was on the other side, my feet were frostbitten because the water was terribly cold, and I did not have a change of socks or shoes. From then on, I was continually plagued with foot problems.

Once I reached the east bank of the river, I turned to look at the forts and saw that there were no carts on the west side. Those who were supposed to lay siege to the forts had all fled, the bandit commander unable to stop them. Meanwhile, there were still lots of carts in the middle of the river. As a consequence, people from the thirteen forts descended in great numbers to chase the outlaws, who abandoned their carts in countless numbers. As soon as my cart got to the top of the bank, the driver, his shirt off, whipped up the horses, and we managed to escape from the tiger's mouth.

Father always had kept strict discipline at home. Except at New Year's and other festivals, I had never been allowed to go anywhere. So I knew nothing except what I had learned from books. Outside, I could not even tell the four directions. Once we were on the other side of the river, I overheard the outlaws' conversation and learned that the thirteen forts on the west bank were all enemies of the outlaws, ready to cut in two those who fell behind. If I had known this earlier, I would not have crossed the river. The outlaws called the thirteen forts the "Old Ox Association," saying that their members would kill anyone on sight. Therefore, even the captives struggled to get across the river.

I learned the origin of the Old Ox Association. They were a group that trained in the tradition of Niu [Ox] Geng. Although Niu Geng had already died, they still called themselves the Old Ox Association because Niu Geng had long been feared by the bandits. When the bandits saw them while on patrol, they would sound the alarm and shout, "Be careful; don't fall asleep; be ready for the Old Ox Association from south of the lake."

On the twenty-ninth, we arrived at the bandits' base camp, a small village with mud walls. There was a gate on the south side and a narrow wooden suspension bridge that could only be used by people on foot. The majority of the people who lived there were of the Jia family, and so the village was called the Jia Family Walled Village. The banner commander had a two-room thatched cottage, where he lived with his wife and his mother in her eighties. His father had been killed by other bandits. When they heard he had returned home, his relatives all came to see him and, on seeing me, asked about my family background. I was so distraught that I could not answer and cried bitterly.

By that time, I had gone for several days without eating much. When the bandits returned home safely, their relatives were joyful and quickly prepared a feast. I saw what actually constituted such a feast—nothing more than white wheat noodles. I recalled that, when I had as a child come home from school, I would not even consider eating noodles like those. Often, I would not even answer my mother when she asked me what I wanted to eat but would merely go to my study. To me, plain noodles were inedible. What a spoiled child I had been! But now that I had nothing else to eat, I sat down gratefully to a bowl of noodles and thought they tasted delicious! After suffering deprivation and hardship, I ate three bowls of them. I realized that I had been picky because I had never experienced genuine hunger. From that time on, I understood how wrong I had been. After I was released by the bandits, there was nothing I would not eat. Everything tasted delicious to me.

Entering that village was like entering a pitch-black prison, where sunlight doesn't penetrate. My heart was burdened with a hundred sorrows and a thousand worries, and I had no relatives to turn to. I do not know how many times a day I was reduced to tears.

The banner chief had captured a boy from Cao County. From a peasant family, he cut grass, cared for horses, and collected firewood, working very diligently. By contrast, I did nothing but sit and eat all day, not even smiling. The banner chief's wife was annoyed by this, but I was able to get the banner chief's mother, who had a kindly nature, to speak on my behalf, so the wife left me alone.

Among the captives was a boy named Fan from Baligang in Tongxu County [Henan]. Younger than me, he had mastered the *Four Books* and their commentaries. Sharing hardship, we became friends. I saw him incessantly call the banner chief "Godfather" and ask for money to buy food. I disdained the way he acted and stopped being friends with him. He left the bandits before me. Later, when I took the provincial examinations, I saw his name on a list of those in the bottom group.

When the bandit chief learned I could read, he looked for books in a dozen or more villages but found only one, which turned out to be a dictionary, a sign of the disorder the bandits had caused.

The commanders of the outlaws were called the chiefs. They were ranked as greater and lesser ones. The great chiefs commanded the great banners, each with specific colors. There were several dozen smaller banners under each command banner. Their colors matched those of their respective commanders. The heads of the smaller banners were called lesser chiefs. Each small banner had three to five cavalrymen and ten to twenty infantrymen. A portion of the booty taken by the outlaws was divided among the greater and lesser chiefs. Another part of it was divided equally among the cavalrymen, at two shares each, and part was given to the infantrymen, at one share each.

The great chiefs whom I knew personally were Sun Kuixin, Zhang Lexing, and Liu Gouzi. The one who captured me was in charge of a lesser unit: his superior was his uncle Yao Deguang. He was away in Huaiyuan County [Anhui] with Gong Xiazi and had his kinsman Yao Hua act on his behalf temporarily. There were many chiefs whose names I did not learn. Since the basic bandit organization had five banners, it had five chiefs as well. Furthermore, each banner was subdivided into units named for the five directions: east, west, center, south, and north, and each of these had a chief. Therefore, the basic bandit organization had twenty-five chiefs. When the bandits, by the tens of thousands, advanced, banners covered the field and dust filled the sky. Their weapons, however, were woefully lacking, and the majority of the rank and file were simply hungry men who joined in order to eat.

Yao Xiu was the son of a great chief. I saw him when he returned home from Huaiyuan. He, for one, did look like a bandit. He had a wife, a daughter, and a young son. Whenever the four lesser chiefs returned with booty, he lived very well. His wife was about fifty and not a simple village woman. Although she was married to a bandit, her domestic discipline was very strict. Yao also had a concubine from Guduiji [Henan], whom he had captured in a raid. She wanted to talk with me, but Yao's wife stopped her. His daughter, Haojie, asked about my family the first time we met. I told her that both of my parents were still alive, which made her sigh deeply. When she inquired about my age, I told her that I was sixteen. She replied that she was seventeen and looked bashful. Her eyes brightened, and she seemed to be thinking of something else. Previously, she had been betrothed to a son of the Wang family, but the Wangs had not joined the bandits, and the two families had subsequently become enemies, so the engagement was broken off. Her mother put an end to our meetings but secretly sent the banner chief to ask me if I was married or engaged and if I would like to settle permanently in the village. I could see they wanted to arrange a marriage between her and me. I answered him frankly, and they did not bring the matter up again.

There was a man named Yao Hu from another village who was of a younger generation than the chief's family. He therefore called Haojie "aunt" and sometimes jokingly addressed her as "old Wang." One day they quarreled over some needlework, and Haojie fell to the ground. The banner chief saw this and immediately banned the unfortunate Yao Hu from the premises. All of these incidents gave me new insight into people.

One day the banner chief's wife made me to go with the boy from Cao County to gather firewood. When I resisted, she said, "Firewood is everywhere. You can cut trees in any village. If anyone asks you who you are or what you are doing, just tell them, 'Yao Deguang told us to do this.' You will not have any trouble." We went to cut some wood from a willow tree, and things went as the chief's wife had predicted. Later she learned that the great chief's wife favored me and so stopped asking me to gather firewood.

My daily fare consisted of noodles made from either beans or sorghum, never wheat. I did not have vegetables very often either, with the occasional exception of large green peppers. I did not feel hungry after eating sorghum noodles, but bean noodles, on the other hand, never really filled me up. Nevertheless, I survived and even came to like the porridge made from beans, as it reminded me of what I ate as a child.

The area from the Fei River to Jia Family Walled Village was open land with mixed vegetation occupied by foxes and rabbits, with no sign of people. After several dozen *li*, one could glimpse an earth mound, which was the village. No family there had more than eight members, as some had been killed by the bandits, others by the government troops. As a result, the people had consolidated several former villages into one new one, around which they built a wall for protection. The land had become uncultivatable, and people had to rely more and more on outside sources for their food supply. Prices rose rapidly; a peck or twelve to thirteen ounces of beans could cost a thousand cash.

In these villages, the worthy people sat and waited to die; the less worthy ones joined the bandits in order to survive. The booty that the bandits collected could never be sold for more than a tiny fraction of its worth. Once, each lesser chief got over twenty thousand from a rich man but spent it all quickly. Even if they spent it all on food, it would not have lasted long. The chiefs would go to every market and spend all of their loot on drinking and horse racing. They also competed with each other in splurging and in this way would squander their money within twenty days. When everything was gone, they would begin pillaging once more. They never used the word "pillage," however. Instead, they employed the euphemism "going out." For several days before such a venture, the chiefs would meet to plan their strategy. This was called "setting of banners": they estimated how many banners would be needed and how they should be deployed.

The Jia Family Walled Village was five *li* from a dry lake. The area north of the lake was occupied by the bandits, south of it by the Old Ox Association. One day the Old Ox Association crossed the lake to hunt. The bandits did not dare to confront them so simply barred their doors for self-protection. The Old Ox Association did not act hostile, so finally a bandit asked them why they had to cross the lake to hunt. A member of the Old Ox Association replied, "South of the lake is mainly cultivated land. It is very difficult for rabbits to hide and burrow there. On the north side of the lake, however, there is a good deal of wilderness. After a short run with our hunting dogs, we should be able to return to our own side with full bags of game." There was a deserted three-room house in one of the abandoned villages. The hunters put a net on the doors and set it on fire, with the result that more than a hundred rabbits came out and were trapped in the net. There is a saying that if animals are allowed to reproduce unchecked, they will fill the universe and there will be no room for people. This certainly appears to be the case.

On the twenty-third day of the twelfth month, the bandits planned a secret attack on the Old Ox Association. Everyone who joined up would get a share of the booty. The banner chief's wife and her cousin Cui wanted to make me go, and I was willing, thinking it might give me an opportunity to escape. Then suddenly my foot problem flared up again. It turned some color between blue and red and gave me unbearable pain. Later the condition was alleviated by bathing the foot in strong alcohol heated on the fire.

During my captivity, the banner chief told me where my father was staying. Zhang Village Fort, New Terrace Market, and so on that he mentioned were all places my father had traveled before. Jia Family Walled Village was only twenty-odd *li* from Zhang Village, but getting between them was challenging. Father knew he could be followed and captured, so he was careful and never entered the main base of the outlaws. He went to Bozhou, where he met a man named Wang Laoyu who owned a secondhand clothes shop and asked him to find out where I was being held. There was an old man, an uncle of the banner chief, who sold clothes to the shop. He had a son with the bandits, and he acted as a go-between to sell the outlaws' booty. Father asked him to carry a letter to me.

When I read the letter Father had written, I could not contain my emotions and broke down and wept. The old man told me that Father was in Bozhou and that he intended to visit me after the New Year. He then brought me a brush and ink to write a reply. As I wrote, the old man stood over me and would let me write only that I was fine and that Father should not worry.

A couple of days later, in the middle of the night, the banner chief brought two horses by. He mounted one and ordered me to mount the other. He said he was taking me home but did not want to leave in the daytime for fear that the great chief would object. I felt both joy and fear and was unsure how to respond. I hurried to follow him and leave the site of my captivity. At dawn on the twenty-seventh or twenty-eighth of the twelfth month, we arrived at New Terrace Market. It was thirty *li* from the village and eighty *li* from Bozhou. The banner chief settled me at a small inn and told the owner to provide me with food and drink, which he would cover. He said, "Your father will come here to pick you up shortly after the New Year. When you see him, tell him the Yaos treated you well, but if he were to try to repay me with so much as a penny, I would not consider myself a human being." We bid farewell with tears in our eyes.

There was a man from Bozhou who purchased secondhand clothes and knew that Father was friendly with Wang Laoyu. He suggested that I leave the inn and go with him at once to meet my father, explaining that my father would not dare venture into a bandit haunt such as this inn. At first I was inclined to agree with him, but then on second thought I was afraid that Father might in fact come to the inn and that we would miss each other. How could I bear it if my escape from the bandits resulted in his getting caught by them? Since I had already endured it all for two months, a few more days shouldn't matter. I therefore turned him down.

On the first day of the first month of the ninth year [1859], the inn owner celebrated the New Year. He brought out rice flour, oil, fuel, and several dozen dumplings and told me to prepare a meal for myself. But I had no experience in cooking and I felt very depressed because it was New Year's Day and I was still separated from my family. Still, I had to eat something, so I poured water into a pot and put the dumplings into it, but the dumplings became all mushy before I even lit the fuel. I did not know that they should be added only after the water had reached boiling. I started to cry and did not eat them but gave them to the firewood boy. I then kneaded the flour to make oil-cakes, but it stuck to my hands and I could not work it properly, which got me upset again. Someone passing by took pity on me and offered to make the oil-cakes, but he forgot to add the salt, and they came out quite tasteless. Still I ate them to avoid starvation. Fortunately, Father was to arrive in a day or two.

On the second, I was looking to the west to watch for Father when the banner chief's uncle arrived from the east and told me, "Your father is at Bozhou and will not come here." He then asked me to go with him. I regretted that I had not listened to the advice of the secondhand clothes dealer. That night we stayed at Zhehe Market, where a lot of people were telling stories and singing. It was crowded, and I cannot remember clearly which ones were outlaws and which were not.

On the third, we arrived at Bozhou, and I was sent directly to Wang Laoyu's. Because Father had not received precise information concerning my whereabouts, he had gone home on the twenty-eighth of the twelfth month to celebrate the New Year. I was once more reduced to tears. Moreover, Wang thought I might be an imposter and quizzed me extensively to make sure that I was who I said I was. Finally, when my words matched the facts, he led me inside and gave the old man silver. Thus I knew I was being ransomed. When I recalled the banner chief's words [about not accepting a cent], I wonder whether he had been lying to me or whether it was the old man.

On the fourth, Wang Laoyu came back and said Mr. Li, the headman of East Gate Compound, had heard that a young boy had escaped from the bandits and ordered that he be assigned to work duty unless ten taels of silver were paid. I could only agree to pay. From that point on, they allowed me to do everything in the same way as the others in the family, including eating with them and not avoiding any of them, treating me like family. Today when I remember this, I still have doubts, not knowing whether or not it was true. I cannot help but be grateful. Still, was the request of the East Gate Compound real or not? There was no way to find out.

Note: Later, after I had passed the provincial exams, my elder brother went to Bozhou on business and investigated. Wang Laoyu had already died, and his widow was living alone, without children.

Although I was not yet home, I had learned that no one in my family had died and the house was not destroyed, so I was calmer, merely awaiting the arrival of Father.

The east gate of Bozhou was usually kept closed. If an enemy came up to it, he would be killed. No one reported this to the officials, or if they did, nothing was done about it. Everything outside the east gate was the outlaws'. An official named Bo had gained the local people's affection. The heads of the gate tower were very powerful. I remember the names of Sun Wulei and Li Zhen.

At that time, the outlaws surrounded the city and attacked it. They used storming shields and scaling ladders, but the guards on the walls drove them back with cannon fire and huge stones. The bodies of the dead bandits filled the moat around the city, yet they did not withdraw. They tried to build a siege tower from which to use their cannon against the walls. But the tower was destroyed by fire even before it was finished. Finally, the outlaws lifted the siege because they concluded that the city was protected by the will of Heaven. Altogether the city was besieged for forty-eight days, during which time the food supplies ran out. If another three days had gone by without the siege being lifted, the defense would have collapsed. That the bandits attributed their failure to Heaven was understandable. Without the goods that the bandits had plundered, there would have been nothing to consume, and if it weren't for the things they used, they wouldn't have taken anything. If this city had fallen, the bandits would have kept their loot while sitting around and waiting to die. After the residents refused to surrender during the weeks-long siege, the bandits would not enter even if the gate was opened and they were invited in.

Now the bandits thought that it was Heaven's intention to protect the city and the tens of thousands of living beings in it. Don't they know that protecting the several tens of thousands of good people in the city was also protecting the several million robbers and bandits of the middle Yangzi region?

Some people asked me, "The way of Heaven is to reward the good and punish the evil. Why then does Heaven not destroy the bandits?" To this I replied that these people were not born to be bandits. They are forced into it because of hunger and cold. When suffering from hunger and cold, they become bandits; when not suffering, they quit being bandits. After being forced by hunger and cold to become bandits, they are not further forced by hunger and cold to die. Those not quite so desperate can wait for a change in fate so that they can go out and beg for their life or pick up a weapon and fight back. That could provide a chance for Heaven to rescue them by plucking them away from amid these swords and spears and letting them live normal domestic life or join a Buddhist establishment. Those who do not accept pacification and become enemies of the government troops are the true bandits. In that situation, they deserve to be executed. Those who do not become enemies of the government army but whose leaders are as evil as Zhang Lexing, they should also not be forgiven. It was never their true intention to be pacified. If their wish was not genuine, then they were true bandits. But how many true bandits are there in fact? The gentleman recognizes that the charitable measures of the Buddhist establishments serve Heaven's intentions. As for the muddle-headed, content Mr. Bo, he cannot be said to be an unworthy official in times of disorder. The ancients had a saying, "Muddling through is difficult to achieve." Mr. Bo is truly capable of muddling through! I regret not knowing his personal name.

On the tenth, Father arrived, and I burst into tears at the sight of him. After a couple days' rest, on the twelfth we rented a small cart to take us home, taking turns riding in it. Although I did not have to walk much, I developed blisters on my feet since the old wounds had not yet fully healed.

On the fifteenth, we arrived at Jidong and saw people repairing the stockade. As we walked along the streets, we could see that half of the houses had been burned down. It certainly looked nothing like it had, and I could not help feeling disheartened. When we got home and I saw Mother, I kowtowed to her with mixed feelings of sorrow and joy. Recalling my miserable experiences with the outlaws, I started to cry all over again. All of our relatives and neighbors came over to see me, but I could not respond to their kindness. My only thought was that I had escaped death.

On the other hand, had I never experienced this travail, I might have been satisfied with myself and concerned only with getting enough to eat. Perhaps I would have become degenerate like young Fan [whom I met while a captive]. Therefore, when I told my story, I recalled my earlier life with tears of regret. There were times when I sighed and asked Heaven why it had been so cruel to me. But on finishing this account, I feel calm and know that I should not complain about my fate. Heaven in fact has been very kind to me. I suffered a harrowing experience but was formed by it. The ancients indeed were not deceiving us [in writing about Heaven].

Recorded by Liu Tang of Fugou in the first month of the *jiachen* year [1859].

SOURCE: Liu Tang 柳堂, *Bijian tang quanji* 筆諫堂全集, reproduced in *Nianjun* 捻軍, ed. Fan Wenlan 范文瀾 et al. (Shanghai: Shenzhou Guoguangshe, 1953), 1:348–55.

Further Reading

Huntington, Rania. "Chaos, Memory, and Genre: Anecdotal Recollections of the Taiping Rebellion." *Chinese Literature, Essays, Articles, Reviews* 27 (2005): 59–91.

Perry, Elizabeth J. *Rebels and Revolutionaries in North China, 1845–1945*. Stanford, CA: Stanford University Press, 1980.

Rowe, William T. *China's Last Empire: The Great Qing*. Cambridge, MA: Harvard University Press, 2009.

Zhang, Daye. *The World of a Tiny Insect: A Memoir of the Taiping Rebellion and Its Aftermath*. Translated by Xiaofei Tian. Seattle: University of Washington Press, 2013.

29

KEEPING FAMILY
MEMBERS INFORMED
Letters to his eldest son by Zeng Guofan
曾國藩 (1811–1872)

Twelve letters written by the eminent scholar-general Zeng Guofan
to his eldest son, Zeng Jize, between 1852 and 1865 let us see him
as a concerned parent even when he was fully engaged in dealing
with urgent political and military matters.

Zeng Guofan became one of the most prominent officials of the mid-nineteenth century. From Hunan, he passed the *jinshi* examination in 1838 and
began his career in the capital, rising through a series of central government
posts. In 1852, he was assigned to be the examiner for the provincial examinations in Jiangxi but on the way there learned that his mother had died,
forcing him to take leave and return to Hunan for the mourning period. This
was just when the Taiping rebellion was making rapid headway in the region.
Soon he was persuaded to return to office and organize a militia in his home
province. Brilliant at organization and planning, he created an army that
proved effective in quelling the rebels. In 1860, he was made governor-gen-
eral and commissioner in charge of suppressing the Taiping, an assignment

that required another four years of often very heavy fighting to complete. Throughout, he remained completely loyal to the Manchu court.

Several hundred of the letters that Zeng Guofan wrote to family members survive, ranging in date from 1840 to 1867. His was a large family, and he wrote not only to his parents and grandparents but also to his uncles, brothers, and sons. He did not address letters to his wife, sisters, or daughters, but if they were living at home, they undoubtedly also read the letters addressed to the men. Unlike the very brief letters written by ordinary people that were found among original documents from the Qin, Han, and Tang periods (see selection 4), these letters are often quite long. Zeng was a highly literate man, and when he was separated from his closest relatives, he often wrote lengthy letters to them. These letters let us see something of the private Zeng Guofan, such as how he handled the business of daily life, managed family relations, balanced work and family, and thought about his commitment to Confucian ideals. A historian trying to get a deeper understanding of Zeng would also want to bring in other personal accounts he wrote, as he also wrote letters to friends and colleagues and kept a diary.

Rather than provide a sample of letters to different relatives, here we include only a selection of the letters he wrote to his eldest son, Zeng Jize (1839–1890). They are arranged chronologically, dating from 1852, when Jize was fourteen *sui* (still twelve by Western counting), to 1865, when he was twenty-seven *sui*. Naturally, Zeng Guofan wrote to his son only when they were apart, so more letters survive from some periods than others. All but the first very long letter are translated here in full.

The father-son relationship was considered fundamental to both the patrilineal family system and Confucian ethics. Most interaction between fathers and sons naturally took place in person and has left no trace in written form. In addition, the documents that historians can draw on most often were written by the son, often after the death of the parent, and so have a retrospective quality. Zeng's letters not only give us the father's perspective but also are more immediate, less edited.

Zeng Guofan's many efforts to shape Jize's moral and intellectual development may deserve some of the credit for Jize's own success as an official responsive to the needs of the time. Jize developed an interest in foreign affairs and became one of the first Qing officials to travel to Europe, serving as ambassador to England, France, and Russia from 1878 to 1886.

To my son Jize,

On the twenty-fifth day of the seventh month, on the road in Taihu County [Jiangsu], I was distraught and grieved on learning of my mother's passing. The same day, I hired a small sedan chair and traveled sixty *li*. I got no sleep that night, writing letters to family members in the capital and making arrangements for everything. You and the other family members, after receiving condolences, should with all speed leave the capital. On the night of the twenty-sixth, I sent a letter to the capital with the Hubei Xizhou correspondence, and on the twenty-seventh, I sent another to the capital with the Fuzhou [Jiangxi] correspondence. The letters are largely the same, but the Jiangxi one gives more detail. It is just that fearing they might not arrive, I sent letters from both places. In the midst of my grief, I haven't been able to think of everything, but here are some tasks I have thought of:

> I estimate that a list of those who owe me money would come to about a thousand [taels?]....
> Hire two mule carts. Your mother and Jihong can ride in one, the wet-nurse and Sister Five and Sister Six can take the other....
> Cotton clothes must be made for the young children. It will definitely be cold traveling in the tenth month, especially while on the boat....
> While on the boat, the greatest fear is robbers. When I was in Jiujiang, Dehua County [both in Jiangxi], I sent someone to act as a guard....
> The eighth day of the eighth month of the second year of the Xianfeng reign [1852], while on a boat in Qizhou [Hubei].

To Jize,

On the eighth, I wrote a letter while on the boat, and on the morning of the eleventh arrived at Huangzhou [Hubei]. Because we were obstructed by the wind for a long time, I hired a small sedan chair to climb up the bank. On the twelfth, at midday, we got to the Hubei provincial seat, where we met an old friend of Chang Nangai's, from whom I learned the news from Hunan, that Changsha was under siege and in danger, that the road was obstructed and travel blocked. I was overcome by grief and distress.

Now I am staying in Wuchang [Hubei] for a while, but at present, family members should definitely not leave the capital. We can discuss this again early next year. After condolences are completed, move to a small house. I will find a way to send you money regularly for your expenses.

Written in haste; I will write again in a day or two.

The twelfth day of the eighth month of the second year of the Xianfeng reign [1852], at night, sent from Wuchang.

To my son Jize,

Hu Er and the others have arrived, bringing your letter. Your calligraphy still has not improved much. This year you are eighteen *sui*, full-grown with your teeth all in, but your studies are not progressing. The son of my relative through marriage Chen Daiyun, called Jisheng, started school this year, and the academy ranked his poem at the top of the class. Since he was born in the *wuxu* year, he is only one year older than you. Because he lost his parents, his family has declined into poverty, which made him work hard at study and achieve a name for himself at a young age. In your case, you have benefited from the privileges accrued by your grandfather and father, you have had plenty of clothes and food and no worries, so you willingly seek careless pleasure and do not apply yourself to reading books or establishing your character. The ancients said, "If one works hard, his mind will turn toward the good; lack of discipline gives rise to excessive desires." Mencius said, "People survive through adversity, perish in ease and comfort." I worry that you go too far in the direction of carelessness.

Your wife just entered our household. She should be instructed to enter the kitchen to cook and to be diligent in spinning and weaving. She should not think that as a child of the rich and high ranking there is nothing she has to do. Are your three younger sisters already able to make large shoes? Your three sisters and your wife should make a pair of shoes for me every year to express their filial and respectful concern. They each should work hard at needlework. Have the cloth they weave made into clothes and sent to me, which will let me see the diligence of those in the women's quarters.

Even while I am with the army, I do not let up studying and both read books and practice calligraphy, never neglecting them for long. Still, I regret that as I grow older I don't improve very much. Since you are still young, time is golden—don't waste any of it! Get someone to sell the fields that were bought in Hengyang [Hunan] two years ago, then send the money to the military camp so that I can pay back the Li family. When one's parents are alive, one should not have private possessions; this is true for both literati and commoners. How much more is this true given that I am a high official!

My skin problem has recurred, but is not as bad as last fall.

Li Ciqing was defeated on the sixteenth in Fuzhou [Jiangxi], which I already related in my letter to Uncle Yuan. I am presently in Chongren [Jiangxi], working on how to handle reorganization. On the thirtieth, we had a victory, but we are short of provisions. The situation is at a critical point, keeping me worried.

Whenever you get a chance, write, and whenever you write, tell me everything going on—don't be too cursory! How grandfather is doing, the news of the whole family, what you have been studying at the academy—give lots of details. Be sure to keep this in mind!

The second day of the tenth month of the sixth year of the Xianfeng reign [1856].

To my son Jize,

On the nineteenth, Zeng Six came to the camp and delivered your letter number five from the seventh along with a poem, letting me know everything. You mentioned that you would enter the examination hall the next day and that everything was ready. So I figure you must have already left the examination hall and returned home. On the eighth, I arrived at the mouth of the river, originally thinking I would enter Fujian via Qian Mountain then attack Chongan [Fujian]. This plan has already been submitted to the imperial court. The Guangze bandits had been causing disturbances in Jiangxi and were reaching the three counties of Luxi, Jinxi, and Anren [Hunan and Jiangxi] and have a base at Anren [Hunan]. On the fourteenth, I sent Zhang Kaizhang to wipe them out. On the fifteenth, I also returned to Yiyang [Jiangxi] to wait until Anren was destroyed, then enter Fujian through the Luxi-Yunji pass.

To my pleasure, I found your poem written in the seven-syllable ancient style to be serene in spirit and confident in language. Generally, one should pay close attention to the tone patterns when writing poetry. I have selected nine authors of five-syllable ancient verse and six authors of the seven-syllable ancient verse whose poems are so euphonic that people can read them hundreds of times without being bored. As to those I did not select—such as the five-syllable ancient verses of Zuo Si (Daichong), Jiang Yan (Wencong), Chen Zi'ang, Liu Zongyuan (Zihou), and the seven-syllable ancient verses of Bao Zhao (Mingyuan), Gao Shi (Dafu), Wang Wei (Mojie), and Lu You (Fangweng)—they are also extraordinary in their tone patterns. If you wish to compose five- or seven-syllable ancient-style poems, you must read dozens of them. First, recite them out loud in order to feel their vitality, then softly chant the verses in order to appreciate their mood. If you do both of these things, you will accustom your own tongue to the tones of the ancients. As a result, when you compose poetry, the tones of your verses will be in harmony with those of the ancients. When you read your poems aloud, you will find them melodious and readable. Gradually, you will develop a keen interest in writing poetry yourself. The ancients said, "After completing and polishing a poem, one should recite it out loud." Furthermore, they said, "Before one completes a poem, he should slowly chant it to himself." From this, you can see that in writing poetry, the ancients put much effort into tone qualities. Word poetry is sounds made by man; wordless poetry is the sounds of nature. If you understand this and can bring together the sounds of man and the sounds of nature, then you have reached the halfway mark in mastering the art of composing poetry.

You wrote that you enjoy practicing your calligraphy. This is a good habit to develop! But lately the color of your ink has not been as smooth and uniform as it was in the spring and summer of last year. From now on, when you write, pay close attention to the quality of your ink. The skillful calligraphers of the past were experts in achieving good ink quality, so that their shiny and glossy calligraphy seemed to float on top of the paper. Diligent practice and concentration made this possible. Furthermore, the age and viscosity of their ink and the speed with which the masters wrote also contributed to the freshness and brightness of their calligraphy.

All my life, I have been ashamed of three things. Although my studies have been wide-ranging, I have no knowledge of astronomy or mathematics. I cannot even recognize the fixed stars and the five latitudes. This is the first thing I am ashamed of. In managing affairs, I have never been able to carry everything through to completion. This is the second thing I am ashamed of. When I was young and practiced calligraphy, I never devoted myself to any single school; therefore, my style is variable and weak. In addition, I write clumsily and slowly, so I cannot write for any practical purpose. And during these last years in the army, I have been negligent and sometimes do not practice at all. This is the third thing that I am ashamed of. If you are a son who is worthy of our family, you should want to help your father make up for these three deficiencies. Although calculation and mathematics are difficult to comprehend, the fixed stars and five latitudes can be easily recognized. There are several books that discuss astronomy, such as the astronomy sections of the seventeen dynastic histories, and the sections on observation of heavenly bodies and calendar making in *The Complete Examination of the Five Rites* (Wuli tongkao). If you can commit to memory two or three fixed stars each night, in a few months you will know them all.

Whatever you do, big or small, simple or difficult, you should see it through to the end. In practicing your calligraphy, it is more important to achieve round and smooth strokes than great speed. If you can write ten thousand words a day in regular script, or at least seven to eight thousand words, then your hand will be able to handle the brush with ease because the more you practice, the more familiar you will get with the strokes. You can make use of this skill in your studies because you will be able to copy numerous books. In the future, in your official life, this skill will enable you to record cases and documents, and there are countless other benefits to be gained from having a smooth and fast hand. If you can accomplish these three things, you will be compensating for my shortcomings.

Since this is your first attempt at the civil service examinations, it does not matter much whether you pass or fail. Afterward, read the commentaries to *The Classic of Poetry* (Shijing). Afterward, you should study the classics and histories together. The books written by the great scholars Gu [Yanwu], Yan [Ruoqu], Jiang [Yong], Dai [Zhen], Duan [Yucai], and Wang [Niansun] should be closely studied and scrutinized.

Every moment is worth a thousand pieces of gold. From now on, when you write to me, let me know what is on your mind, or explain briefly what you have read or studied recently. That way, your letters will let me see how well you are getting on with your studies. Take your time and do not send letters that are too short. This is my wish.

On the twentieth day of the third month of the eighth year of the Xianfeng reign [1858].

To my son Jize,

I have received your letters of the nineteenth and twenty-ninth, so I know that your wedding has taken place and the new bride has been able to gain your mother's approval. This is a blessing for our family.

Our dynasty has had sage emperors one after another, who regularly got up at 4 a.m. This practice hasn't changed for two centuries. In our family, from my great-great-grandfather to my father, all got up early. Great-grand-father and Grandfather both got up before dawn and would sit in the cold winter for an hour before the sky brightened. My father also got up before the sun and, if there were things to do, would not wait for the dawn. Every night, he would rise and take a look a couple of times to check on the time, lest he get up late, something you witnessed yourself. Recently, I have also been getting up before dawn in order to continue the family tradition. Since you have now been capped and have married, you should make getting up early a priority. If you make an effort to do this, you will also be setting an example for your new bride.

All my life, I have had the failing of inconstancy, so that many goals were never accomplished. I am deeply ashamed of the virtues I have not perfected and the tasks I have not completed. Since I began leading troops, which was never part of my original ambition, this failing has gotten worse, to my great regret. If you want to achieve something, you must take to heart the two words "be constant."

I once closely observed how Grandfather's deportment stood out—it can be summed up in the word "weighty." My way of walking is also rather weighty, probably because I model myself on Grandfather. Your deportment is very casual. Since this is a major flaw, you should constantly keep it in mind. Whether you are walking or sitting, you should be serious. Getting up early, being constant, and being serious: these three are all things you need to work on. Getting up early is a family tradition passed down from our forebears. Not following through is my great shame. Not being serious is a shortcoming of yours. For these reasons, I am making the point to earnestly admonish you concerning them.

In my previous letter, I answered three of your questions on changing brushes while doing calligraphy, the phrase "daring to tell the horse to go," and the pluses and minuses of commentaries, going on at some length. Why do you say nothing about that in your letter? From now on, when you get a letter from me that offers instruction, you could respond point by point, not abbreviating. For more advice, see the piece that I sent to Teacher Deng Yinjie on looking, reading aloud, and writing.

The fourteenth day of the tenth month of the ninth year of the Xianfeng reign [1859], handwritten by Disheng [Zeng Guofan's title].

To my sons Jize and Jihong,

I received your mother's and Uncle Cheng's letters on the twenty-ninth day of the tenth month. I also received the padded cotton shoes and two bags of dried melon seeds. From the letters, I know that everyone at home is well and how Jize was stranded in Hankou [Hubei] for six days due to the strong wind. But I suppose he is home by now. Jize should always remember, "In action there must be dignity; in speech there must be deliberation." Do not neglect this even for a moment.

These days, nothing is disturbing my peace. The two armies under Generals Bao and Zhang also are not currently engaged. Zuo Zongtang's army won a victory in Guixi on the twenty-second of last month. And on the twenty-ninth, he won yet another small victory at Dexing [both in Jiangxi]. However, the rebel forces are still strong, and I am very worried about that. They have flocked together to attack Jiande [Zhejiang], where General Pu is stationed. If Generals Zuo and Pu can hold them off, I feel the situation will stabilize everywhere else.

Jize, you have a gift for calligraphy, but your style lacks strength. Therefore, devote some time to practice, because it will be a shame to abandon something you have natural talent for.

Remember everyone in the house, regardless of age, should get up early.

I did not write to Uncle Cheng this time, so please tell him my situation here.

Fourth of the eleventh month of the tenth year of the Xianfeng reign [1860].

To my sons Jize and Jihong,

I received your letters of the twenty-fourth of the first month and know all of you are well. The military situation here has been critical since the eleventh month of last year. But fortunately, we were able to pass through that crisis safely. At present, only Zuo Zongtang's army stationed at Jingdezhen [Jiangxi] is in great danger, but the rest of us are reasonably safe. I will soon move our armies to the Dongliu and Jiande regions [both in Zhejiang].

Enclosed are eight taels; buy some good tea, and send it to me now and then.

Have you begun to plant more bamboo? I hope that you have planted some around the hill behind our house to make it look the way it did in my father's time. I cut down all the bamboo four years ago because I thought it was blocking the sun from shining into our hall. But I have regretted that act ever since because, after it was cut down, the hall was still as dark as ever. That is why I am asking you to plant bamboo again.

Are you keeping in mind those two words: "effort" and "modesty"?

On the fourteenth of the second month of the eleventh year of the Xianfeng reign [1861].

To my son Jize,

Hu Bida and Xie Rongfang arrived here on the twentieth of the eighth month, and from them I received three letters from your uncle Cheng, your mother, and you. In addition, I received *The Works of 103 Scholars of the Han and Wei Dynasties* (Han Wei baisan jia) and three pieces of your calligraphy of *Preface to the Sacred Teachings* (Shengjiao xu). On the twenty-second, Tan Zairong arrived, and from him I received the two letters from your uncle Cheng and you. So I am up-to-date on the latest news from the family.

Cai Yingwu drowned in the Yangzi River at Jingkou [Jiangsu]. His death was unexpected and tragic. In addition to his provision of three taels, I also am sending twenty taels to aid his family, eight taels for the funeral expenses of Zhu Yunsi's mother, and ten taels as a present for Hui's daughter, Yizhen, who is to be married this coming winter. Deliver these to the respective people.

Your elder sister is supposed to get married on the third day of the twelfth month. Have the Yuans agreed on that date yet? I have already set the dowry at two hundred taels; now I am forwarding one hundred taels for your sister to purchase clothes and other articles. The remaining one hundred taels I shall send next time, along with funds to cover the cost of transportation between our house and the Yuans' and the wedding gift for Niece Sixty.

Thrift is the only way to maintain a household over a long period of time. It is particularly important to avoid luxuries during times of social instability. Do not prepare unnecessary clothes, and keep the clothes you buy simple and not overly adorned. Instruct your younger sisters to heed my words, and our family will survive for a long time.

Since Uncle Muyun wishes a post at a private academy, I have written to entrust the matter to Vice Censor-in-Chief Yun for his assistance in the matter. When Uncle Yuan returns to Changsha on leave, ask him to mention this again to him. I do not think there will be any difficulties.

I have been healthy. On the twenty-first day, I wore coarse mourning garments for a funeral. Even though the three days of morning is over, my skin condition is still giving me a lot of discomfort. Every night, I scratch incessantly. Fortunately, it is not infected. Uncle Man was suffering from malaria, but he recovered on the twenty-second.

I did not write to your uncle Cheng this time, so show him this letter from me.

On the twenty-fourth of the eighth month of the eleventh year of the Xianfeng reign [1861].

To Jize,

On the twentieth, I received the letters that you and your uncle Cheng had posted on the second of the fifth month. On the twenty-second, I received a letter from your uncle Cheng posted from Hengzhou [Hunan]. From these letters, I learned that everyone in our household is well and the third daughter's marriage took place.

In your letter, you said you are quite worried about your brother-in-law, Mr. Yuan. I myself never expected him to turn out so bad. I shall write a letter to admonish him. It would not be appropriate for those of you at home to expose your feelings too directly in front of him. A man who still cares for his reputation wants the respect of others. If people show only their high-minded contempt for him, he will no longer care and will place himself in opposition to morally upright people. If he reaches that state, he will be quite beyond any hope of reform. Therefore, everyone in the family, both Zengs and relatives through marriage, both adults and children, must treat Mr. Yuan courteously. If he still shows no improvement in his behavior, I shall take him to my military camp in Anhui and hire a teacher to instruct him.

Generally speaking, children of notable families should not be given a lot of money and clothes. Although these are minor issues, they can have great influence upon them.

The military situation on all fronts is stable. General Duo led his army to assist our soldiers in Shaanxi. Your uncle Yuan's army is now stationed in Jinling [Jiangsu]. I am worried about him because his army is isolated. Huzhou [Zhejiang] was lost to the rebels on the third. General Bao is attacking Ningguo [Jiangxi] but is having difficulty in recapturing it. Anhui has been suffering from severe drought, but just recently rain fell for three days, so the people's morale is getting better. We have been purchasing our rice from Changsha [Hunan], so your uncle Cheng need not worry. Remember to tell him this, since I am not writing to him this time.

Twenty-fourth day of the fifth month of the first year of the Tongzhi reign [1862].

To Jize and Jihong,

I have not received any letters from you recently. I hope everyone in our family is well. With regard to the current military situation, the siege of Jinling was lifted on the fifth, and therefore our camp is quiet. However, Uncle Man has not recovered from his illness. There are three other places where the situation is critical. The first is Ningguo [Jiangxi], where General Bao and General Zhang have their two armies. Their supply lines have been cut by the enemy, and we cannot get reinforcements to them. The second place is Jingde [Anhui], where General Zhu Pinlong's army is quartered. He is also short of supplies and under rebel attack from all sides. The third place is the rebel-occupied Jiufu Island [Jiangsu], where the rebel forces have moved to the north bank, which I am afraid Li Shizhong will not be able to defend. Achieving victory in these three places will be difficult.

I have been worrying a great deal the last two months. Plus, my toothache is very severe and my spirits have been even lower than they were in the spring of the eighth year [1858], when I was at home, and the spring of the tenth year [1860], when I was in Qimen [Anhui]. You will be coming here in the new year; perhaps seeing you will cheer me up.

Do you feel that your walk is more dignified than before? Do you deliberate before you open your mouth to speak? Is Jihong learning to write poetry? Is my son-in-law Mr. Yuan staying home more often? When you come, perhaps you can bring Mr. Yuan and my nephew Jiner with you.

On the twenty-fourth day of the tenth month of the first year of the Tongzhi reign [1862].

To Jize and Jihong,

I sailed from Shaobo [Jiangsu] on the fourth and arrived at Qingjiangpu [Jiangsu] on the eighth. I heard that the three groups of Nian bandits led by Zhang, Ren, and Niu have reached the areas around Meng and Bo [both Anhui]. Ying Fangbo's army has been surrounded by the bandits in Zhiheji [Anhui], and Yi Kaijun's army has been under attack by them on two fronts in Mengcheng [Anhui]. Therefore, it is very difficult to get supplies to them. I have asked Changqi to move the navy from Great Marsh Lake to Linhuai [Anhui]. I am staying here waiting for the arrival of Luo and Liu's armies, and then I shall proceed to Xuzhou [Jiangsu].

When you serve your mother at home, always remember to be industrious and frugal. In your relationships with people, you must be humble and prudent. As a general rule, old families go into decline when members are no longer hardworking and frugal—and this is usually first seen in the women. When I was home, I was quite concerned by the fact that the women of our house tend to want a more opulent lifestyle. Since you two have pledged yourselves to maintain our family's reputation, you must begin by instructing your wives.

I am fairly well except for my ringworm, which is getting slightly worse.

Ninth day of the fifth intercalary month, in the fourth year of the Tongzhi reign [1865].

To Jize,

I received both your letters, from which I learned all the latest news. I am pleased to hear that your mother has recovered from her illness and my grandson in the Luo family is doing well.

I have been in Qingjiang [Jiangsu] for eleven days now. There are disturbances here over unpaid wages, since Liu Songshan has not yet arrived with the payroll. These disturbances have delayed my departure. Lately there has been nothing to be alarmed about in Zhihe and Mengcheng. Luo Maotang and others have already departed by land for Linhuai. I myself plan to leave here by water for Linhuai on the twenty-first if Liu Songshan arrives by then.

My health is fine, but I am greatly worried about the unrest over the unpaid wages in the Hunan army. It is like holding a spear that, if not stopped, will eventually destroy you. This is causing me a great deal of concern day after day. Jiang Zhichun's army has revolted in Hubei, and I am afraid that will help stir up agitation elsewhere and cause unrest in the Xiangxiang region [Hunan]. I still cannot decide on the right policy for punishing those guilty in that revolt.

I have written to Xiaocen that Yiqing should pay fifty taels to Yang Jianshan. I have also written a letter to Yiqing and instructed him to pay my old friend Shao and all the others on a monthly basis. The only person not on that list is Wang Shuxiang, who is to be paid every season. After Liu Boshan's book company is dissolved, I plan to find a post for him. But I have not heard about its final date.

Do not entertain visitors at home. How much do you spend for household expenses each month? Are the wives and daughters spinning and weaving every day? Do they have regular tasks? Report these things to me next time.

Recently I have not been eating meat at dinner. Instead I stew one or two kinds of vegetables in a meat broth until they are quite tender. The taste can't be beat, and it is also good for my health. (One does not have to eat expensive foods. Good taste should be enough to nourish a man.) Try this method, and cook some for your mother. (My grandfather used to pick fresh vegetables at sunset and cook them for dinner. When I ate with him, I found them particularly good. Now I cook the vegetables in a meat broth, but they still do not taste as good as I remember.) The younger generation should not eat meat for the evening meal. Eating vegetables plain without any meat broth is healthy as well as frugal.

Yan Zhitui's *Family Instruction* (Yan shi jiaxun) was written in a time of chaos. Zhang Ying wrote his *Maxims* (Congxunzhai yu) during a time of peace. These two books have detailed instructions for educating every family member. Your brothers should have a copy of each and read them regularly. Then you will make progress every day.

Nineteenth day, fifth month, the fourth year of the Tongzhi reign [1865].

SOURCE: Zeng Guofan 曾國藩, *Zeng Wenzheng gong quanji* 曾文正公全集, 9 vols. (Taipei: Shijie Shuju, 1952), vols. 6 and 7, passim.

Further Reading

Kadar, Daniel Z. *Historical Chinese Letter Writing*. London: Bloomsbury, 2011.

Kuhn, Philip A. *Rebellion and Its Enemies in Late Imperial China: Militarization and Social Structure, 1796–1864*. Cambridge, MA: Harvard University Press, 1970.

Liu, Kwang-Ching. "Education for Its Own Sake: Notes on Tseng Kuo-fan's *Family Letters*." In *Education and Society in Late Imperial China, 1600–1900*, edited by Benjamin A. Elman and Alexander Woodside, 292–339. Berkeley: University of California Press, 1994.

Yang, Binbin. 2017. "A Pictorial Autobiography by Zeng Jifen (1852–1942) and the Use of the 'Exemplary' in China's Modern Transformation." *Nan Nü: Men, Women, and Gender in Early and Imperial China* 19, no. 2 (2017): 263–315. doi:10.1163/15685268–00192P03.

APPENDIX

A Select List of Widely Available Translations of Prose Personal Accounts to 1880

This list is limited to prose works because so much of Chinese poetry is autobiographical that it would be difficult to draw the line on which pieces to include. We have included both short and long pieces, as well as full translations and excerpts from longer works available in anthologies.

Abbreviations

ABI Cook, Constance A., and Paul R. Goldin, eds. *A Source Book of Ancient Chinese Bronze Inscriptions*. Berkeley, California: Society for the Study of Early China, 2016.

ACL Owen, Stephen, ed. and trans. *An Anthology of Chinese Literature: Beginnings to 1911*. New York: W. W. Norton, 1996.

CA Mair, Victor, ed. *The Columbia Anthology of Traditional Chinese Literature*. New York: Columbia University Press, 1994.

CCS Ebrey, Patricia Buckley, ed. *Chinese Civilization: A Sourcebook*. 2nd ed. New York: Free Press, 1993.

CE Pollard, David, ed. *The Chinese Essay*. New York: Columbia University Press, 2000.

CP Wu, Pei-yi. *The Confucian's Progress: Autobiographical Writings in Traditional China*. Princeton, NJ: Princeton University Press, 1989.

EMC Swartz, Wendy, Robert Ford Campany, Yang Lu, and Jessey J. C. Choo, eds. *Early Medieval China: A Sourcebook*. New York: Columbia University Press, 2014.

GCT Mirsky, Jeannette, ed. *The Great Chinese Travelers: An Anthology*. London: Allen & Unwin, 1965.

HR   Mair, Victor H., Nancy S. Steinhardt, and Paul Goldin, eds. *Hawai'i Reader in Traditional Chinese Culture.* Honolulu: University of Hawai'i Press, 2005.

HT   Cai, Zongqi, ed. *How to Read Chinese Prose: A Guided Anthology.* New York: Columbia University Press, 2022.

IL   Strassberg, Richard E. *Inscribed Landscapes: Travel Writing from Imperial China.* Berkeley: University of California Press, 1994.

RB   Idema, Wilt L., and Beata Grant. *The Red Brush: Writing Women of Imperial China.* Cambridge, MA: Harvard University Asia Center, 2004.

SCT   de Bary, William T., and Irene Bloom, eds. *Sources of Chinese Tradition.* Vol. 1. New York: Columbia University Press, 2000.

UCE   Mann, Susan, and Yu-yin Cheng, eds. *Under Confucian Eyes: Writings on Gender in Chinese History.* Berkeley: University of California Press, 2001.

WW   Chang, Kang-i Sun, and Haun Saussy, eds. *Women Writers of Traditional China: An Anthology of Poetry and Criticism.* Stanford, CA: Stanford University Press, 1999.

Zhou Period

Li *Gui* (11th c. BCE), ABI, 11.
Zhong *Xian* (10th c. BCE), ABI, 54.
Hu *Ding* (9th c. BCE), ABI, 130–35.
Duo You *Ding* (8th c. BCE), ABI, 158–59.
Zifan *Bianzhong* (7th c. BCE), ABI, 265.

Qin and Han

Sima Qian (ca. 145–ca. 86 BCE), "Letter to Ren An," ACL, 136–42; SCT, 372; HR, 179–82; HT, 163–6; Stephen Durrant, Wai-yee Li, Michael Nylan, and Hans van Ess, *The Letter to Ren An & Sima Qian's Legacy* (Seattle: University of Washington Press, 2018).
Sima Qian, "The Sacred Duty of the Historian," SCT, 370–71.
Ban Jieyu (48 BCE–2 CE), "Self-Mourning Rhapsody," RB, 80–82.
Ma Dibo (1st c. CE), excerpt from "A Record of the Feng and Shan Sacrifices," IL, 59–62.
Ban Zhao (45–117), "Rhapsody on a Journey to the East," RB, 23–26.
Feng Yan (later Han), "Letter," CCS, 74–75.

Six Dynasties and Tang

Zhuge Liang (181–234), "Memorial on Deploying the Army," HT, 155–7.

Ji Kang (223–262), "Letter to Shan Tao Breaking Off Relations," HT, 168–71.

Li Mi (ca. 225–ca. 290), "Memorial Expressing My Feelings," HT, 157–8.

Shi Chong (249–303), "Preface to the Jingu Garden Poems," EMC, 533–34.

Shi Chong, "Preface to the 'Song of Longing to Return,'" EMC, 534–35.

Ge Hong (283–343), "Autobiography," CCS, 91–96; James Ware, *Alchemy, Medicine, and Religion in China of A.D. 320* (Cambridge, MA: MIT University Press, 1966), 6–21.

Faxian (337–ca. 422), *A Record of Buddhistic Kingdoms: Being an Account by the Chinese Monk Fâ-Hien of His Travels in India and Ceylon (A.D. 399–414) in Search of the Buddhist Books of Discipline*, trans. James Legge (1886; repr., New York: Paragon Book Reprint Corporation, 1965); *Records of Buddhist Countries*, in *Travels of Fah-Hian and Sung-yun: Buddhist Pilgrims from China to India (400 AD and 518 AD)*, trans. Samuel Beal (London: Trübner, 1869), 1–174.

Tao Qian (365–427), "Biography of the Master of Five Willows," EMC, 385–86.

Tao Qian, "Requiem for Myself," CE, 29–30.

Bao Zhao (ca. 414–466), "A Letter to My Younger Sister from the Bank of Thunder Garrison," IL, 74–76.

Yuan Can (421–478), "Biography of the Master of Wonderful Virtue," EMC, 386–87.

Jiang Yan (444–505), "His Own Preface," EMC, 392–95.

Zhang Chong (449–489), "Letter to Wang Jian," EMC, 81–86.

Songyun (Sung-yun, 6th c.), *The Mission of Hwui Seng and Sung Yun to Obtain Buddhist Books in the West*, in *Travels of Fah-Hian and Sung-yun: Buddhist Pilgrims from China to India (400 AD and 518 AD)*, trans. Samuel Beal (London: Trübner, 1869), 175–208.

Yan Zhitui (531–590s), full translations: *Family Instructions for the Yan Clan and Other Works by Yan Zhitui (531–90s)*, trans. Xiaofei Tian (Boston: Walter de Gruyter, 2021); *Family Instructions for the Yen Clan*, trans. Teng Ssu-yü (Brill, 1968). Excerpts: SCT, 541–46; EMC, 499–510.

Wang Bo (ca. 650–ca. 676), "Preface to Poems from the Pavilion of the Prince of T'eng," IL, 106–9.

Li Bo (701–762), "Letter to Han Jingzhou," CA, 556–59.

Lu Yu (733–804), "Autobiography," CA, 699–702.

Han Yu (768–824), "Goodbye to Penury," CE, 35–37.

Bo Juyi (772–846), "Letter to Yuan Zhen," ACL, 603–5.

Liu Zongyuan (773–819), "Eight Pieces from Yung Prefecture," IL, 141–47.

Liao, Song, Jin, and Yuan

Weiming Yuanhao (r. 1032–1048), "Letter to the Song Emperor Renzong," CCS, 140–41.

Ouyang Xiu (1007–1072), "Biography of the Retired Scholar of Six Ones," in *The Literary Works of Ou-yang Hsiu (1007–72)*, by Ronald Egan (Cambridge: Cambridge University Press, 1984), 223–24. Other autobiographical essays translated in this book include "Pleasure Boat Studio," 211–12, "Pavilion of Good Harvests and Joy," 214–15, "The Old Drunkard's Pavilion," 215–17, and "The Three Zithers," 221–22.

Sima Guang (1019–1086), "Account of a Debate at Court," CCS, 151–52.

Su Shi (1037–1101), "Account of Stone Bell Mountain," ACL, 622–24.

Su Shi, "Account of the Terrace 'Passing Beyond,'" ACL, 665–67.

Li Qingzhao (1084–ca. 1151), "Afterword to *Records on Metal and Stone*," ACL, 591–96; CA, 569–72; RB, 207–14; Ronald Egan, *The Burden of Female Talent: The Poet Li Qingzhao and Her Story in China* (Cambridge, MA: Harvard University Asia Center, 2013), 192–99.

Li Qingzhao, "Letter to Qi," RB, 215–16.

Meng Yuanlao (1090–1150), "Preface to *A Record of Dreaming a Dream of Splendors Past in the Eastern Capital*," HT, 275–9.

Lu You (1125–1209), *South China in the Twelfth Century: A Translation of Lu Yu's Travel Diaries, July 3–December 6, 1170*, trans. Chang Chun-shu and Joan Smythe (Hong Kong: Chinese University Press, 1981).

Fan Chengda (1126–1193), *On the Road in Twelfth Century China: The Travel Diaries of Fan Chengda (1126–193)*, trans. James M. Hargett (Stuttgart: Franz Steiner Verlag, 1989).

Fan Chengda, *Riding the River Home: A Complete and Annotated Translation of Fan Chengda's (1126–193) Diary of a Boat Trip to Wu (Wuchuan lu)*, trans. James M. Hargett (Hong Kong: Chinese University Press, 2008). Excerpt in CA, 616–23.

Fan Chengda, *Stairway to Heaven: A Journey to the Summit of Mount Emei*, trans. James M. Hargett (Albany: State University of New York Press, 2006).

Zuqin (1216–1287), "Autobiographical Sermon," HR, 432–36.

Ma Ke (early 13th c.), "Dragon Mountain," IL, 246–50.

Wen Tianxiang (1236–1283), *The Account of the Compass* (excerpts), ACL, 705–20.

Yuanmiao (1238–1295), "A Letter to Master Xueren of Yangshan Expressing Doubts about Succeeding Him," CP, 239–42.

Guo Bi (1280–1335), "A Scholar-Painter's Diary," CCS, 199–201.

Zheng Yunduan (ca. 1327–1356), "Preface to *Suyong ji*," WW, 677–78.

Ming

Zhu Yuanzhang (1328–1398), "Ancestral Instruction," SCT, 780–83.

Zhu Yuanzhang, "Proclamations," CCS, 205–7.

Empress Xu (1362–1407), "Preface to *Nei xun*," WW, 679–81.

Zheng He (1371–1433), "Stone Tablet of the Miracles Performed by T'ien Fei in Ch'ang-lo," trans. Eduard B. Vermeer, in *Chinese Local History: Stone Inscriptions from Fukien in the Sung to Ch'ing Periods* (Boulder: Westview Press, 1991), 112–20.

Xu Yikui (d. ca. 1400), "What the Weaver Said," CCS, 221–22.

Wu Yubi (1392–1469), *The Journal of Wu Yubi: The Path to Sagehood,* trans. Theresa M. Kelleher (Indianapolis, IN: Hackett, 2013). This also includes several of Wu's letters.

Cheng Minzheng (ca. 1446–ca. 1500), "Night Passage over Two Passes," ACL, 625–27.

Gui Youguang (1507–1571), "The Xiangji Studio," CE, 75–77; HT, 366–8.

Gui Youguang et al., *Vignettes from the Late Ming: A Hsiao-p'in Anthology,* trans. Yang Ye (Seattle: University of Washington Press, 1999).

Yang Jisheng (1516–1555), "Final Instructions," UCE, 122–29.

Hu Zhi (1517–1585), "A Record of Learning through Difficulties," CP, 243–51.

Li Zhi (1527–1602), *A Book to Burn and a Book to Keep (Hidden),* trans. Rivi Handler-Spitz, Pauline C. Lee, and Haun Saussy (New York: Columbia University Press, 2016). Particularly autobiographical sections include some of the letters and "A Sketch of Zhuowu: Written in Yunnan," 75–83. For a smaller sample of Li Zhi's letters, see CCS, 258–62.

Hu Shengbao et al. (late 16th to early 17th c.), "Tenant Contracts," CCS, 223–25.

Xu Xiake (1586–1641), *The Travel Diaries of Hsü Hsia-k'o,* trans. Li Chi (Hong Kong: Chinese University Press of Hong Kong, 1974).

Shen Yixiu (1590–1635), "A Biography of My Youngest Daughter Qiongzhang," RB, 400–406.

Gu Ruopu (1592–ca. 1681), "Letter to My Sons," UCE, 151–52.

Gu Ruopu, "Letter to My Younger Brother," HT, 338–39.

Gu Ruopu, "Preface to *Drafts from the Reclining in the Moonlight Studio*," RB, 415–18.

Shang Jinglan (1602–1676), "Preface to the *Remaining Drafts of Zither Tower*," RB, 429–31.

Jizong Xingche (b. 1606), "Autobiographical Account," RB, 464–67.

Qing

Wang Shimin (1592–1680), "Self-Account," CP, 253–62.

Wang Xiuchu (17th c.), *Ten Days in Yangzhou*, CCS, 271–79; ACL, 826–33; Lynn A. Struve, *Voices from the Ming-Qing Cataclysm: China in Tigers' Jaws* (New Haven: Yale University Press, 1998), 32–48.

Mao Xiang (1611–1693), "Reminiscences of the Plum Shadows Convent," in *Plum Shadows and Plank Bridge: Two Memoirs about Courtesans by Mao Xiang and Yu Huai*, ed. and trans. Wai-yee Li (New York: Columbia University Press, 2020), 1–64.

Ji Xian (1614–1683), "Record of Past Karma," UCE, 139–44.

Wu Xiao (mid-17th c.), "Preface to *Xiaoxue an gao*," WW, 690.

Yu Huai (1616–1696), "Miscellaneous Records of the Plank Bridge," in *Plum Shadows and Plank Bridge: Two Memoirs about Courtesans by Mao Xiang and Yu Huai*, ed. and trans. Wai-yee Li (New York: Columbia University Press, 2020), 65–183.

Wang Duanshu (1621–before 1685), "Preface to the *Together with Autumn Poetry Collection* of Xuan Huazi," RB, 449–50.

Yikui Chaozhen (1625–1679), "Autobiography," RB, 457–59.

Qian Fenglun (1644–1703), "A Letter to Lin Yaqing," RB, 483.

Qian Fenglun, "A Letter to My Younger Brother," RB, 485.

Zhang Maozi (mid-17th c.), "A Record of Life beyond My Due," HR, 528–38.

Kangxi (1654–1722), *Emperor of China: Self-Portrait of K'ang-His*, trans. Jonathan D. Spence (New York: Knopf, 1974).

Fang Bao (1668–1749), "Life in Prison," CE, 101–5; Pei-kai Cheng, Michael Lestz, and Jonathan D. Spence, *The Search of Modern China: A Documentary Collection* (New York: Norton, 1999), 54–58.

Xu Si et al. (18th c.), *True Crimes in Eighteenth-Century China: Twenty Case Histories*, trans. Robert E. Hegel. (Seattle: University of Washington Press, 2009).

Shen Fu (1763–1808?). *Six Records of a Floating Life*, trans. Lin Yutang, *The Wisdom of China and Japan* (New York: Random House, 1942), 964–1050; trans. Leonard Pratt and Chiang Su-hui (London: Penguin, 1983); trans. Graham Saunders (London: Hackett, 2011). Excerpts in CA, 709–46 (from Lin Yutang).

Wanyan Yun Zhu (1771–1833), "Preface to *Guochao guixiu zhengshi ji*," WW, 711–12.

Luo Qilan (late 18th c.), "Preface to *Tingqiuguan guizhong tongren ji*," WW, 703–6.

Gong Zizhen (1792–1841), "Passing through Yangzhou Again in the Sixth Month of the Year Jihai," IL, 418–22.

Sample confessions (ca. 1813), in Susan Naquin, *Millenarian Rebellion in China: The Eight Trigrams Uprising of 1813* (New Haven: Yale University Press, 1976), 271–79.

Guangxi Roving Bandit Group (mid-19th c.), "A Statement of Voluntary Surrender," CCS, 320–21.

Hong Daquan (1823–1852), "Confession," trans. Franz H. Michael, in *The Taiping Rebellion: History and Documents*, vol. 2, ed. Franz Michael and Chung-li Chang (Seattle: University of Washington Press, 1971), 187–91.

Shi Dakai (1831–1863), "Confession," trans. Franz H. Michael, in *The Taiping Rebellion: History and Documents*, vol. 3, ed. Franz Michael and Chung-li Chang (Seattle: University of Washington Press, 1971), 1200–1203.

Zhang Daye (b. 1854), *The World of a Tiny Insect: A Memoir of the Taiping Rebellion and Its Aftermath*, trans. Xiaofei Tian (Seattle: University of Washington Press, 2013).

Su Wanlan (19th c.), "Preface to *Guiyin jixiu*," WW, 707–8.

Li Shuyi (19th c.), "Preface to *Shuying lou mingshu baiyong*," WW, 713–14.

INDEX

Emperor Wu (of the Han), 6, 29–32
Emperor Wu (of the Jin), 68
Emperor Wu (of the Liang), 72–76
environmental distress, 166–74. *See also*
  bandits and rebellions; droughts;
  famine; natural disasters
eunuchs, 50, 78, 141
examinations, xi, 9, 78, 142, 143, 214,
  219, 227, 233; Ai Nanying, 146–52;
  preparation and procedures, 146–52,
  185–93; Wang Huizu and, 181,
  186–90, 193, 196–97, 199–203. See
  also *jinshi*; literati; studying
exile, 9, 23, 62, 75, 102–5, 108, 198

family affairs, 51, 123–24, 227–40
family ethics. *See* family instructions
  (*jiaxun*); family relationships; female
  chastity; filial piety; mourning and
  commemoration
family instructions (*jiaxun*), 4, 12–13,
  49–51, 154–65
family relationships, 117, 136, 208, 228.
  See also brother-brother relationship;
  brother-sister relationship; family
  affairs; family ethics; father(-in-
  law)–daughter(-in-law) relationship;
  father-in-law–son-in-law relationship; father-son relationship; filial
  piety; grandmother-granddaughter
  relationship; grandmother-grandson relationship; husband-wife
  relationship; marriage; mother(-in-
  law)–daughter(-in-law) relationship;
  mothers; mother-son relationship;
  uncle-nephew relationship; widows
famine, 12, 39, 166, 169–70, 172–74. *See
  also* droughts
Fan Chengda: *Diary of a Boat Trip*, 9
Fan Zhongyan, 87, 90–92
Fang Bao, 12

father(-in-law)–daughter(-in-law) relationship, 53
father-in-law–son-in-law relationship,
  144, 182, 189–93
father-son relationship, 12, 24–25, 39,
  102, 103, 106, 116, 123, 152, 168,
  187, 225, 228; Cao Cao and Cao Pi,
  59; Zeng Guofan and son, 227–40;
  Zheng Xuan and son, 49–51
female chastity, 117, 119, 153–54, 161,
  198, 203–4. *See also* husband-wife
  relationship; marriage; women
filial piety, 20, 24–26, 144, 153, 155, 157,
  160–61, 187, 204–5, 211, 239–40; un-
  filiality, 24–25, 199, 211–12. *See also*
  ancestors; *The Classic of Filial Piety*
  (Xiaojing); family relationships
"Forms for Sealing and Investigating"
  (Fengzhen shi), 24
friendship, 4, 8, 9, 14, 34, 67, 97, 102,
  105, 108, 123, 129, 209, 212; Bai Juyi,
  78–80; Han Qi and Fan Zhongyan,
  86–87, 89–92; Han Qi and Zhao
  Ziyuan, 92–93; Wang Chong, 39, 41,
  42, 51; Wang Huizu, 183, 199, 202,
  206, 207; Xie Yingfang, 132; Xu Wei,
  142, 143; Zeng Guofan, 228, 229
funerary biographies, 2, 8, 14, 68, 86;
  self-authored, 8, 141–45

grandfather-grandson relationship,
  184–86
grandmother-granddaughter relationship, 136–38
grandmother-grandson relationship,
  183, 188, 192

Han (dynasty), 20, 72, 76, 111, 113, 150;
  autobiographical writing, 2, 3, 4, 9,
  10; Cai Yan, 53–58; Cao Cao, 59–63;
  Cao Pi, 63–66; Emperor Wu of the

poetry, 107–9; travel diary, 111–14; women, 116–20

Song (mountain), 80

Song (state), 44

Southern Song, 111, 112, 117, 121, 122. *See also* Northern Song; Song (dynasty)

Spring and Autumn Annals (Chunqiu), 63, 82, 150

Spring and Autumn period, 31, 40, 43, 45, 49, 50, 68, 76, 114

studying, 46, 66, 82, 99, 151, 182, 185, 211; Cao Cao, 60, 62; Cao Pi, 65; Liu Kai, 98–99; Lu Guimeng, 82–85; Wang Chong, 39–47; Wang Huizu, 185–90, 193, 199; Xu Wei, 142–43; Zeng Guofan, 230–34, 240; Zheng Xuan, 49–51. *See also* examinations; *jinshi*; literati

Su Qin, 43

Su Shi, 9, 105, 150

Su Zhe, 14, 101–4

suicide, 113, 116–19, 141–45

Sun Simiao, 135

Suzhou, 112, 113, 126, 178, 194

Taiping rebels, 213–14, 227; Zeng Guofan and, 230–38

Tan Yunxian, 135–40

Tang (dynasty), 68, 79, 94, 111, 159, 228; autobiographical writing, 1, 8, 9, 10; mourning and commemoration, 86–90; Tan poetry, 107

Tao Qian (Yuanming), 7, 80

tea, 78–79, 81, 84, 148, 149, 216, 235

Three Kingdoms Period, 59. *See also* Cao Cao; Cao Pi

travel, 5, 6, 25–27, 34, 50, 56, 80, 88, 92, 176–79, 211, 212, 228; ambassadorial mission, 111–14, 124–25; and *biji* writing, 101–6; by boat, 84, 105, 113, 125, 126, 133, 168, 178, 186, 187, 194, 197, 203, 229; by carriage, 112–14; diary, 111–14; by horse, 113–14; imperial tour, 177–78; by sedan chair, 80, 92, 229; wartime, 124–27. *See also* Wang Huizu

uncle-nephew relationship, 87–90

violence, 121, 166, 197, 213; testimony, 11–12. *See also* bandits and rebellions; dynastic collapse; war and military campaigns

Wang Chong, 38–39; career and scholarship, 40, 43–45, 47; character, 41–43; family, 39–40, 45–46; old age, 47

Wang Dechen, 101, 102–3

Wang Huizu, 8, 181–207, 208; crime investigation, 197–98; education and examination, 185–89, 193, 195, 199–203; father-in-law, 190–93; filial piety, 205; grandfather, 185–86; illness, 195–96; marriage, 189, 194, 201; parents, 183–84, 187, 189–90, 198–99, 204; *Precepts for Local Administrative Officials* (Zuozhi yaoyan), 207; salary, 206

Wang Xiuchu: "Ten Days in Yangzhou" (Yangzhou shiri), 11

Wang Yangming, 141, 142

Wang Zheng, 208–9, 211–12

war and military campaigns, 21, 29–32, 34–35, 53–58, 74, 91, 119. *See also* bandits and rebellions; dynastic collapse; violence

Warring States period, 49, 50, 62, 81, 114

Wei (dynasty), 59, 236

Wei Ye, 108

Wei Zhongxian, 141, 168

Wen Tianxiang, 8, 12, 121–27

Western Jin, 5, 67. *See also* Jin (dynasty, 3rd–4th centuries)